ॐ – *Oṃ*

# *Śrī Tārā Devī* – Blue *Saraswatī*

*

**Dr. Ramamurthy N.**

M.Sc., B.G.L., CA II B, CCP, DSADP, CISA, PMP, CGBL, Ph.D.

*

Title: *Śrī Tārā Devī* – Blue *Saraswatī*

Series: Two of Ten

First Edition: 2022

Author: **Dr. Ramamurthy N**, Chennai.
http://ramamurthy.jaagruti.co.in/



Number of pages: 174

Price: ₹ 300.00

ISBN (13): 978-93-82237-91-4

Printed at:

Published by:

*****

## Table of Contents

*****

உ

ப்ரஹ்மைவ ஸத்யம்

**SRI SWAYAMPRAKASA AVADHUTHA SADASIVA TRUST**

Sri Sri Judge Swamigal Adhishtanam, East 7th Street,
**PUDUKKOTTAI-622 001**
**Phone: 04322-221440, 222128**
Email: sribhuvaneshwari@gmail.com

# Blessings

Date : 05/08/2022

**ப்ரத்யாலீட4பதா3ர்பிதாங்க்4ரிஶவஹ்ருத்3கோ4ராட்டஹாஸா பரா**
**க2ட்3கே3ந்தீ3வரகர்த்ரிக2ர்பரபு4ஜா ஹுங்காரபீ3ஜோத்3ப4வா**
**க2ர்வா நீலவிஶாலபிங்க3லஜடாஜூடைகநாகை3ர்யுதா**
**ஜாட்3யம் ந்யஸ்ய கபாலகே த்ரிஜக3தாம் ஹந்த்யுக்3ரதாரா ஸ்வயம்**

ஸகல தேவதா ஸ்வரூபிணியாய் மணித்வீபத்தில் வஸித்துக் கொண்டு அனைத்துலகத்தையும் காத்து வருபவளான அன்னை ஸ்ரீ புவனேச்வரி தேவியின் பரிபூர்ண கடாக்ஷத்தினால், நமது ப்ரியசிஷ்யர் ராமமூர்த்தி தாராதேவி குறித்த ஒரு நூலினை வெளியிடப்போவது குறித்து அறிந்ததில் மிக்க மகிழ்ச்சிஅடைகிறேன்.

ஜகன்மாதாவின் தசமஹாவித்யா வடிவங்களுள் இரண்டாவது வடிவாகப் பிரகாசிப்பவள் தாரா தேவி. தோற்றத்தில் காளியை ஒத்திருந்தாலும், தாரா தேவி காளியிடமிருந்து மாறுபட்டவள். இத்தேவி கத்திரிக்கோல், கத்தி, கபாலம், கருங்குவளைப்பூ ஆகியன ஏந்திய நான்கு கரங்கள் கொண்டவள். தரீ என்றால் படகு எனப் பொருள். படகு எவ்வாறு தன்னை நம்பி ஏறி அமர்வோரை தண்ணீரில் மூழ்காமல் காப்பாற்றுகிறதோ அதேபோல் இந்த தாராதேவியும் தன் பக்தர்களை ஸம்ஸார ஸாகரத்தில் மூழ்காமல் காத்து, முக்தியை அருளுபவள். கோரமான ஆபத்துகளிலிருந்து காப்பதால் மஹோக்ரா எனப்படுகிறாள். உணர்வுகள் நசிக்கின்ற பேருணர்வு வடிவே தன் ஸ்வரூபம் என்று உணர்த்தும் முகமாக சிவத்தின் மேல் நின்ற நிலையில் காட்சியளிக்கிறாள்.

பாற்கடலைக் கடைந்த போது சிவபெருமான் ஆலஹால விஷத்தை உண்ட பின் அது தொண்டையில் தங்கி விட்டது. அந்த விஷத்தினால் அவர் மிகவும் அவதிப்பட்டார். அந்த விஷத்தின் கடுமையினால் உடல் முழுவதும் எரியத் துவங்கி சிவபெருமான் மயங்கிச் சோர்ந்தார். தேவர்கள் அனைவரும் அம்பாளை சரணைந்து ப்ரார்த்தனை செய்ய, தாரா தேவி ஆவிர்பவித்து அவரை தன் மடியில் குழந்தையாக்கிப் படுக்க வைத்துக் கொண்டு தனது மார்பில் இருந்து பாலை குடிக்க விட்டாளாம் . அந்த க்ஷீராம்ருதத்தை குடித்தப் பின்னரே ஈசன் மீண்டு வந்தாரென தாரா தந்த்ரம் ஒரு வரலாறைச் சொல்கிறது.

காஷ்மீரில் பிறந்த குழந்தைகளுக்கு, பிறந்து மூன்று நாட்களுக்குள்ளாக தாராவின் ஸ்வரூபமான நீல சரஸ்வதியின் மந்திரத்தை ஜபித்து தேனில் தொட்டு நாவில் எழுதும் மரபு இருந்தது என்று சொல்வதுண்டு. காஷ்மீரி பண்டிட் சிறந்த அறிவுடன் திகழ்ந்ததற்கு இதுவே காரணம் எனவும் கூறப்படுகிறது. திருவண்ணாமலை ஸ்ரீசேஷாத்ரி ஸ்வாமிகளுக்கும் அவரது பால்யத்தில் அவரது பாட்டனாரால் இதே போல் தாரா மந்த்ரம் அபிமந்த்ரணம் செய்யப்பட்ட க்ஷீரத்தைக் கொடுத்தார் என்று அவரது சரித்ரம் கூறுகிறது.

காளீகாண்டம் 12ம் படலத்தில் தாராதேவியின் பெருமைகள் விசேஷமாக பேசப்படுகின்றன. அந்நூல் யோகம் என்பது தாரா யோகமே; ஜபம் என்பதும் தாரா ஜபமே; மஹா மந்த்ரம் என்றால் அது தாரா மந்த்ரமே. இந்த மந்த்ரத்தை உபாஸிப்பவனே மஹாபாக்யவான். அவனே ஞானி. அவனே சீலன். அவனே தீக்ஷை பெற்றவன். அவனே ஆத்ம ஸ்வரூபி. அவனே பிரம்மானந்தத்தில் திளைப்பவன் எனக் கூறப்பட்டுள்ளது.

வஸிஷ்ட மஹரிஷி தாராதேவியின் மஹத்வத்தை அறிந்து. மகாசீனம் எனும் திபெத்திற்குச் சென்று முறையாக தாரா உபாஸனையைக் கற்று காமாக்யா க்ஷேத்ரத்தில் காமபீடம் அருகே உக்ரதாரா பீடத்தை நிறுவியதாக ருத்ரயாமள தந்த்ரம் கூறுகிறது. தாரா மந்த்ரத்தைத் அறிந்து கொள்வதாலேயே ஒருவன் ஜெயமடைவான் - அவனுக்கு வெற்றிகள் குவியும் என ஸ்ரீவித்யார்ணவ தந்த்ரம் கூறுகிறது.

ஸ்ரீ தாரா உபாஸகர்களுக்கு இந்நூல் ஒரு பொக்கிஷமாக ப்ரயோஜனப்படும். இந்நூலை தொகுத்து வழங்கிய முனைவர். N.ராமமூர்த்தி அவர்களுக்கு நமது மனமார்ந்த வாழ்த்துக்களும் ஆசிகளும் உரித்தாகுக! ஜகந்மாதா ஸ்ரீ புவனேச்வரி தேவியின் பரிபூர்ண கடாக்ஷத்தினால், நமது சிஷ்யர் ராமமூர்த்தியின் ஆன்மீகத்தொண்டு தொடரட்டும்.

இந்நூலினை படித்து இன்புறும் எல்லா பக்தர்களும் அம்பிகையின் அருளும், ஸத்குரு ஸ்ரீசாந்தானந்த மஹாஸ்வாமிகளின் அருளும் பெற்று ஸுகானந்த ஸுகவாழ்வு கிடைத்திட ஜகன்மாதா ஸ்ரீ புவனேச்வரி தேவியை பிரார்தித்து ஆசிர்வதிக்கிறேன்.

ஆனந்தம் சுபம் மங்களம் !

ஜய புவனேச்வரி!

**ஸ்ரீ ப்ரணவாநந்த ஸ்வாமின:**
ஸ்ரீ புவனேச்வரி அவதூத வித்யா பீடம்
புதுக்கோட்டை

*****

# Introduction

ॐ श्री गुरुभ्यो नमः । *Oṃ Śrī Gurubhyo Namaḥ* ।

गुरुर्ब्रह्मा गुरुर्विष्णुः गुरुर्देवो महेश्वरः । गुरु साक्षात् परं ब्रह्म तस्मै श्रीगुरवे नमः ॥

*Gururbrahma Gururviṣṇuḥ Gururdevo Maheśvaraḥ* ।
*Guru Sākśāt Parabrahma Tasmai Śrīgurave Namaḥ* ॥

गुरुवे सर्वलोकानां भिषजे भवरोगिनां । निधये सर्व विद्यानां दक्षिणा मूर्तये नमः ॥

*Guruve Sarvloksansam Bhişaje Bhavaroginām* ।

*Nidhaye Sarva Vidhyānām Dakśiṇa Mūrtaye Namaḥ* ॥

सदाशिव समारंभां शङ्कराचार्य मध्यमां। अस्मद आचार्य पर्यन्तां वन्दे गुरु परंपराम्॥

*Sadāshiva Samārambām Śankarāchārya Madhyamām* ।

*Asmad Achārya Paranthām Vande Guru Paramparām* ॥

श्रुति स्मृति पुराणानामालयं करुणालयम् । नमामि भगवत्पादंशंकरंलोकशंकरम् ॥

*Śruti Smruti Purānānām Ālayam Karunālayam* ।
*Namāmi Bhagavatapādam Śankaram Lokaśankaram* ॥

वागर्थाविव सम्प्रुक्तौ वागर्थ प्रतिपत्तये । जगतः पितरौ वन्दे पार्वती परमेश्वरौ ॥

*Vāgarthāviva Sampruktakou Vāgartha Pratipaye* ।

*Jagataḥ Pitarou Vande Pārvati Parameśwarou* ॥

We all originated from *Brahmam*[1]. We reach that *Brahmam* – merge with that *Brahmam*. That is actually *lia-samāti*. This rhythm cannot be exercised without the use or support of an appropriate instructor. The *Upasana* is aimed at an idol. It is both *Suguna* (with qualities) and (without qualities) *Nirguna*. A person is capable of doing *Nirguna Upasana* only after he has attained *Sagunopasana*. Suddenly, it is impossible for one to get involved in *Nirgunobasana* straight away.

As mentioned in *Brahadāranyaka Upanishat* the *Ādhi Moolam*, also called as *Parabrahmam*, does not have any form or qualities. It does not fit within any limitations. However, in order to realise that *Brahmam* without any form, a sort of image worship is suggested. Once the maturity (*Sāloka, Sāmeepya* and *Sāyujya*) is reached, there is no need for any prescriptions

[1] *Brahmam* is different *Brahma*. *Brahma* is the head of all Devas. On the other hand *Brahmam* is *Parabrahmam*, the supreme.

and/ or restrictions to worship gods with different images, fasting, etc. Various *karmas* have to be performed to take us to this *yogic* position.

*Shiva*, *Shakti* and *Vishnu* are all one and the same. These three Gods are without origin. For all other Gods we could read the origin and for some even the end could also be seen in one or other *Purana* or stories.

In the form of *Arddhanāreeshwara* the left half of Lord *Shiva* is *Shakti*. Again, in the form of *Shankaranārāyana*, the left half of Lord *Shiva* is *Vishnu*. This clearly evidences that *Shakti* and *Vishnu* are one and the same and naturally *Shiva* also.

*Brahadāranyaka Upanishat* verses (I–3, I–4), starting from "*Ātmaivetamagra Āseet*" till "*Sa Imamevātmānam Tvetāpātayat Tataḥ*" describes in this manner – the *Parabrahmam* seems to be two as husband and wife.

The energy of the *Parabrahmam* is *Srl Devi* – *Shakti*. Even when the power of that object is within it, the power cannot exist without the entity. Hence, the *Parabrahmam* is the *Shakti* and the *Shakti* is the *Parabrahmam*. Both cannot be different.

In the same manner, if *Eswaran* is considered as *Brahmam*, Goddess Ambika is merged with that *Eswaran*. Can the fragrant and the flower be separate? How about whiteness and the milk? *Ambika* is thus unsplittable from *Eswaran*. *Parameswara* and *Parāshakti* are the earliest/ first couple to be inseparable; They are the mother and father of all living beings. Yet they are one and the same.

*Chāndogya Upanishat* (6:2:1) says "*Ekam Evātvetīyam*" – That is, all the Gods are the same – there is only one God, no two. *Brahma Sootram* says "*Ekam Brahma Dvitīya Nāste Neha Naye Nāste Naya Kinchana*" – there is only one God – no two – not at all two. *Yajur Veda* (32-3) utters – "*Na Tasya Pratimāsti Śutāma Pāpvitam*" – He is so holy and does not have any image.

*Jagadguru Sri Adi Shankara Bhagavat Pada* divided our *Sanatana* Hindu religion into six branches – sub-religions and established *Shanmathas* – *Gānapatyam*, *Koumaram*, *Shaivam*, *Vaishnavam*, *Shaktam* and Souram. *Adi Shankara*, though equally treated all these six sub-religions, he had a distinct admiration for Shaktam-Shakti. She is *Jaganmata* – the mother of this universe – the mother of all living beings.

We are not yet mature enough to realise the formless *Parabrahmam* (no need of writing/ reading this book, if we are that much mature).

Someone has to hold back or attach side wheels until one learns to drive a bicycle. Once he becomes expert these are not needed. We need a boat to cross a river. Once we have reached the other shore, what is the need of a boat.

Therefore, until we all mature enough, we need to worship a God with form – why can't it be the holy mother – is it not that we get that much pleasure when we call mother as '*Amma*'?

When we think of incarnation of God – immediately the 10 incarnations of Lord *Vishnu* (*Dasha avatar*) only come to our mind. If we think a little bit deep, one may be reminded of the 24 incarnations of Lord *Vishnu* as described in *Shrimad Vishnu Bhagavatam* (1.3.6-25).

However, the *Shakta* texts, more importantly Sri Devi Bhagavatam, describe many an incarnation of *Sri Devi*, considered as sister of Lord *Vishnu*. Among them are the ten cosmic forms of the Divine Mother, called the "*Dasha Maha Vidya*"[2], are the most special. He later wrote and published a book on the various forms of *Sri Devi* entitled "Incarnations of Ambika".

The author's Sri Vidya Guru, Head of Pudukkottai Bhuvaneswari Mutt, Pujyasri Pranavananda Saraswathi Avadutha Swamiji, has led the way in writing many books. He asked the author to write a separate book detailing the ten goddesses of "*Dasha Maha Vidya*". In defiance of that order, this Second book is written about *Sri Tārā Devī*.

A few related mantras are also indicated wherever possible. In general, all the *mantras* are supposed to be secretive. All the more about *Shakti* related *mantras*. Hence, they are to be got initiated by an appropriate teacher (*guru*) only, before trying to chant of to do *japam*.

Primarily, the aim of this book is to explain in detail, the incarnation of Sri Devi as *Tārā Devī*, to explain her form and purpose and to explain some of the mantras. It is believed that the devotees will get benefitted by reading and understanding this and worshiping *Sri Tārā Devī* in the right and appropriate way.

---

[2] This author of this book wrote and published a book in 2011, entitled " *Dasha Maha Vidya* " about the ten incarnations in general.

Devotees are advised to consult a qualified scholar or guru, if they have any doubts about any mantras or worshipping methods mentioned in this book. It is highly suggested not to start recitation/ puja with half-knowledge and assuming the rest. Books can only be a reference guide, but cannot act as a teacher (*guru*).

Generally, it is very difficult to read Samskruta words in English with proper pronunciation. It is apt to read them in Samskruta script itself. But to benefit those who cannot read Samskruta script the *mantras* have been given in English also. The Samskruta words, when transliterated in English are given in *italics*. Also, whenever She denotes Goddess *Sri Devi*, it is written as **She** or **Her**. Normally diacritical marks will be used for transliteration of Samskruta words into English. But general readers are not fully conversant with diacritical marks and hence they find it difficult to read. Hence, it not been used in this book in normal texts. But for proper pronunciation it has been completely used in *mantras*.

This book is simultaneously written in Tamil also.

My humble *pranāms* to *Śrīśrī Pranavānanda Saraswathi Swamiji*, for his blessings and some pleasantries about this edition. To enjoy his own wordings it has been given in Tamil itself.

My sincere thanks are due to all those who supported in this noble cause of bring out this book. Attempts have been made to give this book as much error free as possible. Still if there are any errors, apologies are sought. If the errors are given as feedback, it will the next edition to be fault free. Hope the readers would be benefitted by the contents of this book. The readers are requested to feel free to send their feedback and comments.

There is no doubt that *Sri Tārā Devī* will shower her compassion and blessings to all those who read this book.

Our humble *Praṇāms* to all our *Gurus*.

*Om Tat Sat*

Chennai

2022 *Dr. Ramamurthy N*

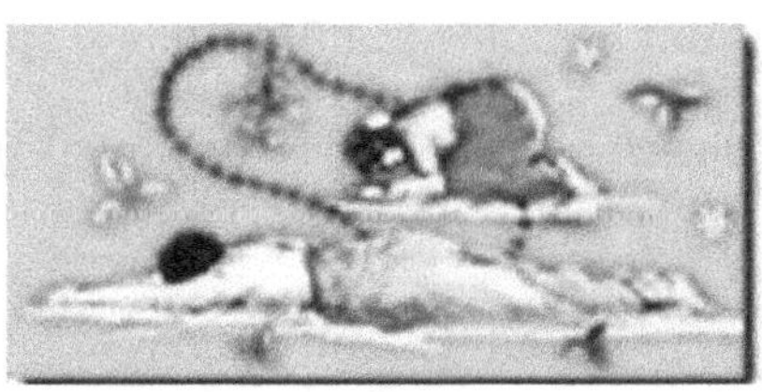

## *Daśa Mahā Vidyā Devis*

There are 'n' number of images of *Devi*-s worshipped by sages for quite a long time. The most significant ten among them are being discussed in this chapter.

Each of these ten *vidya*-s, itself called as *Brahma Vidya. Tantra sastras* describe in detail the worshipping methods of these *Devis.*

Out of these 10 *vidya*-s, the *Tripura Sundari Vidya* also called as *Sri Vidya* is more famous in South India.

The *mantras, yantra, dhyana,* worshipping methods, results, forms, etc., of these ten *vidya*-s can be read in the tantra texts in Samskrutam. Sir Arthur Avalon, has also explained in detail in English.

There are different types, in the worship of *Sri Devi* – like *Vāmāchāra, Dakshināchāra, Samayāchāra* and *Koulachāra. Sri Lalita Sahasranāma* (*Sri Lalitā Sahasranāma* – 98th name – *Samayāchāratatparā,* 441st name – *Koulamārga Tatpara Sevitā*) accepts all these methods.

The destruction of *Daksha*'s *yagna* by *Sati Devi* has been described in the 4th *Skanda* of *Shrimad Bhagavatam.* This has also been described in detail in *Bruhat Dharma Purana.* Once when *Daksha Prajapati* was proceeding towards the *yagna-Shala* (the place where the holy fire was being conducted), Lord *Shiva* (his son-in-law), who was in meditation did not get up as a respect. On account of this *Daksha* got wild and gave a curse that Lord Shiva will not get any share from the *yagna.* From that moment onwards, Lord Shiva does not even see Daksha.

In another instance, Daksha Prajapati himself started a *yagna.* All his daughters were invited with their husbands excepting *Sati Devi.* Knowing this, **she** asked permission from her husband Lord Shiva to attend the *yagna,* executed by her father. When Lord Shiva did not permit her, **she** took the form of *Mahā Kālī.*

Surprised by the most terrified form of peaceful *Sati Devi,* Lord *Shiva* started running from that place. But in whichever direction he ran, *Devi* was before him with the terrified form. The ten forms **She** took in all the ten directions (8 directions + upward + downward) are *Dasha Maha Vidyas* of *Sri Devi.*

Surprised by this Lord Shiva stood stunned. Though *Devi* tried to console him stating that **She** is *Sati Devi* only, Lord *Shiva* could not get away from the fear immediately. Then *Devi* explained the specialties and purposes of all the ten *Vidya*-s to her husband.

Further **She** mentioned – "the *Vedas* and sacred writings (*Agamas*) told by you to this world are my two hands. I wear moveable and immoveable things of this world with those two hands. These ten forms will help to bless the worshippers. People should reach me by secretly following the *mantra*, *yantra*, verses, *kavacha*, etc., as taught by the teacher (Guru). I am telling you with the affection on you. Please permit me to attend the *yagna*" – **She** requested.

After getting his permission, **she** reached the *yagna* place of Daksha, which was protected by Nandi, Brungi and others. **She** could not tolerate the reprimands on Lord Shiva and hence disappeared in the fire of *yoga*. Knowing this Lord Shiva created *Veerabhadra* from his entangled locks of hair and sent him to destroy the *yagna* of Daksha. *Devi* also took the form of *Bhadrakālī* and with the help of *Veerabhadra* destroyed Daksha and all the opponents of Lord Shiva. This is the origin of *Dasha Maha Vidyas*.

The directions in which the ten *Mahavidyas* originated are described in the below diagram.

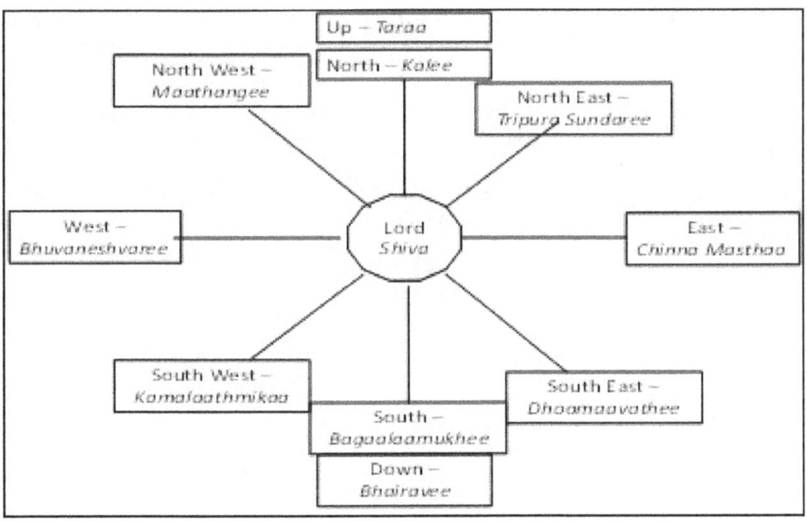


Out of the three qualities of illusion, the pure *sattva* quality related with *Brahmam* (the Supreme Being) is called *Vidya*. Sir Arthur Avalon feels that even in this the fourth and which is beyond any *tattva* is the blissful form of *Devi* is called *Maha Vidya*.

The relation of *Brahmam* to the pure Sattva quality, of the three qualities of *Maya*, is called *Vidya*. The fourth (transcendental) philosophy is the blissful form of the Goddess, which is called *Maha Vidya*. *Chamuṇḍa Tattva* splits these ten *Mahavidyas* into *Mahavidyas, Siddhavidyas* and *Vidyas*. But the text *Shyāmā Rahasya* mentions all these as *Mahavidyas* only. We also follow this and call all the ten as *Mahavidyas*.

The presiding deity(ies) of the 10th Chapter of *Sri Devi Mahatmyam* is said to be these *Dasha Maha Vidyas*.

Let us try to understand a little more about each of these 10 Devis. A book about the first *Devi* Sri *Bhadra Kālī* has already been written. Now this is about the second *Sri Tārā Devi*. We will try to know about other Devis in forthcoming books.

*****

# *Śrī Tārā Devī*

*Adiparasakti, Paradevata, Sarva Loka Jaganmata, Sri Devi* creates, preserves and destroys all the worlds. In addition, she performs the tasks of Anugraham and Tirodanam also, in accordance with one of the names in Sri Lalita Sahasranama "*Pancha Krutya Parayana*". As a *Parabrahma Mahishi*, she, after creating lives, has taken many divine incarnations for the state and has been regularly doing sishta maintenance and evil discipline.

*Shākta tantras* talk about 11 nights; *Kālarātri, Veerarātri, Moharātri, Mahārātri, Krodarātri, Gorarātri, Tārārātri, Abalārātri, Tārunarātri, Shivarātri* and *Divyarātri*.

Out of these, *Tārā* originated in *Kālarātri – Narakachaturdashi* (Diwali) day. The New Moon (*Amāvāsya*) relating to this *Kālarātri* is optimal to *Tārā*. If Tuesday, New Moon and *Kālarātri* fall on a same day, the devotees of *Tārā* feel very happy. That is a very rare occasion.

*Shākta tantras* say that *Tārā Devi* herself incarnated as *Rama* and Lord *Shiva* incarnated as *Sita*. *'Rā'* means *Shakti* and *'Mā'* means *Shiva*. Hence *Rāmā* is the *Parabrahma* form of *Shiva-Shakti*. There is story behind this.

*Rāvanā* was a very great devotee of Lord *Shiva*. Once he shaked and lifted the Mount *Kailash*. Scared of this, *Pārvati* hugged *Shiva*. She was also angry that *Shiva* did not condemn *Rāvanā*. Shiva replied that he was enjoying the hug of his consort. *Pārvati* said that she also wanted to enjoy that feeling. Lord *Shiva* said to *Pārvati* "you incarnate as *Rāmā* and I will incarnate as *Sita*. After the killing of demons *Kara* and others, I will hug you and you will enjoy that feeling".

According to Shrimad Bhagavata, during the dissolution of the universe, Brahma was borne from the naval of Lord Vishnu. Brahma wanted to learn Vedas. Vishnu asked him to worship *Tārā* (*Blue Sarasvati*), who will bestow all the 4 Vedas.

*Shākta tantras* affirm that the *mantras* of *Tārā* will confer all the *Siddhis* – the power of writing poems, the knowledge of all the *Shastras*, in-charge of all the wealth, success in debates and so on. Because she relieves her devotees from heavy (*ugra*) hardships, she is called as *Ugratārā*.

Jains worship *Tārā* as *Padmāvati* or *Prabhāvati*. Buddhists worship her in the name of *Tārā* itself. Chinese worship her as *Mahodrā*.

This *Tārāvidyā* is the second one in *Dasha Mahā Vidyās*. The word *Tārā*, according to the root *"Troo Tarana Plavanayo"*, means a tool to jump or float. The Samskruta word *Tārakā* means star. Star floats in the sky and shines and so as *Tārā Devi*. *Tāree* means cruise. A cruise protects its passengers from drowning into the waters of the ocean. So also, *Tārā Devi* protects her devotees from drowning the ocean of sins and enables them to reach the shore. This is very clear from the verse *"Nāveva Sindum Duritātyagniḥ"* (*Durgā Sooktam* – Rig 1-99-1).

*Tāraponishat* mentions *"Tārayateeti Tārāḥ"* – says Chakreshvara in his book called *Shākta Darshanam*. Shree Shankara Narayanan has proved that worshipping *Tārā* goes back to the *Veda* age (The Ten Great Cosmic Powers).

Devas and demons churned the milky ocean for getting the nectar with Mantara mountain as staff and Vāsuki, the snake king, as a rope. At that time first appeared venom called *kālakooda*. Lord Shiva drank it without any hesitation. *Todala tantra* says that the consort of that Lord Shiva, *Tārā Devi*, made the venom still in the neck of Lord Shiva before going down to his stomach.

Her Bhairava is described as *Akṣobhya* in the *Todala tantra* because he drank the deadly *Halāhala* poison without agitation (*a-kṣobha*). It has been mentioned in *Tārā Rahasya* (secret) that *Akṣobhya* resides on the head of that *Tarā Devi* in the form of a snake. Hence the sage (*Rishi*) for the *Tārā mantra*, according to *tantra shastras* is *Akṣobhya* himself.

*Akshobya Rishi Retasyā Brhatīcchanda Eeritam* (*Mantra Chūdāmani*).

It is clear from Ramana Geeta written by *Ramana Maharishi* that this *Vidyā* was followed by the sages in North India and the sage *Vasishta Ganapathi* was the first to introduce this in South India.

*Dakshine Vindyataḥ Dhakteḥ Tārinyā Ādimā Guruḥ* (Chapter 13)

It is seen that our ancestors worshipped *Tāra Devi* for scholarly learning, expertise in speech and poetic knowledge. The experts in Samskrutam in the areas like Kashmir and Mithila worshipped this, *Devi*.

It is clear from the first *Padala* of *Tārā Tantra* that the sage Vasishta reached the world of stars only by worshipping *Tārā Devi*. Similarly, the sages Doorvāsa, Vyāsa, Vālmeeki, Bharadvāj and others also got benefitted by worshipping *Tārā Devi*.

Her most famous center of worship is the temple and the cremation ground of Tarapith in West Bengal, India.

It is understood from the *tantra* called Rudrayāmala that sage Vasishta having heard of the glory of *Tārā Devi*, for the purpose of reaching her, went to Tibet and learnt and followed it properly. Then he reached Guwahati and established the *Ugra Tārā Peet* at the center.

Sri Tārā Devī is the presiding deity of the first story (first chapter) in Sri Devi Mahatmyam. We worship *Sri Maha Tārā Devī, Sri Maha Lakshmi, Sri Maha Saraswathi Swarupaya Chandika Parameswari* through *Sri Devi Mahatmyam*. *Sri Tārā Devī* is depicted here in the philosophical form of the time. In reality She is beyond all time periods.

We have heard of people in many places, mainly in villages scolding ladies using the words, *Tārā Devī*. They would scold the women, if they had a head scarf or were angry.

In Ramayana, Indra incarnated with his *amsam* as Vāli, king of monkeys in Kishkinta. Tārā Devī also incarnated as his spouse and helped the *vanaras* (monkeys) even after the demise of Vāli.

Durga and Tārā Devī are the same Goddesses in Hinduism. She is considered as a ferocious form of Durga/ Parvati, who is the consort of Lord Shiva. Tārā Devī Ma is simultaneously portrayed as the giver, the one who bestows moksha or liberation and destructor, principally of evil forces. However, in most of the interpretations she is portrayed as ferocious and evil. She is the mother of the world and the treasure-house of compassion.

Among the various incarnations of Sriman Narayanan, as explained by Sri Vishnu Bhagavatam, are the most important *Dasavataras* (Ten incarnations). Similarly, *Devi* originating herself in ten different forms to protect the whole of this world called Dasha *Maha Vidyas*. Out of the ten the *Tārā Devī Vidya* is the second one.

*****

# Form(s) of *Śrī Tārā Devī*

Usually meditative hymns (*dhyana shlokas*) about the gods are figurative of the concerned God or Goddess.

The meditation hymn of *Śrī Tārā Devī*;

ॐ घण्टा शिरः, शूल मसिंकराग्रैः सम्बिभ्रतीं चन्द्रकलावतंसाम् ।
प्रमथ्नतीं पादतले पशुंतां भजे मृदा नील सरस्वतीशाम् ॥

*Gaŋtā Śiraḥ Śūla Masimkarāgraiḥ*
*Sambibhrateem Chandrakalāvatamsām* |
*Pramathnateem Pādatale Paśumtām*
*Bhaje Mrudā Neelasarasvateeśām* ||

*Tārā Devi* stands in a posture with her left leg stretched and her right leg slightly folded. **She** shines with short stature, makes fearful and loud noise, wears white skulls on the head, the skin of a tiger as dress, has a skull and a dark lily flower in left hands and knife and scissors in right hands. **She** has entangled locks of hair and a snake called Akshobya on it. With all these **She** sees her devotees with her compassionate eyes.

The commonly known origin of *Tārā Devi* is from the 17th chapter of the *Rudrayāmala*. She is also described as the form of the *Atharva Veda* (*Atharva Veda Śākhinī*).

**Various other forms of *Tārā Devi***;

In the first *Taranga* of the book called *Tārā Bhakti Sudhārnava* written by Narasimha Pandit, her three most famous forms are Ekajaṭā, Ugratara, and Nīlasarasvatī (Neela Saraswati). **She** playfully bestows the art of speech and hence *Neela Sarasvati*. Since **She** bestows happiness and bliss, **She** is *Tārā*. **She** protects from very serious (*ugra*) dangers and hence *Ugra Tārā*.

Kali and Tara are similar in appearance. They both are described as standing upon a supine corpse sometimes identified with Shiva. However, while Kali is described as black, Tara is described as blue. Both wear minimal clothing, however Tara wears a tiger-skin skirt, while Kali wears only a girdle of severed human arms. Both wear a garland of severed human heads. Both have a lolling tongue, and blood oozes from their mouths. Their appearances are so strikingly similar that it is easy to mistake one for the other. Tara is shown standing in the *pratyalidha* stance (in which the left foot is forward). Her Bhairava (consort) is *Akṣobhya*, a form of Shiva who is in the form of a Naga (serpent) coiled around her matted hair. She wears a crown made of 5 skulls connected with plates of bone. Eight forms of Tara are attested in the Māyātantra quoted in the tantric compendium Tantrasāra and the names are Ekajaṭa, Ugra-Tara, Mahogra, Kameshvari-Tara, Chamunda, Nila-Sarasvati (Neelasaraswati or 'Blue Saraswati'), Vajra-Tara and Bhadrakali.

The below picture shows the similarity between Kali and Tara Devis;

The 12th *padala* of *Neelatantra* says that there are eight other names for *Tārā Devi, – "Tārā, Chokra, Mahāgrasa, Vajra, Neela, Saraswathi, Kāmeshvari, Badrakāli"*. In addition, *Tārā Devi* is worshipped in different forms according to various *tantras*.

During the *Maha Pralaya* time – the entire universe is dissolute and destructed. The whole world is like a cemetery. Tārā Devī is the only one who is and hence immortal.

To gain the best results one should chant and worship the Goddess properly, by getting initiated through an appropriate guru. Let us all worship her and exploit her benefits.

## *Śrī Tārā Devī Mantras*

*Tārā Devī* indicates the *kriya shakti* (operative energy) in the breathing of the human beings. Isn't that breath being the one which is non-stop right from the birth? Human beings could do any action only with its help. This breath is praised as *jyeshtar* (elder or senior) or *sreshtar* (famous or high positioned) by *Vedas* (*Ca*-2.5.1.). It is also ordered to worship the air that is in-charge for the breath, as '*Samvargga*' art. The important worshipping method is to breathe thinking that *Tārā Devī* is not different from our breath.

Chanting *Mantras* create vibrations in the human body, which can only be felt by the individuals and cannot be explained in words. For instance, if anyone asks how sugar will taste, it can be said that it is sweet. On the other hand, is someone asks how will be sweet, no one can explain. It has to be enjoyed individually. In the same way the vibrations of the mantras can be only be felt. However, to get complete result, it should be chant with proper pronunciation with clear words entirely focusing on the deity and not as a routine.

### *Srī Tārā Devī Vidyā*

In Samskrutam, in general *Vidyā* means mantra. Vidya means knowledge. Here is a very powerful *Srī Tārā Devī Mantra.*

*Om Asya Shree Tārā* (*Neela Saraswatee*) *Mahā Mantrasya* I
*Akṣobhya Rishiḥ* I *Bruhatee Chandaḥ* I
*Tārā Neela Saraswatee Devatā* I
*Hreem Beejam, Hoom Shaktiḥ Streem Keelakam* I

*Hrām Akila Vāg Roopinyai* *Angushtābhyām Namaḥ* I
*Hreem Akila Vāg Roopinyai* *Darjaneebhyām Namaḥ* I
*Hroom Akila Vāg Roopinyai* *Madhymābhyām Namaḥ* I
*Hraim Akila Vāg Roopinyai* *Anāmikābhyām Namaḥ* I
*Hroum Akila Vāg Roopinyai* *Kanishtikābhyām Namaḥ* I
*Hraha Akila Vāg Roopinyai* *Karatala Karabrushtābhyām Namaḥ* I I

*Hrām Akila Vāg Roopinyai* *Hrudayāya Namaḥ* I
*Hreem Akila Vāg Roopinyai* *Sirase Svāhā* I
*Hroom Akila Vāg Roopinyai* *Shikāyai Vashat* I
*Hraim Akila Vāg Roopinyai* *Kavachāya Hoom* I
*Hroum Akila Vāg Roopinyai* *Netratrayāya Voushat* I
*Hraha Akila Vāg Roopinyai* *Astrāyapaṭ* I

*Bhurbhuvasvarom Iti Dig Bandaḥ* I I

### *Tārā (Neela Saraswatee) Dhyānam*

ॐ घण्टा शिरः शूल मसिंकराग्रैः सम्बिभ्रतीं चन्द्रकलावतंसाम् ।
प्रमथ्नतीं पादतले पशुंतां भजे मृदा नील सरस्वतीशाम् ॥

*Gaṇtā Śiraḥ Śūla Masimkarāgraiḥ*
*Sambibhrateem Chandrakalāvatamsām* |
*Pramathnateem Pādatale Paśumtām*
*Bhaje Mrudā Neelasarasvateeśām* ||

*Lam Pritviyātmikāyai Gandham Samarpayāmi* |
*Ham Ākashātmikāyai Pushpaiḥ Poojayāmi* |
*Yam Vaivātmikāyai Dhoopam Agrāpayāmi* |
*Ram Vahniyātmikāyai Dheepam Dharshayāmi* |
*Vam Amrutātmikāyai Amrutam Mahāneivedhyam Nivedayāmi* |
*Sam Sarvātmikāyai Sarvopachāra Poojām Samarpayāmi* ||

### *Tārā (Neela Saraswatee) Moola mantra*

ॐ ह्रीं स्त्रीं हुं फट् तारी तुत्तारे तुरे (स्वाहा) ।
*Om Hreem Streem Hum Phat Tare Tutthāre Ture* (*Svāhā*) |

This is a very powerful mantra dedicated to Mother Goddess Tara who gives everything. To get the best results, this mantra should be chant every morning between 4 a.m. and 6 a.m., meditate on Goddess Tara with body and mind and pray 108 to 1,008 mantras. If it is chant like this for 48 days or 1 mandala, all the desires will be fulfilled. Sudden fortunes will occur. Devotees will get success in government matters. This mantra has to be chant after getting initiated by an appropriate *guru*.

The *beejāksharam* (root letter) of *Tārā Devī* is –

'*Strīm*' is the root letter (*beejāksharam*) of *Tārā Devī*.
*Strīm* = *St* + *ra* + *īm* – The bright form of *Shakti*, who gives liberation (*moksham*).

The best time to chant the '*Strīm*' mantra is early in the morning, *Ushadkalam*, in *Brahma Muhurtha*, before sunrise (4:30 – 6:00 am). Always chant before meals and not after meals. When this mantra is chant in groups, it gives more powerful results.

**Results of worshipping *Tārā Devi*;**

One can attain enjoyment and liberation with this *mantra*. This is an easy way importantly to get art of speech, poetic ability, appreciation from government, wealth and position. And at last liberation can also be reached with the knowledge of *Vedāntas*. Is it not that her form protects the three worlds by burning the innocence and putting it in the skulls?

*Jātyam Nyasya Kabālake Trijagatām Sandygra Tārā Svayam*

**Prescribed process**:

There are *Ashtotra* and two different *Sahasranāmas* on *Tārā*. Other texts like *Tārā tantra* and *Tārā Upanishad* are also famous on *Tārā Devi*.

One should never tell a lie. Always should talk only the truth. *Vedas* should be practiced. One should absorb equal sound – whether others talk ill or praise of us, unrelated poems or sentences, crying or song, etc. One can easily get the above-mentioned fruits by following the rules and worshipping *Tarā Devi* after getting initiated the same from an appropriate (*guru*) teacher.

*Om*, the *pranava mantra*, is an important letter (*akshara*) in the *mantra* of *Tārā Devi*. Hence, **She** is praised as *Akshara Vidyā* (*Br. Up*.11.8) and *Udgeeta Vidyā* (*cha*. 2.1.1). *Vedas* will not protect a person who does not recognise the *Brahmam*, which is the meaning of *pranava*. Similarly, other *mantras* will not protect the person who does not know *Tārā Mantra*.

Thus, we can see that Tārā Devī's boon is won when man confronts or accepts her and the realities, she dramatically conveys to him. The image of Tārā Devī, in a variety of ways, teaches man that pain, sorrow, decay, death, and destruction cannot be conquered by denying them or explaining them away. For man to realize the fullness of his being, for man to exploit his potential as a human being, he must finally accept this dimension of existence and in return gain Tārā Devī's boon of freedom, the freedom of the mankind to revel in the moment.

However, to gain best results one should chant and worship the Goddess properly.

A few points should thus be kept in mind;

- Chanting should be started with respect, faith and honesty.

- Though one can pray any time during the day, the best time of day is 2 hours before sunrise. This is a time when one's home and neighborhood would mostly be quiet and he can focus and concentrate without distractions.
- One should be fresh without any association with meat, alcohol, etc.
- As one gets into a routine of chanting, he may begin to feel a fine vibration. The mantras start to fill one with strength and courage, which makes him more powerful than the problems he is facing and helps to solve them quickly. Reciting these, hence, brings stability to life and helps people to decide what is right and wrong in their lives.

Ten commandments – Simple Strategy to Summon the Inner Strength. These are not rules, but recommended tips for beginners. By pointing us toward those parts of ourselves that we have rejected, Goddess Tārā Devī inspires us to transform and find inner strength.

1. *Say Oṁ* – Say three *Oms*, with the intention of creating a space of sacredness.

2. Contemplate – Spend a few moments in contemplation, recalling the symbology of Tārā Devī. Because the psyche responds to symbols and images far more readily than to words, it can often be found that invoking this archetypal imagery can open up realms of the personal unconscious that are otherwise unavailable.

3. Summon Tārā Devī – With a notebook and pen close by, close your eyes and summon Tārā Devī inwardly. Ask that the Tārā Devī energy within you be present. Say, "Let me speak to Tārā Devī."

4. Feel Tārā Devī – At this point, drop inside and notice what is invoked in you by this request. Let yourself feel the energy of the Tārā Devī within you. If it feels natural, you might even begin to speak out loud as Tārā Devī.

5. Start a Dialogue – With your dominant hand, write, "Who are you?" or "Tell me about yourself." Then take the pen in your other hand and write an answer. With your dominant hand, write, "What do you want to express?" With the nondominant hand, write your answer.

6. Continue the Dialogue – Continue the dialogue as long as it has energy. You can always come back to it later.

7. Be Aware of Your Breath – When the dialogue feels finished, sit quietly for a few moments, being present with the breath. Notice the spaces between the in-breath and the out-breath, the out-breath and the in-breath. Without holding your breath, see if you can be aware of how the breath arises and subsides from stillness. This open space is the essential nature of the Tārā Devī energy.

8. Thank Tārā Devī – Thank your inner Tārā Devī. Place the picture or image of Tārā Devī where you can see it every day.

9. Do Tārā Devī-like Activities – Take an action that feels connected to the Tārā Devī energy you've accessed. Tārā Devī-like activities might include wild dancing or kicking, speaking a truth you have been afraid to voice, asserting a preference, doing something you never did before.

10. Be Introspective – Pay close attention and note any dreams, insights, or shifts that arise in the next few days.

Tārā Devī is the fast track, often on a bumpy road, to problem solution and spiritual advancement. When called by mantras that carry her vibrations, Tārā Devī responds with a direct power that often leads right through some cherished part of our ego attachments. Her power tools are the Kundalini Shakti (the power of spiritual electricity); the Kriya Shakti, the power to creatively affect the universe; and Iccha Shakti, the power of will that personally compels our physical movements and actions, while in the universe it causes the galaxies to rush away from one another into cosmic night. Although she puts 'effective' before 'gentle', it should also be noted that even in the midst of the sometimes-turbulent effects she produces, Tārā Devī is a repository of great compassion.

Let us all get initiated with these mantras from an appropriate guru and get all the benefits.

Progress is the only in the life, if the grace of Tārā Devī is given to a devotee. Motivation comes naturally in the actions that are done. There is nothing he cannot achieve by her grace. She is interested in removing the sins of her devotees and showing him the right way. She lovingly bestows grace on those who are active, solid, and engaged in worship.

# Śrī Tārā Devī Yantram

It is usual to worship Gods through *mantras*, *tantras* and *yantras*. Worshipping through *mantras* is called *Māntrīka* method. Worshipping through *tantras* is called *Tāntrīca* method. Worshipping through *yantras* is called *Vaidhīka* method. Whichever be the method *mantras* are definitely used to worship. But which is predominant is to be considered.

***Mantras***, the sound form of deities, are integral to *Sādhanas* (worship). *Mantra* pertaining to each God/ Goddess will have different number of letters called *chandas*. Similarly, each God/ Goddess will have various *mantras* – probably each one for a particular purpose/ satiating a desire.

***Tantras*** (Looms or Weavings) refer to numerous and varied scriptures pertaining to any of several esoteric traditions rooted in philosophy of the religion. The religious culture of the *Tantras* is essentially *Tāntric* material can be shown to have been derived from earlier *Vedic* sources. And although *Tantras* of different religions have many similarities from the outside, internally they do have some clear distinctions.

***Yantras*** are some mathematical drawings/ patterns used for worship. There are mathematical construction methods explaining the drawing of *yantras*. *Yantras* mean originally the mechanical, mnemonic and musical contraption in the macrocosm. It is a graphic symbol of the contemplative meditation in the tradition, which was intended to be unified with the Gods/ goddesses. *Yantras* area also called as *cakras*. In a human body itself we have seven cakras thought to be an energy point or node in the subtle body viz., *Mūlādhārā, Swādhiṣṭānā, Maṇipūrakā, Anāhatā, Viśuddha, Agjnā* and *Sahasrārā*.

Usually when consecrating an idol of a deity, it is customary to place the *yantras* of the respective deities beneath the respective idols, duly drawn on copper, five-metals, silver, gold, etc. Properly drawn *yantras* emit micro-vibrations. Those vibrations are not feelable by human beings. However, they have a huge impact on our body, mainly positive impact. It is customary to worship the concerned deity alongwith the respective *chakras/ yantras*.

*Yantras* are great cosmic conductors of energy, an antenna of Nature, a powerful tool for harmony, prosperity, success, good health, yoga and meditation. *Yantras* are usually made out of copper and consist of a series of geometric patterns. The eyes and mind concentrate at the center of the yantra to achieve higher levels of consciousness.

*Śrī Tārā Devī Yantram*

*Tara Yantra* should be installed and worshipped to make oneself free from sins and problems by the blessings of Goddess Tara who is considered as the most compassionate Goddess. Goddess Tara is also popularly known as Tarini means the one who takes us safely across the impermanent ocean of existence (Samsara).

The Goddess *Tara* is the almighty Goddess of Shakti decimates all malevolent, is invulnerable and expels idleness, numbness and haziness from the lover's life.

The word Tara means 'star' and it symbolizes light. Thus, Goddess *Tara* as 'light' is known to guide, carry over, overcome and conquer hurdles for acquiring knowledge, attain powerful speech and acquire the qualities of learning.

Goddess Tara is known to offer the ultimate knowledge and salvation. She is also known as Neel Saraswathi. Her weapons are Khadka, Sword, and pair of scissors. Goddess Tara is one of the oldest deities Who is worshipped in modern times as well.

Also known as the mother creator, Goddess Tara represents the eternal life force that fuels all our lives. Even Great Yogis like Vasishta, Vishwamitra, Ravan, Gorakhnath is known to worship her.

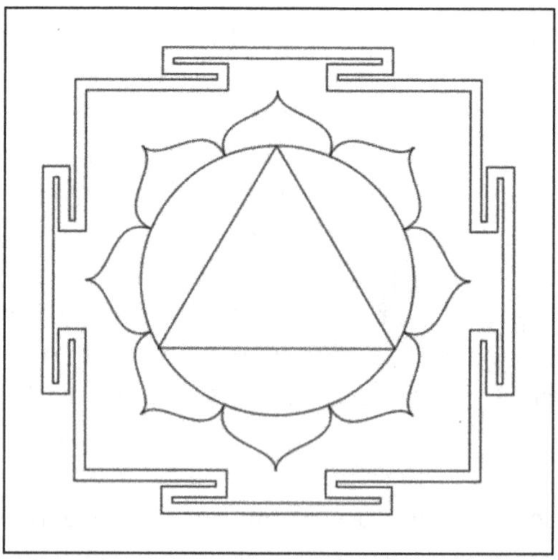

The square is the fundamental format of Tara yantras. There is a significant, well thought out logic behind it. The phenomenal world extends into four directions. These four directions represent the totality of space, and they bind the earth in order.

The square is the simplest and perfect manifestation of the number four, by virtue of the four perfect, equal lines bounding its form. Hence it is visualized as the perfect symbol to denote the terrestrial world. This mundane, physical world is the one which must be transcended by spiritual practice.

The square pattern has four gates, one in each of the cardinal directions. They are known as cosmic doors because it is through them that the aspirant symbolically enters the yantra. They represent the passage from the earthly realm to the 'inner', sacred space of the yantra.

These gates are an initiatory threshold which simultaneously opposes the phenomenal and embraces the noumenal. It is further believed that these gateways themselves are guarded by divine forces which protect the sacred precinct within, from negative and disintegrating forces.

When we look at the Tara Yantra, it can be noticed that certain symbols that are engraved.

Within the *Yantra*, the two circles symbolize birth and death. The petals inside symbolize the lotus blossom, the eight *chakras* and *Tārā Devī* as nurturer. The five layers of the triangle symbolize the five sheaths of the human condition including the physical sheath, the life force, the emotional sheath, wisdom, and bliss. The downward-facing triangle symbolizes the yoni *yantra*, which signifies the Mother Goddess and female regenerative power and the point in the middle of the triangle is the *Bindu*, which symbolizes new life and new birth.

This Tārā Devī Yantra is a very powerful tool that emits the divine power of Goddess Tārā Devī. This radiates occult powers that nullify, the ill-effects of black magic, freeing the native from the bad influences of spirits and ghosts. This yantra also eliminates the harmful effects of malefic planets, especially Saturn, which is usually responsible for misfortunes, sufferings and sorrows in life. This Yantra bestows spiritual power, results in fulfillment of desires, increases in wealth and comforts.

Worshipping this *Tārā Devī Yantra* bestows spiritual power and results in fulfilment of desires, increase in wealth and comforts of life. This *Yantra* is also a remedy against chronic diseases like blood pressure, paralysis and nervous disorders. It also bestows longevity to the person who worship this *Yantra* regularly.

This Yantra can also be used for meditating over Goddess Tārā Devī. It will help in making the person more focused and mentally stable. This yantra will also aid in attaining union with Goddess through geometric visualization. This yantra is a window through which one can align with divine energy. Through resonance, it connects the devotee to the energy present in the macrocosm.

The powers of this Yantra thrives on the reverberation of cosmic energies. Focusing at the center of the Yantra inclines the mind towards the creative force. The centermost point of the yantra is where the energy normally flows from. Also, placing the yantra in the right direction is important. Yantra is the ultimate solution for establishing a vibration of a large amplitude or resonance with the cosmos benefic energies. Thus, the vibration generated gets the devotees in contact with highly elevated energies and entitle, which put the devotee on a spiritual path resonant with the principles of the deity of the Yantra.

*Beeja Mantra* of *Tara Yantram – Oṁ Hreem Streem Hum Phat*

This powerful Yantra resonates with the positive energies of Goddess Tara and blesses the worshipper with prosperity, wisdom and great communication skills.

Yantra Worship Guidelines;

- One has to purify the body and start with a clear and positive mind frame
- Light incense or candle and offer fruits and flowers
- Place Yantra along with the image of the deity of Yantra and the 'Ishta' God
- Take some water mixed with pure water with a mango leaf from any tree and sprinkle the water on self and followed by sprinkling the water on the Yantra.
- Surrender oneself completely in devotion to God and chant 21 times the mantra.
- Take the water with a mango leaf and sprinkle the water on yourself, followed by sprinkling the water on the Yantra
- Close the eyes and concentrate on the deity to bless with wishes. Now with all sincerity, ask the gods of nine planets for whatever the wish is.

- The yantra may be placed in East direction facing West or in the Puja altar in the East direction
- It may be kept it with silk frame or without a frame
- Ritual worship is not compulsory and is up to the worshipper as per the spiritual discipline followed.
- Many have seen its power by meditating on the tip of the Yantra
- Worship it by gazing at it and saying the prayers
- It works by manifesting the prayers through the power of the mantra embedded in it

Let us all get initiated by an appropriate Guru in meditating and worshipping with *Tārā Devī Yantra*, perform the worship properly and regularly, and exploit the benefits.

*****

# *Śrī Tārā Devī Stotram*

*Śrī Nīla Sarasvatī Stotram*

*Śrī Gaṇeśāya Namaḥ* ||

*Ghorarūpe Mahārāve Sarvaśatruvaśaṅkarī* |

*Bhaktebhyo Varade Devi Trāhi Māṃ Śaraṇāgatam* || 1

*Surā'surārcite Devi Siddhagandharvasevite* |

*Jāḍyapāpahare Devi Trāhi Māṃ Śaraṇāgatam* || 2

*Jaṭājūṭasamāyukte Lolajihvānukāriṇī* |

*Drutabuddhikare Devi Trāhi Māṃ Śaraṇāgatam* || 3

*Saumyarūpe Ghorarūpe Caṇḍarūpe Namo'stu Te* |

*Dṛṣṭirūpe Namastubhyaṃ Trāhi Māṃ Śaraṇāgatam* || 4

*Jaḍānāṃ Jaḍatāṃ Hanti Bhaktānāṃ Bhaktavatsale* |

*Mūḍhatāṃ Hara Me Devi Trāhi Māṃ Śaraṇāgatam* || 5

*Hrūṃ Hrūṃkāramaye Devi Balihomapriye Namaḥ* |

*Ugratāre Namastubhyaṃ Trāhi Māṃ Śaraṇāgatam* || 6

*Buddhiṃ Dehi Yaśo Dehi Kavitvaṃ Dehi Dehi Me* |

*Kubuddhiṃ Hara Me Devi Trāhi Māṃ Śaraṇāgatam* || 7

*Indrādideva Sadvṛndavandite Karuṇāmayī* |

*Tāre Tārādhināthāsye Trāhi Māṃ Śaraṇāgatam* || 8

|| *Atha Phalaśrutiḥ* ||

*Aṣṭamyāṃ Ca Caturdaśyāṃ Navamyāṃ Yaḥ Paṭhennaraḥ* |

*Ṣaṇmāsaiḥ Siddhimāpnoti Nā'tra Kāryā Vicāraṇā* || 1

*Mokṣārthī Labhate Mokṣaṃ Dhanārthī Dhanamāpnuyāt* I

*Vidyārthī Labhate Vidyāṃ Tarkavyākaraṇādikām* II 2

*Idaṃ Stotraṃ Paṭhedyastu Satataṃ Śraddhayānvitaḥ* I

*Tasya Śatruḥ Kṣayaṃ Yāti Mahāprajñā Ca Jāyate* II 3

*Pīḍāyāṃ Vāpi Saṅgrāme Japye Dāne Tathā Bhaye* I

*Ya Idaṃ Paṭhati Stotraṃ Śubhaṃ Tasya Na Saṃśayaḥ* II 4

*Stotreṇānena Deveśi Stutvā Devīṃ Sureśvarīm* I

*Sarvakāmamavāpnoti Sarvavidyānidhirbhavet* II 5

*Iti Te Kathitaṃ Divyaṃ Stotraṃ Sārasvatapradam* I

*Asmātparataraṃ Nāsti Stotraṃ Tantre Maheśvarī* II 6

*Iti Bṛhannilatantre Dvitīyapaṭale Tāriṇīnīlasarasvatīstotraṃ Samāptam* II

## श्री नील सरस्वती स्तोत्रम्

श्री गणेशाय नमः ॥

घोररूपे महारावे सर्वशत्रुवशङ्करी ।
भक्तेभ्यो वरदे देवि त्राहि मां शरणागतम् ॥ १

सुराऽसुरार्चिते देवि सिद्धगन्धर्वसेविते ।
जाड्यपापहरे देवि त्राहि मां शरणागतम् ॥ २

जटाजूटसमायुक्ते लोलजिह्वानुकारिणी ।
द्रुतबुद्धिकरे देवि त्राहि मां शरणागतम् ॥ ३

सौम्यरूपे घोररूपे चण्डरूपे नमोऽस्तु ते ।
दृष्टिरूपे नमस्तुभ्यं त्राहि मां शरणागतम् ॥ ४

जडानां जडतां हन्ति भक्तानां भक्तवत्सले ।
मूढतां हर मे देवि त्राहि मां शरणागतम् ॥ ५

हूं हूंकारमये देवि बलिहोमप्रिये नमः ।
उग्रतारे नमस्तुभ्यं त्राहि मां शरणागतम् ॥ ६

बुद्धिं देहि यशो देहि कवित्वं देहि देहि मे ।
कुबुद्धिं हर मे देवि त्राहि मांशरणागतम् ॥ ७

इन्द्रादिदेव सद्वृन्दवन्दिते करुणामयी ।
तारे ताराधिनाथास्ये त्राहि मां शरणागतम् ॥ ८

॥ अथ फलश्रुतिः ॥

अष्टम्यां च चतुर्दश्यां नवम्यां यः पठेन्नरः ।
षण्मासैः सिद्धिमाप्नोति नाऽत्र कार्या विचारणा ॥ १

मोक्षार्थी लभते मोक्षं धनार्थी धनमाप्नुयात् ।
विद्यार्थी लभते विद्यां तर्कव्याकरणादिकाम् ॥ २

इदं स्तोत्रं पठेद्यस्तु सततं श्रद्धयान्वितः ।
तस्य शत्रुः क्षयं याति महाप्रज्ञा च जायते ॥ ३

पीडायां वापि सङ्ग्रामे जप्ये दाने तथा भये ।
य इदं पठति स्तोत्रं शुभं तस्य न संशयः ॥ ४

स्तोत्रेणानेन देवेशि स्तुत्वा देवीं सुरेश्वरीम् ।
सर्वकाममवाप्नोति सर्वविद्यानिधिर्भवेत् ॥ ५

इति ते कथितं दिव्यं स्तोत्रं सारस्वतप्रदम् ।
अस्मात्परतरं नास्ति स्तोत्रं तन्त्रे महेश्वरी ॥ ६

॥ इति बृहन्निलतन्त्रे द्वितीयपटले तारिणीनीलसरस्वतीस्तोत्रं समाप्तम्॥

## *Śrī Tārā Kavacham*

A *Kavacam* is a shield protecting the body. This is a mantra shield to protect our body, mind and soul. We chant *Kavachams* on various lords like, *Skanda Shashti Kavacham* (about Lord Kumara), *Kavacham Kavacham, Sri Devi Kavacham*, etc. Among them, this *Tārā Devī Kavacam* is an infallible weapon to receive the blessings of *Sri Tārā Devī* and to protect one's body and home. This Kavacha can be read daily and the results can be seen by self, how effective it is.

*Śrī Tārā Kavacam*

*Oṃ Śrīgaṇeśāya Namaḥ* I

*Īśvara Uvāca* I

*Koṭitantreṣu Gopyā Hi Vidyātibhayamocinī* I

*Divyaṃ Hi Kavacaṃ Tasyāḥ Śṛṇuṣva Sarvakāmadam* II 1

*Asya Tārākavacasya Akṣobhya Ṛṣiḥ , Triṣṭup Chandaḥ ,*

*Bhagavatī Tārā Devatā , Sarvamantrasiddhisamṛddhaye Jape Viniyogaḥ* I

*Praṇavo Me Śiraḥ Pātu Brahmarūpā Maheśvarī* I

*Lalāṭe Pātu Hrīṃkāro Bījarūpā Maheśvarī* II 2

*Strīṃkāro Vadane Nityaṃ Lajjārūpā Maheśvarī* I

*Hūṁkāraḥ Pātu Hṛdaye Bhavānīrūpaśaktidhṛk* II 3

*Phaṭkāraḥ Pātu Sarvāṅge Sarvasiddhiphalapradā* I

*Kharvā Māṃ Pātu Deveśī Gaṇḍayugme Bhayāpahā* II 4

*Nimnodarī Sadā Skandhayugme Pātu Maheśvarī* I

*Vyāghracarmāvṛtā Kaṭyāṃ Pātu Devī Śivapriyā* II 5

*Pīnonnatastanī Pātu Pārśvayugme Maheśvarī* I

*Raktavartulanetrā Ca Kaṭideśe Sadā'vatu* II 6

*Lalajihvā Sadā Pātu Nābhau Māṃ Bhuvaneśvarī* I

*Karālāsyā Sadā Pātu Liṅge Devī Harapriyā* II 7

*Piṅgograikajaṭā Pātu Jaṅghāyāṃ Vighnanāśinī* ।
*Pretakharparabhṛddevī Jānucakre Maheśvarī* ॥ 8

*Nīlavarṇā Sadā Pātu Jānunī Sarvadā Mama* ।
*Nāgakuṇḍaladhartrī Ca Pātu Pādayuge Tataḥ* ॥ 9

*Nāgahāradharā Devī Sarvāṅgaṃ Pātu Sarvadā* ।
*Nāgakaṅkadharā Devī Pātu Prāntaradeśataḥ* ॥ 10

*Caturbhujā Sadā Pātu Gamane Śatrunāśinī* ।
*Khaḍgahastā Mahādevī Śravaṇe Pātu Sarvadā* ॥ 11

*Nīlāmbaradharā Devī Pātu Māṃ Vighnanāśinī* ।
*Kartrihastā Sadā Pātu Vivāde Śatrumadhyataḥ* ॥ 12

*Brahmarūpadharā Devī Saṅgrāme Pātu Sarvadā* ।
*Nāgakaṅkaṇadhartrī Ca Bhojane Pātu Sarvadā* ॥ 13

*Śavakarṇā Mahādevī Śayane Pātu Sarvadā* ।
*Vīrāsanadharā Devī Nidrāyāṃ Pātu Sarvadā* ॥ 14

*Dhanurbāṇadharā Devī Pātu Māṃ Vighnasaṅkule* ।
*Nāgāñcitakaṭī Pātu Devī Māṃ Sarvakarmasu* ॥ 15

*Chinnamuṇḍadharā Devī Kānane Pātu Sarvadā* ।
*Citāmadhyasthitā Devī Māraṇe Pātu Sarvadā* ॥ 16

*Dvīpicarmadharā Devī Putradāradhanādiṣu* ।
*Alaṅkārānvitā Devī Pātu Māṃ Haravallabhā* ॥ 17

*Rakṣa Rakṣa Nadīkuñje Hūṃ Hūṃ Phaṭ Susamanvite* ।
*Bījarūpā Mahādevī Parvate Pātu Sarvadā* ॥ 18

*Maṇibhṛdvajriṇī Devī Mahāpratisare Tathā* ।
*Rakṣa Rakṣa Sadā Hūṃ Hūṃ Oṃ Hrīṃ Svāhā Maheśvarī* ॥ 19

*Puṣpaketurajārheti Kānane Pātu Sarvadā* ।
*Oṃ Hrīṃ Vajrapuṣpaṃ Huṃ Phaṭ Prāntare Sarvakāmadā* ॥ 20

*Oṃ Puṣpe Puṣpe Mahāpuṣpe Pātu Putrānmaheśvarī* I
*Hūṃ Svāhā Śaktisaṃyuktā Dārān Rakṣatu Sarvadā* II 21

*Oṃ Āṃ Hūṃ Svāhā Maheśānī Pātu Dyūte Harapriyā* I
*Oṃ Hrīṃ Sarvavighnotsāriṇī Devī Vighnānmāṃ Sadā'vatu* II 22

*Oṃ Pavitravajrabhūme Huṃphaṭsvāhā Samanvitā* I
*Pūrikā Pātu Māṃ Devī Sarvavighnavināśinī* II 23

*Oṃ Āḥ Surekhe Vajrarekhe Huṃphaṭsvāhāsamanvitā* I
*Pātāle Pātu Sā Devī Lākinī Nāmasaṃjñikā* II 24

*Hrīṃkārī Pātu Māṃ Pūrve Śaktirūpā Maheśvarī* I
*Strīṃkārī Pātu Deveśī Vadhūrūpā Maheśvarī* II 25

*Hūṃsvarūpā Mahādevī Pātu Māṃ Krodharūpiṇī* I
*Phaṭsvarūpā Mahāmāyā Uttare Pātu Sarvadā* II 26

*Paścime Pātu Māṃ Devī Phaṭsvarūpā Harapriyā* I
*Madhye Māṃ Pātu Deveśī Hūṃsvarūpā Nagātmajā* II 27

*Nīlavarṇā Sadā Pātu Sarvato Vāgbhavā Sadā* I
*Bhavānī Pātu Bhavane Sarvaiśvaryapradāyinī* II 28

*Vidyādānaratā Devī Vaktre Nīlasarasvatī* I
*Śāstre Vāde Ca Saṅgrāme Jale Ca Viṣame Girau* II 29

*Bhīmarūpā Sadā Pātu Śmaśāne Bhayanāśinī* I
*Bhūtapretālaye Ghore Durgamā Śrīghanā'vatu* II 30

*Pātu Nityaṃ Maheśānī Sarvatra Śivadūtikā* I
*Kavacasya Māhātmyaṃ Nāhaṃ Varṣaśatairapi* II 31

*Śaknomi Gadituṃ Devi Bhavettasya Phalaṃ Ca Yat* I
*Putradāreṣu Bandhūnāṃ Sarvadeśe Ca Sarvadā* II 32

*Na Vidyate Bhayaṃ Tasya Nṛpapūjyo Bhavecca Saḥ* I
*Śucirbhūtvā'śucirvāpi Kavacaṃ Sarvakāmadam* II 33

*Prapaṭhan Vā Smaranmartyo Duḥkhaśokavivarjitaḥ* I

*Sarvaśāstre Maheśāni Kavirāḍ Bhavati Dhruvam* II 34

*Sarvavāgīśvaro Martyo Lokavaśyo Dhaneśvaraḥ* I

*Raṇe Dyūte Vivāde Ca Jayastatra Bhaved Dhruvam* II 35

*Putrapautānvito Martyo Vilāsī Sarvayoṣitām* I

*Śatravo Dāsatāṃ Yānti Sarveṣāṃ Vallabhaḥ Sadā* II 36

*Garvī Kharvī Bhavatyeva Vādī Skhalati Darśanāt* I

*Mṛtyuśca Vaśyatāṃ Yāti Dāsāstasyāvanībhujaḥ* II 37

*Prasaṅgātkathitaṃ Sarvaṃ Kavacaṃ Sarvakāmadam* I

*Prapaṭhanvā Smaranmartyaḥ Śāpānugrahaṇe Kṣamaḥ* II 38

*Ānandavṛndasindhūnāmadhipaḥ Kavirāḍ Bhavet* I

*Sarvavāgiśvaro Martyo Lokavaśyaḥ Sadā Sukhī* II 39

*Guroḥ Prasādamāsādya Vidyāṃ Prāpya Sugopitām* I

*Tatrāpi Kavacaṃ Devi Durlabhaṃ Bhuvanatraye* II 40

*Gururdevo Haraḥ Sākṣāttatpatnī Tu Harapriyā* I

*Abhedena Bhajedyastu Tasya Siddhidūrataḥ* II 41

*Mantrācārā Maheśāni Kathitāḥ Pūrvavatpriye* I

*Nābhau Jyotistathā Raktaṃ Hṛdayopari Cintayet* II 42

*Aiśvaryaṃ Sukavitvaṃ Ca Mahāvāgiśvaro Nṛpaḥ* I

*Nityaṃ Tasya Maheśāni Mahilāsaṅgamaṃ Caret* II 43

*Pañcācārarato Martyaḥ Siddho Bhavati Nānyathā* I

*Śaktiyukto Bhavenmartyaḥ Siddho Bhavati Nānyathā* II 44

*Brahmā Viṣṇuśca Rudraśca Ye Devāsuramānuṣāḥ* I

*Taṃ Dṛṣṭvā Sādhakaṃ Devi Lajjāyuktā Bhavanti Te* II 45

*Svarge Martye Ca Pātāle Ye Devāḥ Siddhidāyakāḥ* I

*Praśaṃsanti Sadā Devi Taṃ Dṛṣṭvā Sādhakottamam* II 46

*Vighnātmakāśca Ye Devāḥ Svarge Martye Rasātale* I

*Praśaṃsanti Sadā Sarve Taṃ Dṛṣṭvā Sādhakottamam* II 47

*Iti Te Kathitaṃ Devi Mayā Samyakprakīrtitam* I

*Bhuktimuktikaraṃ Sākṣātkalpavṛkṣasvarūpakam* II 48

*Āsādyādyaguruṃ Prasādya Ya Idaṃ Kalpadrumālambanaṃ*

*Mohenāpi Madena Cāpi Rahito Jāḍyena Vā Yujyate* I

*Siddho'sau Bhuvi Sarvaduḥkhavipadāṃ Pāraṃ Prayātyantake*

*Mitraṃ Tasya Nṛpāśca Devi Vipado Naśyanti Tasyāśu Ca* II 49

*Tadgātraṃ Prāpya Śastrāṇi Brahmāstrādīni Vai Bhuvi* I

*Tasya Gehe Sthirā Lakṣmīrvāṇī Vaktre Vased Dhruvam* II 50

*Idaṃ Kavacamajñātvā Tārāṃ Yo Bhajate Naraḥ* I

*Alpāyurnirddhano Mūrkho Bhavatyeva Na Saṃśayaḥ* II 51

*Likhitvā Dhārayedyastu Kaṇṭhe Vā Mastake Bhuje* I

*Tasya Sarvārthasiddhiḥ Syādyadyanmanasi Vartate* II 52

*Gorocanākuṅkumena Raktacandanakena Vā* I

*Yāvakairvā Maheśāni Likhenmantraṃ Samāhitaḥ* II 53

*Aṣṭamyāṃ Maṅgaladine Caturddaśyāmathāpi Vā* I

*Sandhyāyāṃ Devadeveśi Likhedyantraṃ Samāhitaḥ* II 54

*Maghāyāṃ Śravaṇe Vāpi Revatyāṃ Vā Viśeṣataḥ* I

*Siṃharāśau Gate Candre Karkaṭasthe Divākare* II 55

*Mīnarāśau Gurau Yāte Vṛścikasthe Śanaiścare* I

*Likhitvā Dhārayedyastu Uttarābhimukho Bhavet* II 56

*Śmaśāne Prāntare Vāpi Śūnyāgāre Viśeṣataḥ* I

*Niśāyāṃ Vā Likhenmantraṃ Tasya Siddhiracañcalā* II 57

*Bhūrjapatre Likhenmantraṃ Guruṇā Ca Maheśvari* I

*Dhyānadhāraṇayogena Dhārayedyastu Bhaktitaḥ* II 58

*Acirattasya Siddhiḥ Syānnātra Kāryā Vicāraṇā* II 59

II *Iti Śrīrudrayāmale Tantre Ugratārākavacaṃ Sampūrṇam* II

## श्री तारा कवचम्

ॐ श्री गणेशाय नमः ।

ईश्वर उवाच ।

कोटितन्त्रेषु गोप्या हि विद्यातिभयमोचिनी ।
दिव्यं हि कवचं तस्याः शृणुष्व सर्वकामदम् ॥ १

अस्य ताराकवचस्य अक्षोभ्य ऋषिः , त्रिष्टुप् छन्दः ,
भगवती तारा देवता , सर्वमन्त्रसिद्धिसमृद्धये जपे विनियोगः ।

प्रणवो मे शिरः पातु ब्रह्मरूपा महेश्वरी ।
ललाटे पातु ह्रींकारो बीजरूपा महेश्वरी ॥ २

स्त्रींकारो वदने नित्यं लज्जारूपा महेश्वरी ।
हूँकारः पातु हृदये भवानीरूपशक्तिधृक् ॥ ३

फट्कारः पातु सर्वाङ्गे सर्वसिद्धिफलप्रदा ।
खर्वा मां पातु देवेशी गण्डयुग्मे भयापहा ॥ ४

निम्नोदरी सदा स्कन्धयुग्मे पातु महेश्वरी ।
व्याघ्रचर्मावृता कट्यां पातु देवी शिवप्रिया ॥ ५

पीनोन्नतस्तनी पातु पार्श्वयुग्मे महेश्वरी ।
रक्तवर्तुलनेत्रा च कटिदेशे सदाऽवतु ॥ ६

ललजिह्वा सदा पातु नाभौ मां भुवनेश्वरी ।
करालास्या सदा पातु लिङ्गे देवी हरप्रिया ॥ ७

पिङ्गोग्रैकजटा पातु जङ्घायां विघ्ननाशिनी ।
प्रेतखर्परभृद्देवी जानुचक्रे महेश्वरी ॥ ८

नीलवर्णा सदा पातु जानुनी सर्वदा मम ।
नागकुण्डलधर्त्री च पातु पादयुगे ततः ॥ ९

नागहारधरा देवी सर्वाङ्गं पातु सर्वदा ।
नागकङ्कधरा देवी पातु प्रान्तरदेशतः ॥ १०

चतुर्भुजा सदा पातु गमने शत्रुनाशिनी ।
खड्गहस्ता महादेवी श्रवणे पातु सर्वदा ॥ ११

नीलाम्बरधरा देवी पातु मां विघ्ननाशिनी ।
कर्त्रिहस्ता सदा पातु विवादे शत्रुमध्यतः ॥ १२

ब्रह्मरूपधरा देवी सङ्ग्रामे पातु सर्वदा ।
नागकङ्कणधर्त्री च भोजने पातु सर्वदा ॥ १३

शवकर्णा महादेवी शयने पातु सर्वदा ।
वीरासनधरा देवी निद्रायां पातु सर्वदा ॥ १४

धनुर्बाणधरा देवी पातु मां विघ्नसङ्कुले ।
नागाञ्चितकटी पातु देवी मां सर्वकर्मसु ॥ १५

छिन्नमुण्डधरा देवी कानने पातु सर्वदा ।
चितामध्यस्थिता देवी मारणे पातु सर्वदा ॥ १६

द्वीपिचर्मधरा देवी पुत्रदारधनादिषु ।
अलङ्कारान्विता देवी पातु मां हरवल्लभा ॥ १७

रक्ष रक्ष नदीकुञ्जे हूं हूं फट् सुसमन्विते ।
बीजरूपा महादेवी पर्वते पातु सर्वदा ॥ १८

मणिभृद्वज्रिणी देवी महाप्रतिसरे तथा ।
रक्ष रक्ष सदा हूं हूं ॐ ह्रीं स्वाहा महेश्वरी ॥ १९

पुष्पकेतुरजार्हेति कानने पातु सर्वदा ।
ॐ ह्रीं वज्रपुष्पं हुं फट् प्रान्तरे सर्वकामदा ॥ २०

ॐ पुष्पे पुष्पे महापुष्पे पातु पुत्रान्महेश्वरी ।
हूं स्वाहा शक्तिसंयुक्ता दारान् रक्षतु सर्वदा ॥ २१

ॐ आं हूं स्वाहा महेशानी पातु द्यूते हरप्रिया ।
ॐ ह्रीं सर्वविघ्नोत्सारिणी देवी विघ्नान्मां सदाऽवतु ॥ २२

ॐ पवित्रवज्रभूमे हुंफट्स्वाहा समन्विता ।
पूरिका पातु मां देवी सर्वविघ्नविनाशिनी॥ २३

ॐ आः सुरेखे वज्ररेखे हुंफट्स्वाहासमन्विता ।
पाताले पातु सा देवी लाकिनी नामसंज्ञिका ॥ २४

ह्रींकारी पातु मां पूर्वे शक्तिरूपा महेश्वरी ।
स्त्रींकारी पातु देवेशी वधूरूपा महेश्वरी ॥ २५

हूंस्वरूपा महादेवी पातु मां क्रोधरूपिणी ।
फट्स्वरूपा महामाया उत्तरे पातु सर्वदा ॥ २६

पश्चिमे पातु मां देवी फट्स्वरूपा हरप्रिया ।
मध्ये मां पातु देवेशी हूंस्वरूपा नगात्मजा ॥ २७

नीलवर्णा सदा पातु सर्वतो वाग्भवा सदा ।
भवानी पातु भवने सर्वैश्वर्यप्रदायिनी ॥ २८

विद्यादानरता देवी वक्त्रे नीलसरस्वती ।
शास्त्रे वादे च सङ्ग्रामे जले च विषमे गिरौ ॥ २९

भीमरूपा सदा पातु श्मशाने भयनाशिनी ।
भूतप्रेतालये घोरे दुर्गमा श्रीघनाऽवतु ॥ ३०

पातु नित्यं महेशानी सर्वत्र शिवदूतिका ।
कवचस्य माहात्म्यं नाहं वर्षशतैरपि ॥ ३१

शक्नोमि गदितुं देवि भवेत्तस्य फलं च यत् ।
पुत्रदारेषु बन्धूनांसर्वदेशे च सर्वदा ॥ ३२

न विद्यते भयं तस्य नृपपूज्यो भवेच्च सः ।
शुचिर्भूत्वाऽशुचिर्वापि कवचं सर्वकामदम् ॥ ३३

प्रपठन् वा स्मरन्मर्त्यो दुःखशोकविवर्जितः ।
सर्वशास्त्रे महेशानि कविराड् भवति ध्रुवम् ॥ ३४

सर्ववागीश्वरो मर्त्यो लोकवश्यो धनेश्वरः ।
रणे द्यूते विवादे च जयस्तत्र भवेद् ध्रुवम् ॥ ३५

पुत्रपौतान्वितो मर्त्यो विलासी सर्वयोषिताम् ।
शत्रवो दासतां यान्ति सर्वेषां वल्लभः सदा ॥ ३६

गर्वी खर्वी भवत्येव वादी स्खलति दर्शनात् ।
मृत्युश्च वश्यतां याति दासास्तस्यावनीभुजः ॥ ३७

प्रसङ्गात्कथितं सर्वं कवचं सर्वकामदम् ।
प्रपठन्वा स्मरन्मर्त्यः शापानुग्रहणे क्षमः ॥ ३८

आनन्दवृन्दसिन्धूनामधिपः कविराड् भवेत् ।
सर्ववागिश्वरो मर्त्यो लोकवश्यः सदा सुखी ॥ ३९

गुरोः प्रसादमासाद्य विद्यां प्राप्य सुगोपिताम् ।
तत्रापि कवचं देवि दुर्लभं भुवनत्रये ॥ ४०

गुरुर्देवो हरः साक्षात्तत्पत्नी तु हरप्रिया ।
अभेदेन भजेद्यस्तु तस्य सिद्धिदूरतः ॥ ४१

मन्त्राचारा महेशानि कथिताः पूर्ववत्प्रिये ।
नाभौ ज्योतिस्तथा रक्तं हृदयोपरि चिन्तयेत् ॥ ४२

ऐश्वर्यं सुकवित्वं च महावागिश्वरो नृपः ।
नित्यं तस्य महेशानि महिलासङ्गमं चरेत्॥ ४३

पञ्चाचाररतो मर्त्यः सिद्धो भवति नान्यथा ।
शक्तियुक्तो भवेन्मर्त्यः सिद्धो भवति नान्यथा ॥ ४४

ब्रह्मा विष्णुश्च रुद्रश्च ये देवासुरमानुषाः ।
तं दृष्ट्वा साधकं देवि लज्जायुक्ता भवन्ति ते ॥ ४५

स्वर्गे मर्त्ये च पाताले ये देवाः सिद्धिदायकाः ।
प्रशंसन्ति सदा देवि तं दृष्ट्वा साधकोत्तमम् ॥ ४६

विघ्नात्मकाश्च ये देवाः स्वर्गे मर्त्ये रसातले ।
प्रशंसन्ति सदा सर्वे तं दृष्ट्वा साधकोत्तमम् ॥ ४७

इति ते कथितं देवि मया सम्यक्प्रकीर्तितम् ।
भुक्तिमुक्तिकरं साक्षात्कल्पवृक्षस्वरूपकम् ॥ ४८

आसाद्याद्यगुरुं प्रसाद्य य इदं कल्पद्रुमालम्बनं
मोहेनापि मदेन चापि रहितो जाड्येन वा युज्यते ।

सिद्धोऽसौ भुवि सर्वदुःखविपदां पारं प्रयात्यन्तके
मित्रं तस्य नृपाश्च देवि विपदो नश्यन्ति तस्याशु च ॥ ४९

तद्गात्रं प्राप्य शस्त्राणि ब्रह्मास्त्रादीनि वै भुवि ।
तस्य गेहे स्थिरा लक्ष्मीर्वाणी वक्त्रे वसेद् ध्रुवम् ॥ ५०

इदं कवचमज्ञात्वा तारां यो भजते नरः ।
अल्पायुर्निर्द्धनो मूर्खो भवत्येव न संशयः ॥ ५१

लिखित्वा धारयेद्यस्तु कण्ठे वा मस्तके भुजे ।
तस्य सर्वार्थसिद्धिः स्याद्यद्यन्मनसि वर्तते ॥ ५२

गोरोचनाकुङ्कुमेन रक्तचन्दनकेन वा ।
यावकैर्वा महेशानि लिखेन्मन्त्रं समाहितः ॥ ५३

अष्टम्यां मङ्गलदिने चतुर्दश्यामथापि वा ।
सन्ध्यायां देवदेवेशि लिखेद्यन्त्रं समाहितः ॥ ५४

मघायां श्रवणे वापि रेवत्यां वा विशेषतः ।
सिंहराशौ गते चन्द्रे कर्कटस्थे दिवाकरे ॥ ५५

मीनराशौ गुरौ याते वृश्चिकस्थे शनैश्चरे ।
लिखित्वा धारयेद्यस्तु उत्तराभिमुखो भवेत् ॥ ५६

श्मशाने प्रान्तरे वापि शून्यागारे विशेषतः ।
निशायां वा लिखेन्मन्त्रं तस्य सिद्धिरचञ्चला ॥ ५७

भूर्जपत्रे लिखेन्मन्त्रं गुरुणा च महेश्वरि ।
ध्यानधारणयोगेन
धारयेद्यस्तु भक्तितः ॥ ५८

अचिरात्तस्य सिद्धिः
स्यान्नात्र कार्या विचारणा ॥
५९

॥ इति श्रीरुद्रयामले तन्त्रे
उग्रताराकवचं सम्पूर्णम् ॥

*****

## *Śrī Tārā Karpūra Stotram*

*Oṃ Namastāriṇyai* I

*Śrīkaṇṭhāmṛtakeśavarṇaghaṭitaṃ Candrārdhacūḍojjvalaṃ*
*Bījaṃ Yatparamaṃ Guṇatrayamayaṃ Kāmapradaṃ Muktidam* I
*Mātaḥ! Śaṅkaravallabhe! Pratidinaṃ Dhyāyanti Ye Ye Sadā*
*Te Te Yānti Cidātmakaṃ Hariharabrahmādisāmyaṃ Mudā* II 1

*Vyomārṇaṃ Vāmanetrānvitamanalayutaṃ Bindu Candrārdha Yuktaṃ*
*Bījaṃ Te Guhyametattribhuvanajanani! Trikṣaṇe Ye Japanti* I
*Teṣāṃ Vaktrāravinde Viharati Madhurā Gadyapadyāvalī Gī-*
*Rmātaścandrārdhacūḍe! Sakalabhayahare! Siddhibhājāṃ Narāṇām* II 2

*Śukrārṇaṃ Pūtanāsthaṃ Kalitaśaśikalābindubhūṣaṃ Savahni*
*Bhrājadvāmākṣiyuktaṃ Janani! Tava Vadhūbījametajjapanti* I
*Te Te Lolekṣaṇānāṃ Vigalitarasanāpīnavakṣojavāsaḥ*
*Keśānāṃ Cittamāśu Smaraharamahile! Mohayanti Prakāmam* II3

*Īśānaṃ Vāmakarṇollasitaśaśikalābinduyuktaṃ Suguhyaṃ*
*"bījaṃ Mātastvadīyāṃ Yadi Japati Jano Vāramekaṃ Jaḍātmā* I
*Cañcatpañcāśadugragrathitanaraśiromālikākrāntakaṇṭhe!*
*Mātaḥ Śailendraputri! Tribhuvanamapi Sa Kṣobhayatyeva Śīghram* II 4

*Paścādastraṃ Tadanyatpuraharamahile! Bījamatyantaguhyaṃ*
*Bhālodyatpañcamudre Prakaṭavikaṭadaṃṣṭrogravakrāravinde* I
*Nityaṃ Ye Bhāvayanti Pratidinamamale! Ghorarūpāṭṭahāse!*
*Te Nūnaṃ Bhāvayanti Trijagadaghahare! Cakravadviśvametat* II5

*Māyāstrīkūrcabījairnavatapanaharitsārdhacandrāṃśuvarṇe*
*Mātarnīlākhyametattava Manumaniśaṃ Ye Prakāmaṃ Japanti* I

*Vitte Vitteśatulyāḥ Śukagurusadṛśāstarkakāvyāgamādau*

*Te Te Nīlāmbudālīruciruciratano! Kāmatulyā Bhavanti* || 6

*Bhavānyebhirbijairhimagirisute! Cāstrasahitai-*

*Rnigūḍhaṃ Ye Mātarmanumanujapantyekajaṭile!* |

*Triyāmānāthārdhapravilasitabhāle! Trinayane!*

*Gṛhe Teṣāṃ Nityaṃ Nivasati Sadā Sindhutanayā* || 7

*Amībhirbījaiste Praṇavasahitaiḥ Śailatanaye!*

*Nijasvānte Cāstraṃ Parijapati Pañcākṣaramiti* | (*5 Aksharas – Oṃ Hrīṃ Strīṃ Hūṃ Phaṭ*)

*Sa Sākṣātte Nyāsī Sa Tu Puraharo'sau Muraharaḥ*

*Sa Dhātā Yaṃ Mukto Bhavati Hi Cidānandarasike!* || 8

*Śavāsīnāṃ Kaṇṭhākalitanṛkaroṭīṃ Karalasat*

*Kapālāsiśyāmotpalarucirakartrīṃ Trinayanām* |

*Navāmbhodaśyāmānvikaṭaradabhīmānpṛthukucāṃ*

*Sadaiva Tvāṃ Dhyāyan Janani! Ca Jaḍo Vākpatisamaḥ* || 9

*Taṭe Nadyāḥ Sindhorgiriśirasi Mālūragahane*

*Śmaśāne Goṣṭhe Vā Giriśabhavane Śūnyasadane* |

*Haviṣyāśī Lakṣaṃ Prajapati Vaśī Bhāvanaparaḥ*

*Sa Sarvajño Vāgmī Bhavati Sughanāpīnajaghane!* || 10

*Mudā Mātaḥ Śuddhodakaruciragandhāḍhyasalilaiḥ*

*Svayambhūpuṣpasrakkulatanubhagacchālana Jalaiḥ* |

*Śive! Tvāṃ Sandhyāyan Haramahiṣi! Santarpayati Yaḥ*

*Sa Daivastrīvṛndaṃ Vaśayati Sa Vidyādharapatiḥ* || 11

*Japāpuṣpairbilvairmarubakulavargaiśca Kusumaiḥ*

*Sugandhaiḥ Karpūrairagarusahitairdhūpanikaraiḥ* |

*Pradīpairujjvālairghṛtaracitanaivedyanikarai-*

*Stavārcāṃ Yaḥ Kuryātsa Bhavati Kavīndraḥ Kṣititale* || 12

*Sadūrvābhiḥ Padmaistrimadhulalitaiḥ Śrīphaladalai-*

*Rghṛtairgavyai Raktaiḥ Sukulabhagaliṅgāmṛtarasaiḥ* I

*Trikoṇe Kuṇḍe Yo Hutavahamakhe Homavidhinā*

*Juhoti Tvāṃ Mātaḥ! Sa Bhavati Kavīndraḥ Kṣitipatiḥ* II 13

*Niśīthe Kalyāṇi! Pramuditamanā Yaḥ Pitṛvane*

*Baliṃ Te Meṣādyaiḥ Sanaramahiṣairvā Paricaret* I

*Sa Rājānaṃ Kṣipraṃ Vaśayati Mṛgākṣīsamudayaṃ*

*Trilokīṃ Vā Bhūmau Sa Bhavati Janaḥ Satkavivaraḥ* II 14

*Mahāpūjāṃ Mātastava Vitanute Yastu Madhunā*

*Tathā Māṃsairmatsyairvividhanavamudrādibhirapi* I

*Varastrībhiḥ Sārdhaṃ Nidhuvanavinodena Mudito*

*Niśīthe Saṃsārātsa Bhavati Vimuktaḥ Paśubhayāt* II 15

*Trikoṇe Pīṭhe Tvāṃ Varanidhuvanāsaṅgahṛdayāṃ*

*Mahākālenodyatpulakanicayāṃ Smeravadanām* I

*Svayaṃ Naktaṃ Kāntāratirasasamāsaktahṛdayo*

*Manuṣyo Yo Dhyāyedbhavati Śivatulyaḥ Sa Dharaṇau* II 16

*Samuttuṅgāpīnastanajaghanarājatkulavadhū-*

*Vyavāyavyāsakto Japati Tava Bhakto Yadi Manum* I

*Galadvāsaḥkeśo Janani! Manujo Medinitale*

*Sa Siddhīśaḥ Śaktyā Jayati Suciraṃ Sarvasujanam* II 17

*Bhavāni ! Śrīrmātarnijagalitavīryāptacikura-*

*Matha Premṇā Labdhvā Vacanabhuvaneśīyutamanum* I

*Samuccārya Kṣoṇītanayadivase Pretasadane*

*Sa Dīrghāyurvāgmī Bhavati Śatahomātkṣititale* II 18

*Ajasraṃ Yo Mantraṃ Tava Japati Bhūmīdharasute*

*Vicintyāgre Mātaḥ! Kusumalalitaṃ Mārabhavanam* I

*Dharaṇyāṃ Kandarpapratimatanubhūtaḥ Sa Sakalā-*

*Nnijeṣṭānāpnoti Praviśati Mudā Tāriṇipadam* II 19

*Tamograste Candre Yadi Japati Lokastava Manuṃ*
*Navamyāṃ Vā Mātardharaṇidharakanye! Vitanute* I
*Tathā Sūrye Pṛthvīvalayatilakaḥ Kāvyataṭinī*
*Payodhiḥ Siddhīnāṃ Bhavati Bhavanaṃ Sarvaviditaḥ* II 20

*Sadā Pādāmbhoje Bhajatu Hṛdayaṃ Bhṛṅga Iva Me*
*Sadā Pāṇidvandvaṃ Paricaratu Karṇastava Kathām* I
*Śṛṇotu Tvakīrtiṃ Haramahiṣi! Gīrgāyatu Sadā*
*Sadā Dṛṣṭirbhūyādbhavadanucarālokanaparā* II 21

*Kadākāle Śaileśvaratanubhave! Pādayugalaṃ*
*Mudā Drakṣye Brahmapramukhavibudhānāṃ Pariṇutam* I
*Kṛpāpārāvāre! Bhavajananabhītaikaśaraṇe!*
*Śaraṇye! Kāruṇyaṃ Mayi Vitara Dīne Bhagavati!* II 22

*Sadaiva Stotraṃ Yaḥ Paṭhati Muditaḥ Sādhakavaro*
*Na Dāridryaṃ Tasya Prabhavati Kadācitkṣititale* I
*Trivargo Haste Syājjagadakhilametacca Vaśagaṃ*
*Ciraṃ Jīvannante Janani! Labhate Mokṣapadavīm* II 23

*Idaṃ Stotraṃ Mātaḥ Prapaṭhati Divārātrimaniśaṃ*
*Sa Sarvajño Yogīśvaranikaracūḍāmaṇisame!* I
*Jaḍo'pi Tvadrūpaṃ Japati Yadi Sañcitya Manasā*
*Tvadagre Bhūyoccaiḥ Kṣitipatisamānaḥ Kṣititale* II 24

*Mahāpuṇyaṃ Dhanyaṃ Sakalapuruṣārthaikanilayaṃ*
*Yaśasyaṃ Cāyuṣyaṃ Satatabhavatāpāpahamidam* I
*Rahasyaṃ Prākāśyanna Hi Khalu Kadācitpaśujane*
*Paṭhetpūjākāle Janani! Labhate Mokṣapadavīm* II 25

II *Iti Śrīphetkārītantre Tārākarpūrastotram* II

# तारा कर्पूर स्तोत्रम्

ॐ नमस्तारिण्यै ।

श्रीकण्ठामृतकेशवर्णघटितं चन्द्रार्धचूडोज्ज्वलं
बीजं यत्परमं गुणत्रयमयं कामप्रदं मुक्तिदम् ।
मातः ! शङ्करवल्लभे ! प्रतिदिनं ध्यायन्ति ये ये सदा
ते ते यान्ति चिदात्मकं हरिहरब्रह्मादिसाम्यं मुदा ॥ १

व्योमार्णं वामनेत्रान्वितमनलयुतं बिन्दुचन्द्रार्धयुक्तं
बीजं ते गुह्यमेतत्त्रिभुवनजननि ! त्रिक्षणे ये जपन्ति ।
तेषां वक्त्रारविन्दे विहरति मधुरा गद्यपद्यावली गी-
र्मातश्चन्द्रार्धचूडे ! सकलभयहरे ! सिद्धिभाजां नराणाम् ॥ २

शुक्रार्णं पूतनास्थं कलितशशिकलाबिन्दुभूषं सवह्नि
भ्राजद्वामाक्षियुक्तं जननि ! तव वधूबीजमेतज्जपन्ति ।
ते ते लोलेक्षणानां विगलितरसनापीनवक्षोजवासः
केशानां चित्तमाशु स्मरहरमहिले ! मोहयन्ति प्रकामम् ॥ ३

ईशानं वामकर्णोल्लसितशशिकलाबिन्दुयुक्तं सुगुह्यं
बीजं मातस्त्वदीयं यदि जपति जनो वारमेकं जडात्मा ।
चञ्चत्पञ्चाशदुग्रग्रथितनरशिरोमालिकाक्रान्तकण्ठे
मातः शैलेन्द्रपुत्रि ! त्रिभुवनमपि स क्षोभयत्येव शीघ्रम् ॥ ४

पश्चादस्त्रं तदन्यत्पुरहरमहिले! बीजमत्यन्तगुह्यं
भालोद्यत्पञ्चमुद्रे प्रकटविकटदंष्ट्रोग्रवक्त्रारविन्दे ।
नित्यं ये भावयन्ति प्रतिदिनममले! घोररूपाट्टहासे!
ते नूनं भावयन्ति त्रिजगदघहरे ! चक्रवद्विश्वमेतत् ॥ ५

मायास्त्रीकूर्चबीजैर्नवतपनहरित्सार्धचन्द्रांशुवर्णे
मातर्नीलाख्यमेतत्तव मनुमनिशं येप्रकामं जपन्ति ।
वित्ते वित्तेशतुल्याः शुकगुरुसदृशास्तर्ककाव्यागमादौ
ते ते नीलाम्बुदालीरुचिरुचिरतनो! कामतुल्या भवन्ति ॥ ६

भवान्येभिर्बिजैर्हिमगिरिसुते ! चास्त्रसहितै-
र्निगूढं ये मातर्मनुमनुजपन्त्येकजटिले!।

त्रियामानाथार्धप्रविलसितभाले ! त्रिनयने!
गृहे तेषां नित्यं निवसति सदा सिन्धुतनया ॥ ७

अमीभिर्बीजैस्ते प्रणवसहितैः शैलतनये
निजस्वान्ते चास्त्रं परिजपति पञ्चाक्षरमिति। (5 *Aksharas* ॐ ह्रीं स्त्रीं हूं फट्)
स साक्षात्ते न्यासी स तु पुरहरोऽसौ मुरहरः
स धाता यं मुक्तो भवति हि चिदानन्दरसिके ! ॥ ८

शवासीनां कण्ठाकलितनृकरोटीं करलसत्
कपालासिश्यामोत्पलरुचिरकर्त्रीं त्रिनयनाम् ।
नवाम्भोदश्यामान्विकटरदभीमान्पृथुकुचां
सदैव त्वां ध्यायन् जननि! च जडो वाक्पतिसमः ॥ ९

तटे नद्याः सिन्धोर्गिरिशिरसि मालूरगहने
श्मशाने गोष्ठे वा गिरिशभवने शून्यसदने ।
हविष्याशी लक्षं प्रजपति वशी भावनपरः
स सर्वज्ञो वाग्मी भवति सुघनापीनजघने! ॥ १०

मुदा मातः शुद्धोदकरुचिरगन्धाढ्यसलिलैः
स्वयम्भूपुष्पस्रक्कुलतनुभगच्छालन जलैः ।
शिवे ! त्वां सन्ध्यायन् हरमहिषि ! सन्तर्पयति यः
स दैवस्त्रीवृन्दं वशयति स विद्याधरपतिः ॥ ११

जपापुष्पैर्बिल्वैर्मरुबकुलवर्गैश्च कुसुमैः
सुगन्धैः कर्पूरैरगरुसहितैर्धूपनिकरैः ।
प्रदीपैरुज्ज्वालैर्घृतरचितनैवेद्यनिकरै-
स्तवार्चां यः कुर्यात्स भवति कवीन्द्रः क्षितितले ॥ १२

सदूर्वाभिः पद्मैस्त्रिमधुललितैः श्रीफलदलै-
र्घृतैर्गव्यै रक्तैः सुकुलभगलिङ्गामृतरसैः ।
त्रिकोणे कुण्डे यो हुतवहमखे होमविधिना
जुहोति त्वां मातः! स भवति कवीन्द्रः क्षितिपतिः ॥ १३

निशीथे कल्याणि ! प्रमुदितमना यः पितृवने
बलिं ते मेषाद्यैः सनरमहिषैर्वा परिचरेत् ।

स राजानं क्षिप्रं वशयति मृगाक्षीसमुदयं
त्रिलोकीं वा भूमौ स भवति जनः सत्कविवरः ॥ १४

महापूजां मातस्तव वितनुते यस्तु मधुना
तथा मांसैर्मत्स्यैर्विविधनवमुद्रादिभिरपि ।
वरस्त्रीभिः सार्धं निधुवनविनोदेन मुदितो
निशीथे संसारात्स भवति विमुक्तः पशुभयात् ॥ १५

त्रिकोणे पीठे त्वां वरनिधुवनासङ्गहृदयां
महाकालेनोद्यत्पुलकनिचयां स्मेरवदनाम् ।
स्वयं नक्तं कान्तारतिरससमासक्तहृदयो
मनुष्यो यो ध्यायेद्भवति शिवतुल्यः स धरणौ ॥ १६

समुत्तुङ्गापीनस्तनजघनराजत्कुलवधू
व्यवायव्यासक्तो जपति तव भक्तो यदि मनुम् ।
गलद्वासःकेशो जननि ! मनुजो मेदिनितले
स सिद्धीशः शक्त्या जयति सुचिरं सर्वसुजनम् ॥ १७

भवानि ! श्रीमार्तर्निजगलितवीर्याप्तचिकुर-
मथ प्रेम्णा लब्ध्वा वचनभुवनेशीयुतमनुम् ।
समुच्चार्य क्षोणीतनयदिवसे प्रेतसदने
स दीर्घायुर्वाग्मी भवति शतहोमात्क्षितितले ॥ १८

अजस्रं यो मन्त्रं तव जपति भूमीधरसुते
विचिन्त्याग्रे मातः ! कुसुमललितं मारभवनम् ।
धरण्यां कन्दर्पप्रतिमतनुभूतः स सकला-
न्निजेष्टानाप्नोति प्रविशति मुदा तारिणिपदम् ॥ १९

तमोग्रस्ते चन्द्रे यदि जपति लोकस्तव मनुं
नवम्यां वा मातर्धरणिधरकन्ये ! वितनुते ।
तथा सूर्ये पृथ्वीवलयतिलकः काव्यतटिनी
पयोधिः सिद्धीनां भवति भवनं सर्वविदितः ॥ २०

सदा पादाम्भोजे भजतु हृदयं भृङ्ग इव मे
सदा पाणिद्वन्द्वं परिचरतु कर्णस्तव कथाम् ।

शृणोतु त्वकीर्तिं हरमहिषि ! गीर्गायतु सदा
सदा दृष्टिर्भूयाद्भवदनुचरालोकनपरा ॥ २१

कदाकाले शैलेश्वरतनुभवे ! पादयुगलं
मुदा द्रक्ष्ये ब्रह्मप्रमुखविबुधानां परिणुतम् ।
कृपापारावारे ! भवजननभीतैकशरणे!
शरण्ये ! कारुण्यं मयि वितर दीने भगवति ! ॥ २२

सदैव स्तोत्रं यः पठति मुदितः साधकवरो
न दारिद्र्यं तस्य प्रभवति कदाचित्क्षितितले ।
त्रिवर्गो हस्ते स्याज्जगदखिलमेतच्च वशगं
चिरं जीवन्नन्ते जननि ! लभते मोक्षपदवीम् ॥ २३

इदं स्तोत्रं मातः प्रपठति दिवारात्रिमनिशं
स सर्वज्ञो योगीश्वरनिकरचूडामणिसमे ।
जडोऽपि त्वद्रूपं जपति यदि सञ्चित्य मनसा
त्वदग्रे भूयोच्चैः क्षितिपतिसमानः क्षितितले ॥ २४

महापुण्यं धन्यं सकलपुरुषार्थैकनिलयं
यशस्यं चायुष्यं सततभवतापापहमिदम् ।
रहस्यं प्राकाश्यन्न हि खलु कदाचित्पशुजने
पठेत्पूजाकाले जननि ! लभते मोक्षपदवीम् ॥ २५

॥ इति श्रीफेत्कारीतन्त्रे ताराकर्पूरस्तोत्रम् ॥

*****

## *Śrīmad Ugratārā Hrudaya Stotram*

*Śrīmadugratārāhṛdayastotram*

*Śrīśiva Uvāca* I

*Śṛṇu Pārvati Bhadraṃ Te Lokānāṃ Hitakārakam* I
*Kathyate Sarvadā Gopyaṃ Tārāhṛdayamuttamam* II 1

*Śrīpārvatyuvāca* I

*Stotraṃ Kathaṃ Samutpannaṃ Kṛtaṃ Kena Purā Prabho* I
*Kathyatāṃ Sarvasadvṛttaṃ(Sad Vṛttaṃ) Kṛpāṃ Kṛtvā Mamopari* II2

*Śrīśiva Uvāca* I

*Raṇe Devāsure Pūrvaṃ Kṛtamindreṇa Supriye* I
*Duṣṭaśatruvināśārthaṃ Balavṛddhiyaśaskaram* II 3

*Viniyogaḥ* I

*Oṃ Asya Śrīmadugratārāhṛdayastotramantrasya Śrībhairavaṛṣiḥ* I
*Anuṣṭup Chandaḥ* I *Śrīmadugratārādevatā* I *Strīṃ Bījam* I
*Hūṃ Śaktiḥ* I *Namaḥ Kīlakam* I
*Sakalaśatruvināśārthe Pāṭhe Viniyoga* II

II *Ṛṣyādinyāsaḥ* II

*Śrībhairava Ṛṣaye Namaḥ Śirasi* I
*Anuṣṭupchandase Namaḥ Mukhe* I
*Śrīmadugratārā Devatāyai Namaḥ Hṛdi* I
*Strīṃ Bījāya Namaḥ Guhye* I

*Hūṃ Śaktaye Namaḥ Nābhau* ।

*Namaḥ Kīlakāya Namaḥ Pādayoḥ* ।

*Sakala Śatruvināśārthe Pāṭhe Viniyogāya Namaḥ Añjalau* ॥

॥ *Atha Karanyāsaḥ* ॥

*Oṃ Strīṃ Aṅguṣṭhābhyāṃ Namaḥ* ।

*Oṃ Hrīṃ Tarjanībhyāṃ Namaḥ* ।

*Oṃ Hūṃ Madhyamābhyāṃ Namaḥ* ।

*Oṃ Trīṃ Anāmikābhyāṃ Namaḥ* ।

*Oṃ Aiṃ Kaniṣṭhikābhyāṃ Namaḥ* ।

*Oṃ Haṃsaḥ Karatala Karapṛṣṭhābhyāṃ Namaḥ* ॥

॥ *Atha Hṛdayādiṣaḍaṅganyāsaḥ* ॥

*Oṃ Strīṃ Hṛdayāya Namaḥ* ।
*Oṃ Hrīṃ Śirase Svāhā* ।

*Oṃ Hūṃ Śikhāyai Vaṣaṭ* ।
*Oṃ Trīṃ Kavacāya Hum* ।

*Oṃ Aiṃ Netratrayāya Vauṣaṭ* ।
*Oṃ Haṃsaḥ Astrāya Phaṭ* ॥

॥ *Atha Dhyānam* ॥

*Oṃ Dhyāyetkoṭidivākaradyutinibhāṃ Bālenduyukśekharāṃ*
*Raktāṅgīṃ Rasanāṃ Suraktavasanāṃ Pūrṇendubimbānanām* ।
*Pāśaṃ Kartrīmahāṅkuśādi Dadhatīṃ Dorbhiścaturbhiryutāṃ*
*Nānābhūṣaṇabhūṣitāṃ Bhagavatīṃ Tārāṃ Jagattāriṇīm* ॥ 4

*Evaṃ Dhyātvā Śubhāṃ Tārāṃ Tatasyu Hṛdayaṃ Paṭhet* ॥

*Tāriṇī Tattvaniṣṭhānāṃ Sarvatattvaprakāśikā* ।
*Rāmābhinnā Parāśaktiḥ Śatrunāśaṃ Karotu Me* ॥ 5

*Sarvadā Śatrusaṃrambhe Tārā Me Kurutāṃ Jayam* I
*Strīṃ Trīṃsvarūpiṇī Devī Triṣu Lokeṣu Viśrutā* II 6

*Tava Snehānmayākhyātaṃ Na Paiśunyaṃ Prakāśyatām* I
*Śṛṇudevi Tava Snehāt Tārānāmāni Tattvataḥ* II 7

*Varṇayiṣyāmi Guptāni Durlabhāni Jagattraye* I
*Tāriṇī Taralā Tārā Trirūpā Taraṇiprabhā* II 8

*Sattvarūpā Mahāsādhvī Sarvasajjanapālikā* I
*Ramaṇīyā Rajorūpā Jagatsṛṣṭikarī Parā* II 9

*Tamorūpā Mahāmāyā Ghorarāvāṃ Bhayānakā* I
*Kālarūpā Kālikākhyā Jagadvidhvaṃsakārikā* II 10

*Tattvajñānaparānandā Tattvajñānapradā'naghā* I
*Raktāṅgī Raktavastrā Ca Raktamālāpraśobhitā* II 11

*Siddhilakṣmīśca Brahmāṇī Mahākālī Mahālayā* I
*Nāmānyetāni Ye Marttyāḥ Sarvadaikāgramānasāḥ* II 12

*Prapaṭhanti Priye Teṣāṃ Kiṅkaratvaṃ Karomyaham* I
*Tārāṃ Tāraparāṃ Devīṃ Tārakeśvarapūjitām* II 13

*Tāriṇīṃ Bhavapāthodherugratārāṃ Bhajāmyaham* I
*Strīṃ Hrīṃ Hūṃ Trīṃ Phaṭ Mantreṇa Jalaṃ Japtvā'bhiṣecayet* II 14

*Sarve Rogāḥ Praṇaśyanti Satyaṃ Satyaṃ Vadāmyaham* I
*Trīṃ Svāhāntairmahāmantraiścandanaṃ Sādhayettataḥ* II 15

*Tilakaṃ Kurute Prajño Loko Vaśyo Bhavetpriye* I
*Strīṃ Hrīṃ Trīṃ Svāhā Mantreṇa Śmaśānaṃ Bhasmamantrayet* II16

*Śatrorgṛhe Pratikṣiptvā Śatrormṛtyurbhaviṣyati* ।
*Hrīṃ Hūṃ Strīṃ Phaḍantamantraiḥ Puṣpaṃ Saṃśodhya Saptadhā* ॥

*Uccāṭanaṃ Nayatyāśu Ripūṇāṃ Naiva Saṃśayaḥ* ।
*Strīṃ Trīṃ Hrīṃ Mantravaryeṇa Akṣatāścābhimantritāḥ* ॥ 18

*Tatpratikṣepamātreṇa Śīghramāyāti Māninī* ।
*(Haṃsaḥ Oṃ Hrīṃ Strīṃ Hūṃ Haṃsaḥ)*
*Iti Mantreṇa Japtena Śodhitaṃ Kajjalaṃ Priye* ॥ 19

*Tasyaiva Tilakaṃ Kṛtvā Jaganmohaṃ Samācaret* ।
*Tārāyāḥ Hṛdayaṃ Devi Sarvapāpapraṇāśanam* ॥ 20

*Vājapeyādiyajñānāṃ Koṭikoṭiguṇottaram* ।
*Gaṅgādisarvatīrthānāṃ Phalaṃ Koṭiguṇātsmṛtam* ॥ 21

*Mahāduḥkhe Mahāroge Saṅkaṭe Prāṇasaṃśaye* ।
*Mahābhaye Mahāghore Paṭhetstotraṃ Mahottamam* ॥ 22

*Satyaṃ Satyaṃ Mayoktaṃ Te Pārvati Prāṇavallabhe* ।
*Gopanīyaṃ Prayatnena Na Prakāśyamidaṃ Kvacit* ॥ 23

॥ *Iti Śrībhairavītantre Śivapārvatīsamvāde Śrīmadugratārāhṛdayaṃ Sampūrṇam* ॥

## श्रीमदुग्रताराहृदयस्तोत्रम्

श्रीशिव उवाच ।

शृणु पार्वति भद्रं ते लोकानां हितकारकम् ।
कथ्यते सर्वदा गोप्यं ताराहृदयमुत्तमम् ॥ १

श्रीपार्वत्युवाच ।

स्तोत्रं कथं समुत्पन्नं कृतं केन पुरा प्रभो।
कथ्यतां सर्वसद्वृत्तं(सद् वृत्तं) कृपां कृत्वा ममोपरि॥ २

श्रीशिव उवाच।

रणे देवासुरे पूर्वं कृतमिन्द्रेण सुप्रिये।
दुष्टशत्रुविनाशार्थं बलवृद्धियशस्करम्॥ ३

विनियोगः।

ॐ अस्य श्रीमदुग्रताराहृदयस्तोत्रमन्त्रस्य श्रीभैरवऋषिः।
अनुष्टुप् छन्दः। श्रीमदुग्रतारादेवता। स्त्रीं बीजम्। हूं शक्तिः।
नमः कीलकम्। सकलशत्रुविनाशार्थे पाठे विनियोग॥

॥ ऋष्यादिन्यासः॥

श्रीभैरव ऋषये नमः शिरसि। अनुष्टुप्छन्दसे नमः मुखे।
श्रीमदुग्रतारा देवतायै नमः हृदि। स्त्रीं बीजाय नमः गुह्ये।
हूं शक्तये नमः नाभौ। नमः कीलकाय नमः पादयोः।
सकल शत्रुविनाशार्थे पाठे विनियोगाय नमः अञ्जलौ॥

॥ अथ करन्यासः॥

ॐ स्त्रीं अङ्गुष्ठाभ्यां नमः। ॐ ह्रीं तर्जनीभ्यां नमः।
ॐ हूं मध्यमाभ्यां नमः। ॐ त्रीं अनामिकाभ्यां नमः।
ॐ ऐं कनिष्ठिकाभ्यां नमः। ॐ हंसः करतल करपृष्ठाभ्यां नमः॥

॥ अथ हृदयादिषडङ्गन्यासः॥

ॐ स्त्रीं हृदयाय नमः। ॐ ह्रीं शिरसे स्वाहा।
ॐ हूं शिखायै वषट्। ॐ त्रीं कवचाय हुम्।
ॐ ऐं नेत्रत्रयाय वौषट्। ॐ हंसः अस्त्राय फट्॥

॥ अथ ध्यानम्॥

ॐ ध्यायेत्कोटिदिवाकरद्युतिनिभां बालेन्दुयुक्शेखरां
रक्ताङ्गीं रसनां सुरक्तवसनां पूर्णेन्दुबिम्बाननाम्।

पाशं कर्त्रीमहाङ्कुशादि दधतीं दोर्भिश्चतुर्भिर्युतां
नानाभूषणभूषितां भगवतीं तारां जगत्तारिणीम् ॥ ४

एवं ध्यात्वा शुभां तारां ततस्तु हृदयं पठेत् ॥

तारिणी तत्त्वनिष्ठानां सर्वतत्त्वप्रकाशिका ।
रामाभिन्ना पराशक्तिः शत्रुनाशं करोतु मे ॥ ५

सर्वदा शत्रुसंरम्भे तारा मे कुरुतां जयम् ।
स्त्रीं त्रींस्वरूपिणी देवी त्रिषु लोकेषु विश्रुता ॥ ६

तव स्नेहान्मयाख्यातं न पैशुन्यं प्रकाश्यताम् ।
शृणुदेवि तव स्नेहात् तारानामानि तत्त्वतः ॥ ७

वर्णयिष्यामि गुप्तानि दुर्लभानि जगत्त्रये ।
तारिणी तरला तारा त्रिरूपा तरणिप्रभा ॥ ८

सत्त्वरूपा महासाध्वी सर्वसज्जनपालिका ।
रमणीया रजोरूपा जगत्सृष्टिकरी परा ॥ ९

तमोरूपा महामाया घोररावां भयानका ।
कालरूपा कालिकाख्या जगद्विध्वंसकारिका ॥ १०

तत्त्वज्ञानपरानन्दा तत्त्वज्ञानप्रदाऽनघा ।
रक्ताङ्गी रक्तवस्त्रा च रक्तमालाप्रशोभिता ॥ ११

सिद्धिलक्ष्मीश्च ब्रह्माणी महाकाली महालया ।
नामान्येतानि ये मर्त्याः सर्वदैकाग्रमानसाः ॥ १२

प्रपठन्ति प्रिये तेषां किङ्करत्वं करोम्यहम् ।
तारां तारपरां देवीं तारकेश्वरपूजिताम् ॥ १३

तारिणीं भवपाथोधेरुग्रतारां भजाम्यहम् ।
स्त्रीं ह्रीं हूं त्रीं फट् मन्त्रेण जलं जप्त्वाऽभिषेचयेत् ॥ १४

सर्वे रोगाः प्रणश्यन्ति सत्यं सत्यं वदाम्यहम् ।
त्रीं स्वाहान्तैर्महामन्त्रैश्चन्दनं साधयेत्ततः ॥ १५

तिलकं कुरुते प्राज्ञो लोको वश्यो भवेत्प्रिये ।
स्त्रीं ह्लीं त्रीं स्वाहा मन्त्रेण श्मशानं भस्ममन्त्रयेत् ॥ १६

शत्रोर्गृहे प्रतिक्षिप्त्वा शत्रोर्मृत्युर्भविष्यति ।
ह्लीं हूं स्त्रीं फडन्तमन्त्रैः पुष्पं संशोध्य सप्तधा ॥ १७

उच्चाटनं नयत्याशु रिपूणां नैव संशयः ।
स्त्रीं त्रीं ह्लीं मन्त्रवर्येण अक्षताश्चाभिमन्त्रिताः ॥ १८

तत्प्रतिक्षेपमात्रेण शीघ्रमायाति मानिनी । (हंसः ॐ ह्लीं स्त्रीं हूं हंसः)
इति मन्त्रेण जप्तेन शोधितं कज्जलं प्रिये ॥ १९

तस्यैव तिलकं कृत्वा जगन्मोहं समाचरेत् ।
तारायाः हृदयं देवि सर्वपापप्रणाशनम् ॥ २०

वाजपेयादियज्ञानां कोटिकोटिगुणोत्तरम् ।
गङ्गादिसर्वतीर्थानां फलं कोटिगुणात्स्मृतम् ॥ २१

महादुःखे महारोगे सङ्कटे प्राणसंशये ।
महाभये महाघोरे पठेत्स्तोत्रं महोत्तमम् ॥ २२

सत्यं सत्यं मयोक्तं ते पार्वति प्राणवल्लभे।
गोपनीयं प्रयत्नेन न प्रकाश्यमिदं क्वचित् ॥ २३

॥ इति श्रीभैरवीतन्त्रे शिवपार्वतीसम्वादे श्रीमदुग्रताराहृदयं सम्पूर्णम् ॥

*****

## Tāropanishat Atharvavedīya

*Oṃ Atha Tāropaniṣat ।*

*Oṃ Tatsat । Brahmatadrūpaṃ Prakṛtiparaṃ Gagananābhaṃ Tatparaṃ Paramaṃ Mahatsatyaṃ Tadahaṃ Hrīṅkāraṃ Raktavarṇaṃ Mannābhistrīṅkāraṃ Piṅgalābhaṃ Hūṅkāraṃ Maddhṛdayarūpaṃ Viśadābhaṃ Bhūmaṇḍalaṃ Phaṭkāraṃ Dhūmravarṇaṃ Madkhaḍgamoṅkārajvaladrūpaṃ Me Mastakaṃ Vedā Maddhastāścandrārkānalā Mannetre Divānaktaṃ Matpādau Sandhye Matkarṇau Saṃvatsaro Madudaraṃ Śvetakṛṣṇapakṣau Matpārśvai Vārartavo Madaṅgulyo Vidyā Mannakhāḥ Pāvako Manmukhaṃ Mahī Madrasanā Dyaurmanmukhaṃ Gaganaṃ Madhṛdayaṃ Bhaktirmama Carmarasaṃ Madrudhiraṃ Cānnaṃ Vāsāṃsi Phalāni Nirahaṅkārā Asthīni Sudhāmanmajjā Sthāvarāṇi Madromāṇi Pātālādilokau Matkucau Brahmanādaṃ Mannāḍyo Jñānaṃ Manmanaḥ Kṣamābuddhiḥ Śūnyaṃ Madāsanaṃ Nakṣatrāṇi Madbhūṣaṇāni ॥*

*Etadvairāṭakaṃ Madvapuḥ । Madujvalaṃ Sattvaṃ Bindusvarūpaṃ Mahoṅkārasvarūpajjyotirmayaṃ Viddhi । Śira Ugratārāṃ Mahogrāṃ Nīlāṃ Ghanāmekajaṭāṃ Mahāmāyāṃ Prakṛtiṃ Māṃ Viditvā Yo Japati Madrūpāṇi Yo Vetti Manmantraṃ Yo Japati Madrūpakalpitāṃ Yo Japati Madrūpāṇi Yo Vetti Manmantraṃ Yo Japati Madrūpakalpatāṃ Yo Japati Bhagaṃ Bhajati Nirvikalpaḥ Sādhakaḥ Sadā Madrūpo Bhavati ॥*

*Sarvāṇi Karmāṇi Sādhyāni (Kṛtvā) Nirbhayo Bhavati । Gurunnatvā Vastrabhūṣaṇāni Dattvā Imānupaniṣadvidyāṃ Prāpya Māṃ Yo Japati Sa Jīvanmukto Bhavati ॥*

*Ityatharvavede Saubhāgyakāṇḍe Tāropaniṣatsamāptā ॥*

तारोपनिषत् अथर्ववेदीय

ॐ अथ तारोपनिषत् ।

ॐ तत्सत् । ब्रह्मतद्रूपं प्रकृतिपरं गगननाभं तत्परं परमं महत्सत्यं तदहं ह्रीङ्कारं रक्तवर्णं मन्नाभिस्त्रीङ्कारं

पिङ्गलाभं हूङ्कारं मद्धृदयरूपं विशदाभं भूमण्डलं
फट्कारं धूम्रवर्णं मद्खड्गमोङ्कारज्वलद्रूपं मे मस्तकं
वेदा मद्धस्ताश्चन्द्रार्कानला मन्नेत्रे दिवानक्तं मत्पादौ सन्ध्ये
मत्कर्णौ संवत्सरो मदुदरं श्वेतकृष्णपक्षौ मत्पार्श्वे
वारर्तवो मदङ्गुल्यो विद्या मन्नखाः पावको मन्मुखं मही मद्रसना
द्यौर्मन्मुखं गगनं मधृदयं भक्तिर्मम चर्मरसं मद्रुधिरं
चान्नं वासांसि फलानि निरहङ्कारा अस्थीनि सुधामन्मज्जा स्थावराणि
मद्रोमाणि पातालादिलोकौ मत्कुचौ ब्रह्मनादं मन्नाड्यो ज्ञानं मन्मनः
क्षमाबुद्धिः शून्यं मदासनं नक्षत्राणि मद्भूषणानि ॥

एतद्वैराटकं मद्वपुः । मदुज्वलं सत्त्वं बिन्दुस्वरूपं
महोङ्कारस्वरूपज्ज्योतिर्मयं विद्धि । शिर उग्रतारां महोग्रां नीलां
घनामेकजटां महामायां प्रकृतिं मां विदित्वा यो जपति मद्रूपाणि
यो वेत्ति मन्मन्त्रं यो जपति मद्रूपकल्पितां यो जपति मद्रूपाणि यो
वेत्ति मन्मन्त्रं यो जपति मद्रूपकल्पतां यो जपति भगं भजति
निर्विकल्पः साधकः सदा मद्रूपो भवति ॥

सर्वाणि कर्माणि साध्यानि (कृत्वा) निर्भयो भवति । गुरुन्नत्वा
वस्त्रभूषणानि दत्त्वा इमानुपनिषद्विद्यां प्राप्य मां यो जपति स
जीवन्मुक्तो भवति ॥

इत्यथर्ववेदे सौभाग्यकाण्डे तारोपनिषत्समाप्ता ॥

*****

## *Śrī Tārā Devī Aṣṭakam*

*Tārāstotram Athavā Tārāṣṭakaṃ Athavā Śrīnīlasarasvatīstotram*

*Śrīgaṇeśāya Namaḥ* I

*Mātarnīlasarasvati Praṇamatāṃ Saubhāgyasampatprade*
*Pratyālīḍhapadasthite Śavahṛdi Smerānanāmbhoruhe* I
*Phullendīvaralocane Trinayane Kartrīkapālotpale Khaḍgaṃ*
*Cādadhatī Tvameva Śaraṇaṃ Tvāmīśvarīmāśraye* I I 1

*Vācāmīśvari Bhaktikalpalatike Sarvārthasiddhiśvari*
*Gadyaprākṛtapadyajātaracanāsarvārthasiddhiprade* I
*Nīlendīvaralocanatrayayute Kāruṇyavārānnidhe*
*Saubhāgyāmṛtavardhanena Kṛpayāsiñca Tvamasmādṛśam* I I 2

*Kharve Garvasamūhapūritatano Sarpādiveṣojvale*
*Vyāghratvakparivītasundarakaṭivyādhūtaghaṇṭāṅkite* I
*Sadyaḥkṛttagaladrajaḥparimilanmuṇḍadvayīmūrddhaja-*
*Granthiśreṇinṛmuṇḍadāmalalite Bhīme Bhayaṃ Nāśaya* I I 3

*Māyānaṅgavikārarūpalalanābindvarddhacandrāmbike*
*Huṃphaṭkāramayi Tvameva Śaraṇaṃ Mantrātmike Mādṛśaḥ* I
*Mūrtiste Janani Tridhāmaghaṭitā Sthūlātisūkṣmā*
*Parā Vedānāṃ Nahi Gocarā Kathamapi Prājñairnutāmāśraye* I I 4

*Tvatpādāmbujasevayā Sukṛtino Gacchanti Sāyujyatāṃ*
*Tasyāḥ Śrīparameśvaratrinayanabrahmādisāmyātmanaḥ* I
*Saṃsārāmbudhimajjane Paṭutanurdevendramukhyāsurān*
*Mātaste Padasevane Hi Vimukhān Kiṃ Mandadhīḥ Sevate* I I 5

*Mātastvatpadapaṅkajadvayarajomudrāṅkakoṭīriṇaste*
*Devā Jayasaṅgare Vijayino Niḥśaṅkamaṅke Gatāḥ* I
*Devo'haṃ Bhuvane Na Me Sama Iti Sparddhāṃ Vahantaḥ Pare*
*Tattulyāṃ Niyataṃ Yathā Śaśiravī Nāśaṃ Vrajanti Svayam* I I 6

*Tvannāmasmaraṇātpalāyanaparāndraṣṭuṃ Ca Śaktā Na Te*
*Bhūtapretapiśācarākṣasagaṇā Yakṣaśca Nāgādhipāḥ* I
*Daityā Dānavapuṅgavāśca Khacarā Vyāghrādikā Jantavo*
*Ḍākinyaḥ Kupitāntakaśca Manujān Mātaḥ Kṣaṇaṃ Bhūtale* II 7

*Lakṣmīḥ Siddhigaṇaśca Pādukamukhāḥ Siddhāstathā Vairiṇāṃ*
*Stambhaścāpi Varāṅgane Gajaghaṭāstambhastathā Mohanam* I
*Mātastvatpadasevayā Khalu Nṛṇāṃ Siddhyanti Te Te Guṇāḥ*
*Klāntaḥ Kāntamanobhavo'tra Bhavati Kṣudro'pi Vācaspatiḥ* II 8

*Tārāṣṭakamidaṃ Puṇyaṃ Bhaktimān Yaḥ Paṭhennaraḥ* I
*Prātarmadhyāhnakāle Ca Sāyāhne Niyataḥ Śuciḥ* II 9

*Labhate Kavitāṃ Vidyāṃ Sarvaśāstrārthavidbhavet*
*Lakṣmīmanaśvarāṃ Prāpya Bhuktvā Bhogānyathepsitān* I
*Kīrtiṃ Kāntiṃ Ca Nairujyaṃ Prāpyānte Mokṣamāpnuyāt* II 10

II *Iti Śrīnīlatantre Tārāstotraṃ Athavā Tārāṣṭakaṃ Sampūrṇam* II

श्रीताराष्टकम्

मातर्नीलसरस्वति प्रणमतां सौभाग्यसम्पत्प्रदे
प्रत्यालीढपदस्थिते शिवहृदि स्मेराननाम्भोरूहे ।
फुल्लेन्दीवरलोचनत्रययुते कर्त्री कपालोत्पले खंगे
चादधती त्वमेव शरणं त्वामीश्वरीमाश्रये ॥ 1

वाचामीश्वरि भक्तकल्पलतिके सर्वार्थसिद्धिप्रदे
गद्यप्राकृतपद्यजातरचना सर्वत्र सिद्धिप्रदे ।
नीलन्दीवरलोचनत्रययुते कारुण्यवारां निधे
सौभाग्यामृतवर्षणेन कृपया सिंच त्वमस्मादृशम् ॥ 2

शर्वे गर्वसमूहपूरिततनो सर्पादिवेषोज्ज्वले
व्याघ्रत्वक्परिवीतसुंदरकटिव्याधूतघंटांकिते ।

सद्य: कृत्तगलद्रज: परिमिलन्मुंडद्वयीमूर्धज
ग्रन्थिश्रेणिनृमुंडदामललिते भीमे भयं नाशय।। 3

मायानंगविकारुपललनाबिन्द्वर्धचन्द्रात्मिके
हुंफट्कारमयि त्वमेव शरणं मंत्रात्मिके माद्रश: ।
मूर्तिस्ते जननि त्रिधामघटिता स्थूलाऽतिसूक्ष्मा
परा वेदानां न हि गोचरा कथमपि प्राप्तां तु तामाश्रये ।।4

यत्पादाम्बुजसेवया सुयमिनो गच्छन्ति सायुज्यतां
तस्य स्त्री परमेश्वरी त्रिनयनब्रह्मादिसाम्यात्मन: ।
संसारांबुधिमज्जने पटुतनून्देवेन्द्रमुख्यान्सुरान्मात
स्त्वपदसेवने हि विमुखो यो मंदधी: सेवते ।।5

मातस्त्वत्पदपंकजद्वयरजोमुद्रांककोटिरिणस्ते
देवा जयसंगरे विजयिनो नि:शंकमंके गता: ।
देवोऽहं भुवने न मे सम इति स्पर्धावहंत:
परं तत्तुल्यं नियतं यथासुभिरमी नाशं व्रजंति स्वयम् ।।6

त्वन्नामस्मरणात्पलायनपरा द्रष्टुं च शक्ता
न ते भूतप्रेतपिशाचराक्षसगणा यक्षाश्च नागाधिपा: ।
दैत्या दानवपुंगवाश्च खचरा व्याघ्रादिका
जंतवो डाकिन्य: कुपितांतकाश्च मनुजं मात: क्षणंभूतले ।। 7

लक्ष्मी: सिद्धगणाश्च पादुकमुखा: सिद्धास्तथा
चारणा: स्तम्भश्चापि रणांगणे गजघटास्तम्भस्तथा मोहनम् ।
मातस्त्वत्पदसेवया खलु नृणां सिद्धयन्ति ते
ते गुणा: कान्ति: कान्तमनोभवस्य भवति क्षुद्रोपि वाचस्पति: ।।8

ताराष्टकमिदं रम्यं भक्तिमान् य: पठेन्नर: ।
प्रातर्मध्याह्न्काले च सायाह्ने नियत: शुचि: ।। 9

लभते कथितां दिव्यां सर्वशास्त्रार्थविद्भवेत् ।
लक्ष्मीमनश्वरां प्राप्य भुक्त्वा भोगान यथेप्सितान् ।। 10

कीर्ति कान्तिं च नैरुज्यं सर्वेषां प्रियतां व्रजेत् ।
विख्यातिं चापि लोकेषु प्राप्यांते मोक्षमापनुयात् ।।11

श्रीताराष्टकम् समाप्ता ।।

*****

## Śrī Tārā Śatanāma Stotram

*Śrīśiva Uvāca ||*

*Oṃ Tāriṇī Taralā Tanvī Tārā Taruṇavallarī |*

*Tīvrarūpā Tarī Śyāmā Tanukṣīṇapayodharā || 1*

*Turīyā Taralā(Taruṇā) Tīvragamanā Nīlavāhinī |*

*Ugratārā Jayā Caṇḍī Śrīmadekajaṭāśirāḥ || 2*

*Taruṇī Śāmbhavīchinnabhālā Ca Bhadratāriṇī |*

*Ugrā Cograprabhā Nīlā Kṛṣṇā Nīlasarasvatī || 3*

*Dvitīyā Śobhanā Nityā Navīnā Nityanūtanā |*

*Caṇḍikā Vijayārādhyā Devī Gaganavāhinī || 4*

*Aṭṭahāsyā Karālāsyā Carāsyā Ditipūjitā |*

*Saguṇā Saguṇārādhyā Harīndradevapūjitā || 5*

*Raktapriyā Ca Raktākṣī Rudhirāsyavibhūṣitā |*

*Balipriyā Baliratā Durgā Balavatī Balā || 6*

*Balapriyā Balaratā Balarāmaprapūjitā |*

*Ardhakeśeśvarī Keśā Keśavāsavibhūṣitā || 7*

*Padmamālā Ca Padmākṣī Kāmākhyā Girinandinī |*

*Dakṣiṇā Caiva Dakṣā Ca Dakṣajā Dakṣiṇe Ratā || 8*

*Vajrapuṣpapriyā Raktapriyā Kusumabhūṣitā |*

*Māheśvarī Mahādevapriyā Pañcavibhūṣitā || 9*

*Iḍā Ca Piṅgalā Caiva Suṣumnā Prāṇarūpiṇī |*

*Gāndhārī Pañcamī Pañcānanādi Paripūjitā || 10*

*Tathyavidyā Tathyarūpā Tathyamārgānusāriṇī |*

*Tattvapriyā Tattvarūpā Tattvajñānātmikā'naghā || 11*

*Tāṇḍavācārasantuṣṭā Tāṇḍavapriyakāriṇī* I
*Tāladānaratā Krūratāpinī Taraṇiprabhā* II 12

*Trapāyuktā Trapāmuktā Tarpitā Tṛptikāriṇī* I
*Tāruṇyabhāvasantuṣṭā Śaktirbhaktānurāgiṇī* II 13

*Śivāsaktā Śivaratiḥ Śivabhaktiparāyaṇā* I
*Tāmradyutistāmrarāgā Tāmrapātraprabhojinī* II 14

*Balabhadrapremaratā Balibhugbalikalpinī* I
*Rāmarūpā Rāmaśaktī Rāmarūpānukāriṇī* II 15

*Ityetatkathitaṃ Devi Rahasyaṃ Paramādbhutam* I
*Śrutvā Mokṣamavāpnoti Tārādevyāḥ Prasādataḥ* II 16

*Ya Idaṃ Paṭhati Stotraṃ Tārāstutirahasyakam* I
*Sarvasiddhiyuto Bhūtvā Viharet Kṣitimaṇḍale* II 17

*Tasyaiva Mantrasiddhiḥ Syānmamasiddhiranuttamā* I
*Bhavatyeva Mahāmāye Satyaṃ Satyaṃ Na Saṃśayaḥ* II 18

*Mande Maṅgalavāre Ca Yaḥ Paṭhenniśi Saṃyataḥ* I
*Tasyaiva Mantrasiddhissyādgāṇapatyaṃ Labheta Saḥ* II 19

*Śraddhayā'śraddhayā Vāpi Paṭhettārārahasyakam* I
*So'cireṇaiva Kālena Jīvanmuktaḥ Śivo Bhavet* II 20

*Sahasrāvartanāddevi Puraścaryāphalaṃ Labhet* I
*Evaṃ Satatayuktā Ye Dhyāyantastvāmupāsate* I
*Te Kṛtārthā Maheśāni Mṛtyusaṃsāravartmanaḥ* II 21

*Iti Svarṇamālātantre Tārāśatanāmastotraṃ Samāptam* II

And

*Iti Muṇḍamālātantre Harapārvatī-Saṃvāde*

*Trayodaśapaṭalāntargataṃ Tārāśatanāmastotraṃ Sampūrṇam* ||

Verses 1-10 are in *Mundamalatantra* 13th *Patala* Verses 3-12 as *Tarashatanamastotram* with little variations|

For example, the following lines come between 4-1 and 4-2 above.

*Raudrā Raudramayī Mūrtirviśokā Śokanāśinī* || 51

*Śivapūjyā Śivārādhyā Śivadhyeyā Sanātanī*
*Brahmavidyā Jagaddhātrī Nirguṇā Guṇa-Pūjitā* || 52

श्रीताराशतनामस्तोत्रम्

श्रीशिव उवाच ॥

ॐ तारिणी तरला तन्वी तारा तरुणवल्लरी ।
तीव्ररूपा तरी श्यामा तनुक्षीणपयोधरा ॥ १

तुरीया तरला(तरुणा) तीव्रगमना नीलवाहिनी ।
उग्रतारा जया चण्डी श्रीमदेकजटाशिराः ॥ २

तरुणी शाम्भवीछिन्नभाला च भद्रतारिणी ।
उग्रा चोग्रप्रभा नीला कृष्णा नीलसरस्वती ॥ ३

द्वितीया शोभना नित्या नवीना नित्यनूतना ।
चण्डिका विजयाराध्या देवी गगनवाहिनी ॥ ४

अट्टहास्या करालास्या चरास्या दितिपूजिता ।
सगुणा सगुणाराध्या हरीन्द्रदेवपूजिता ॥ ५

रक्तप्रिया च रक्ताक्षी रुधिरास्यविभूषिता ।
बलिप्रिया बलिरता दुर्गा बलवती बला ॥ ६

बलप्रिया बलरता बलरामप्रपूजिता ।
अर्धकेशेश्वरी केशा केशवासविभूषिता ॥ ७

पद्ममाला च पद्माक्षी कामाख्या गिरिनन्दिनी ।
दक्षिणा चैव दक्षा च दक्षजा दक्षिणे रता ॥ ८

वज्रपुष्पप्रिया रक्तप्रिया कुसुमभूषिता ।
माहेश्वरी महादेवप्रिया पञ्चविभूषिता ॥ ९

इडा च पिङ्गला चैव सुषुम्ना प्राणरूपिणी ।
गान्धारी पञ्चमी पञ्चाननादि परिपूजिता ॥ १०

तथ्यविद्या तथ्यरूपा तथ्यमार्गानुसारिणी ।
तत्त्वप्रिया तत्त्वरूपा तत्त्वज्ञानात्मिकाऽनघा ॥ ११

ताण्डवाचारसन्तुष्टा ताण्डवप्रियकारिणी ।
तालदानरता क्रूरतापिनी तरणिप्रभा ॥ १२

त्रपायुक्ता त्रपामुक्ता तर्पिता तृप्तिकारिणी ।
तारुण्यभावसन्तुष्टा शक्तिर्भक्तानुरागिणी ॥ १३

शिवासक्ता शिवरतिः शिवभक्तिपरायणा ।
ताम्रद्युतिस्ताम्ररागा ताम्रपात्रप्रभोजिनी ॥ १४

बलभद्रप्रेमरता बलिभुग्बलिकल्पिनी ।
रामरूपा रामशक्ती रामरूपानुकारिणी ॥ १५

इत्येतत्कथितं देवि रहस्यं परमाद्भुतम् ।
श्रुत्वा मोक्षमवाप्नोति तारादेव्याः प्रसादतः ॥ १६

य इदं पठति स्तोत्रं तारास्तुतिरहस्यकम् ।
सर्वसिद्धियुतो भूत्वा विहरेत् क्षितिमण्डले ॥ १७

तस्यैव मन्त्रसिद्धिः स्यान्ममसिद्धिरनुत्तमा ।
भवत्येव महामाये सत्यं सत्यं न संशयः ॥ १८

मन्दे मङ्गलवारे च यः पठेन्निशि संयतः ।
तस्यैव मन्त्रसिद्धिस्स्याद्गाणपत्यं लभेत सः ॥ १९

श्रद्धयाऽश्रद्धया वापि पठेत्तारारहस्यकम् ।
सोऽचिरेणैव कालेन जीवन्मुक्तः शिवो भवेत् ॥ २०

सहस्रावर्तनाद्देवि पुरश्चर्याफलं लभेत् ।
एवं सततयुक्ता ये ध्यायन्तस्त्वामुपासते ।
ते कृतार्था महेशानि मृत्युसंसारवर्त्मनः ॥ २१

इति स्वर्णमालातन्त्रे ताराशतनामस्तोत्रं समाप्तम् ॥

and

इति मुण्डमालातन्त्रे हरपार्वती-संवादे त्रयोदशपटलान्तर्गतं
ताराशतनामस्तोत्रं सम्पूर्णम् ॥

Verses 1-10 are in *Mundamalatantra* 13th *Patala* Verses 3-12 as *Tarashatanamastotram* with little variations।

For example, the following lines come between 4-1 and 4-2 above.

रौद्रा रौद्रमयी मूर्तिर्विशोका शोकनाशिनी ॥ ५१

शिवपूज्या शिवाराध्या शिवध्येया सनातनी
ब्रह्मविद्या जगद्धात्री निर्गुणा गुण-पूजिता ॥ ५२

*****

# Śrī Tārā Devī Aṣṭottara Śata Nāmāvaliḥ

| | | |
|---|---|---|
| 1 | *Oṁ Tāriṇyai Namaḥ* । | ॐ तारिण्यै नमः । |
| 2 | *Oṁ Taralāyai Namaḥ* । | ॐ तरलायै नमः । |
| 3 | *Oṁ Tanvyai Namaḥ* । | ॐ तन्व्यै नमः । |
| 4 | *Oṁ Tārāyai Namaḥ* । | ॐ तारायै नमः । |
| 5 | *Oṁ Taruṇa-Vallaryai Namaḥ* । | ॐ तरुणवल्लर्यै नमः । |
| 6 | *Oṁ Tīra-Rūpāyai Namaḥ* । | ॐ तीररूपायै नमः । |
| 7 | *Oṁ Taryai Namaḥ* । | ॐ तर्यै नमः । |
| 8 | *Oṁ Śyāmāyai Namaḥ* । | ॐ श्यामायै नमः । |
| 9 | *Oṁ Tanu-Kṣīṇa-Payodharāyai Namaḥ* । | ॐ तनुक्षीणपयोधरायै नमः । |
| 10 | *Oṁ Turīyāyai Namaḥ* । | ॐ तुरीयायै नमः। |
| 11 | *Oṁ Tarunāyai Namaḥ* । | ॐ तरुनायै नमः। |
| 12 | *Oṁ Tīvra-Gamanāyai Namaḥ* । | ॐ तीव्रगमनायै नमः। |
| 13 | *Oṁ Nīla-Vāhinyai Namaḥ* । | ॐ नीलवाहिन्यै नमः। |
| 14 | *Oṁ Ugra-Tārāyai Namaḥ* । | ॐ उग्रतारायै नमः। |
| 15 | *Oṁ Jayāyai Namaḥ* । | ॐ जयायै नमः। |
| 16 | *Oṁ Caṇḍyai Namaḥ* । | ॐ चण्ड्यै नमः। |
| 17 | *Oṁ Śrīmad-Ekajaṭā-Śirāyai Namaḥ* । | ॐ श्रीमदेकजटाशिरायै नमः। |
| 18 | *Oṁ Taruṇyai Namaḥ* । | ॐ तरुण्यै नमः। |
| 19 | *Oṁ Śāmbhavyai Namaḥ* । | ॐ शाम्भव्यै नमः। |

| | | |
|---|---|---|
| 20 | *Oṁ Chinna-Bhālāyai Namaḥ* \| | ॐ छिन्नभालायै नमः। |
| 21 | *Oṁ Bhadra-Tāriṇyai Namaḥ* \| | ॐ भद्रतारिण्यै नमः। |
| 22 | *Oṁ Ugrāyai Namaḥ* \| | ॐ उग्रायै नमः। |
| 23 | *Oṁ Ugra-Prabhāyai Namaḥ* \| | ॐ उग्रप्रभायै नमः। |
| 24 | *Oṁ Nīlāyai Namaḥ* \| | ॐ नीलायै नमः। |
| 25 | *Oṁ Kṛṣṇāyai Namaḥ* \| | ॐ कृष्णायै नमः। |
| 26 | *Oṁ Nīla-Sarasvatyai Namaḥ* \| | ॐ नीलसरस्वत्यै नमः। |
| 27 | *Oṁ Dvitīyāyai Namaḥ* \| | ॐ द्वितीयायै नमः। |
| 28 | *Oṁ Śobhanāyai Namaḥ* \| | ॐ शोभनायै नमः। |
| 29 | *Oṁ Nityāyai Namaḥ* \| | ॐ नित्यायै नमः। |
| 30 | *Oṁ Navīnāyai Namaḥ* \| | ॐ नवीनायै नमः। |
| 31 | *Oṁ Nitya-Nūtanāyai Namaḥ* \| | ॐ नित्यनूतनायै नमः। |
| 32 | *Oṁ Caṇḍikāyai Namaḥ* \| | ॐ चण्डिकायै नमः। |
| 33 | *Oṁ Vijay-Ārādhyāyai Namaḥ* \| | ॐ विजयाराध्यायै नमः। |
| 34 | *Oṁ Devyai Namaḥ* \| | ॐ देव्यै नमः। |
| 35 | *Oṁ Gagana-Vāhinyai Namaḥ* \| | ॐ गगनवाहिन्यै नमः। |
| 36 | *Oṁ Aṭṭa-Hāsyāyai Namaḥ* \| | ॐ अट्टहास्यायै नमः। |
| 37 | *Oṁ Karālāsyāyai Namaḥ* \| | ॐ करालास्यायै नमः। |
| 38 | *Oṁ Carāsyāyai Namaḥ* \| | ॐ चरास्यायै नमः। |
| 39 | *Oṁ Aditi-Pūjitāyai Namaḥ* \| | ॐ अदितिपूजितायै नमः। |

| | | |
|---|---|---|
| 40 | *Oṁ Saguṇāyai Namaḥ* I | ॐ सगुणायै नमः। |
| 41 | *Oṁ Asaguṇāyai Namaḥ* I | ॐ असगुणायै नमः। |
| 42 | *Oṁ Ārādhyāyai Namaḥ* I | ॐ आराध्यायै नमः। |
| 43 | *Oṁ Harīndra-Deva-Pūjitāyai Namaḥ* I | ॐ हरीन्द्रदेवपूजितायै नमः। |
| 44 | *Oṁ Rakta-Priyāyai Namaḥ* I | ॐ रक्तप्रियायै नमः। |
| 45 | *Oṁ Raktākṣyai Namaḥ* I | ॐ रक्ताक्ष्यै नमः। |
| 46 | *Oṁ Rudhirāsya-Vibhūṣitāyai Namaḥ* I | ॐ रुधिरास्यविभूषितायै नमः। |
| 47 | *Oṁ Bali-Priyāyai Namaḥ* I | ॐ बलिप्रियायै नमः। |
| 48 | *Oṁ Bali-Ratāyai Namaḥ* I | ॐ बलिरतायै नमः। |
| 49 | *Oṁ Durdhāyai Namaḥ* I | ॐ दुर्धायै नमः। |
| 50 | *Oṁ Balavatyai Namaḥ* I | ॐ बलवत्यै नमः। |
| 51 | *Oṁ Balāyai Namaḥ* I | ॐ बलायै नमः। |
| 52 | *Oṁ Bala-Priyāyai Namaḥ* I | ॐ बलप्रियायै नमः। |
| 53 | *Oṁ Bala-Ratāyai Namaḥ* I | ॐ बलरतायै नमः। |
| 54 | *Oṁ Balarāma-Prapūjitāyai Namaḥ* I | ॐ बलरामप्रपूजितायै नमः। |
| 55 | *Oṁ Ardha-Keśeśvaryai Namaḥ* I | ॐ अर्धकेशेश्वर्यै नमः। |
| 56 | *Oṁ Keśāyai Namaḥ* I | ॐ केशायै नमः। |
| 57 | *Oṁ Keśavāyai Namaḥ* I | ॐ केशवायै नमः। |
| 58 | *Oṁ Savi-Bhūṣitāyai Namaḥ* I | ॐ सविभूषितायै नमः। |
| 59 | *Oṁ Padma-Mālayai Namaḥ* I | ॐ पद्ममालयै नमः। |

| | | |
|---|---|---|
| 60 | *Oṁ Padmākṣyai Namaḥ* \| | ॐ पद्माक्ष्यै नमः। |
| 61 | *Oṁ Kāmākhyāyai Namaḥ* \| | ॐ कामाख्यायै नमः। |
| 62 | *Oṁ Giri-Nandinyai Namaḥ* \| | ॐ गिरिनन्दिन्यै नमः। |
| 63 | *Oṁ Dakṣiṇāyai Namaḥ* \| | ॐ दक्षिणायै नमः। |
| 64 | *Oṁ Dakṣāyai Namaḥ* \| | ॐ दक्षायै नमः। |
| 65 | *Oṁ Dakṣajāyai Namaḥ* \| | ॐ दक्षजायै नमः। |
| 66 | *Oṁ Dakṣiṇe-Ratāyai Namaḥ* \| | ॐ दक्षिणेरतायै नमः। |
| 67 | *Oṁ Vajra-Puśpa-Priyāyai Namaḥ* \| | ॐ वज्रपुश्पप्रियायै नमः। |
| 68 | *Oṁ Rakta-Priyāyai Namaḥ* \| | ॐ रक्तप्रियायै नमः। |
| 69 | *Oṁ Kusuma-Bhūṣitāyai Namaḥ* \| | ॐ कुसुमभूषितायै नमः। |
| 70 | *Oṁ Māheśvaryai Namaḥ* \| | ॐ माहेश्वर्यै नमः। |
| 71 | *Oṁ Mahādeva-Priyāyai Namaḥ* \| | ॐ महादेवप्रियायै नमः। |
| 72 | *Oṁ Pañca-Vibhūṣitāyai Namaḥ* \| | ॐ पञ्चविभूषितायै नमः। |
| 73 | *Oṁ Iḍāyai Namaḥ* \| | ॐ इडायै नमः। |
| 74 | *Oṁ Pingalāyai Namaḥ* \| | ॐ पिन्गलायै नमः। |
| 75 | *Oṁ Suṣumnā-Prāṇa-Rūpiṇyai Namaḥ* \| | ॐ सुषुम्नाप्राणरूपिण्यै नमः |
| 76 | *Oṁ Gāndharyai Namaḥ* \| | ॐ गान्धर्यै नमः। |
| 77 | *Oṁ Pañcamyai Namaḥ* \| | ॐ पञ्चम्यै नमः। |
| 78 | *Oṁ Pañcānanādi-Paripūjitāyai Namaḥ* \| | ॐ पञ्चाननादिपरिपूजितायै नमः। |

| | | |
|---|---|---|
| 79 | *Oṁ Tathya-Vidyāyai Namaḥ* ǀ | ॐ तथ्यविद्यायै नमः। |
| 80 | *Oṁ Tathya-Rūpāyai Namaḥ* ǀ | ॐ तथ्यरूपायै नमः। |
| 81 | *Oṁ Tathya-Mārg-Ānusāriṇyai Namaḥ* ǀ | ॐ तथ्यमार्गानुसारिण्यै नमः। |
| 82 | *Oṁ Tattva-Rūpāyai Namaḥ* ǀ | ॐ तत्त्वरूपायै नमः। |
| 83 | *Oṁ Tattva-Priyāyai* | ॐ तत्त्वप्रियायै |
| 84 | *Oṁ Tattva-Jñānātmikāyai Namaḥ* ǀ | ॐ तत्त्वज्ञानात्मिकायै नमः। |
| 85 | *Oṁ Anaghāyai Namaḥ* ǀ | ॐ अनघायै नमः। |
| 86 | *Oṁ Tāṇdavā-Cāra-Santuṣṭāyai Namaḥ* ǀ | ॐ ताण्दवाचारसन्तुष्तायै नमः। |
| 87 | *Oṁ Tāṇdava-Priyakārinyai Namaḥ* ǀ | ॐ ताण्दवप्रियकारिन्यै नमः। |
| 88 | *Oṁ Tāla-Nāda-Ratāyai Namaḥ* ǀ | ॐ तालनादरतायै नमः। |
| 89 | *Oṁ Krūra-Tāpinyai Namaḥ* ǀ | ॐ क्रूरतापिन्यै नमः। |
| 90 | *Oṁ Taraṇi-Prabhāyai Namaḥ* ǀ | ॐ तरणिप्रभायै नमः। |
| 91 | *Oṁ Trapā-Yuktāyai Namaḥ* ǀ | ॐ त्रपायुक्तायै नमः। |
| 92 | *Oṁ Trapā-Muktāyai Namaḥ* ǀ | ॐ त्रपामुक्तायै नमः। |
| 93 | *Oṁ Tarpitāyai Namaḥ* ǀ | ॐ तर्पितायै नमः। |
| 94 | *Oṁ Tṛpti-Kāriṇyai Namaḥ* ǀ | ॐ तृप्तिकारिण्यै नमः। |
| 95 | *Oṁ Tāruṇya-Bhāva-Santuṣṭāyai Namaḥ* ǀ | ॐ तारुण्यभावसन्तुष्टायै नमः। |
| 96 | *Oṁ Śakti-Bhakt-Ānurāgiṇyai Namaḥ* ǀ | ॐ शक्तिभक्तानुरागिण्यै नमः। |
| 97 | *Oṁ Śiv-Āsaktāyai Namaḥ* ǀ | ॐ शिवासक्तायै नमः। |
| 98 | *Oṁ Śiva-Ratyai Namaḥ* ǀ | ॐ शिवरत्यै नमः। |

| | | |
|---|---|---|
| 99 | *Oṁ Śiva-Bhakti-Parāyaṇāyai Namaḥ* \| | ॐ शिवभक्तिपरायणायै नमः। |
| 100 | *Oṁ Tāmra-Dyutyai Namaḥ* \| | ॐ ताम्रद्युत्यै नमः। |
| 101 | *Oṁ Tāmra-Rāgāyai Namaḥ* \| | ॐ ताम्ररागायै नमः। |
| 102 | *Oṁ Tāmra-Pātra-Prabhodhinyai Namaḥ* \| | ॐ ताम्रपात्रप्रभोधिन्यै नमः। |
| 103 | *Oṁ Balabhadra-Prema-Ratāyai Namaḥ* \| | ॐ बलभद्रप्रेमरतायै नमः। |
| 104 | *Oṁ Bali-Bhujyai Namaḥ* \| | ॐ बलिभुज्यै नमः। |
| 105 | *Oṁ Bali-Kalpinyai Namaḥ* \| | ॐ बलिकल्पिन्यै नमः। |
| 106 | *Oṁ Rāma-Rūpāyai Namaḥ* \| | ॐ रामरूपायै नमः। |
| 107 | *Oṁ Rāma-Śaktyai Namaḥ* \| | ॐ रामशक्त्यै नमः। |
| 108 | *Oṁ Rāma-Rūp-Ānurāgiṇyai Namaḥ* \| | ॐ रामरूपानुरागिण्यै नमः। |

*Śrī Tārā Devī Aṣṭottaraśata Nāmāvaliḥ Sampūrṇam* |

*****

# *Śrī Tārā Sahasranāma Stotram*

1000 divine names of *Sri Tārā Devī*.

*Tārāsahasranāmastotram Bṛhannīlatantrārgatam*

*Śrīdevyuvāca |*

*Deva Deva Mahādeva Sṛṣṭisthityantakāraka |*
*Prasaṅgena Mahādevyā Vistaraṃ Kathitaṃ Mayi* || 1

*Devyā Nīlasarasvatyāḥ Sahasraṃ Parameśvara |*
*Nāmnāṃ Śrotuṃ Maheśāna Prasādaḥ Kriyatāṃ Mayi |*
*Kathayasva Mahādeva Yadyahaṃ Tava Vallabhā* || 2

*Śrībhairava Uvāca |*

*Sādhu Pṛṣṭaṃ Mahādevi Sarvatantreṣu Gopitam |*
*Nāmnāṃ Sahasraṃ Tārāyāḥ Kathituṃ Naiva Śakyate* || 3

*Prakāśāt Siddhihāniḥ Syāt Śriyā Ca Parihīyate |*
*Prakāśayati Yo Mohāt Ṣaṇmāsād Mṛtyumāpnuyāt* || 4

*Akathyaṃ Parameśāni Akathyaṃ Caiva Sundari |*
*Kṣamasva Varade Devi Yadi Sneho'sti Māṃ Prati* || 5

*Sarvasvaṃ Śṛṇu He Devi Sarvāgamavidāṃ Vare |*
*Dhanasāraṃ Mahādevi Goptavyaṃ Parameśvari* || 6

*Āyurgopyaṃ Gṛhacchidraṃ Gopyaṃ Na Pāpabhāg Bhavet |*
*Sugopyaṃ Parameśāni Gopanāt Siddhimaśnute* || 7

*Prakāśāt Kāryahāniśca Prakāśāt Pralayaṃ Bhavet |*
*Tasmād Bhadre Maheśāni Na Prakāśyaṃ Kadācana* || 8

*Iti Devavacaḥ Śrutvā Devī Paramasundarī |*
*Vismitā Parameśānī Viṣaṇā Tatra Jāyate* || 9

*Śṛṇu He Parameśāna Kṛpāsāgarapāraga |*
*Tava Sneho Mahādeva Mayi Nāstyatra Niścitam* || 10

*Bhadraṃ Bhadraṃ Mahādeva Iti Kṛtvā Maheśvarī |*
*Vimukhībhūya Deveśī Tatrāste Śailajā Śubhā* || 11

*Vilokya Vimukhīṃ Devīṃ Mahādevo Maheśvaraḥ |*
*Prahasya Parameśānīṃ Pariṣvajya Priyāṃ Kathām* || 12

*Kathayāmāsa Tatraiva Mahādevyai Maheśvari |*
*Mama Sarvasvarūpā Tvaṃ Jānīhi Naganandini ||* 13

*Tvāṃ Vināhaṃ Mahādevi Pūrvoktaśavarūpavān |*
*Kṣamasva Paramānande Kṣamasva Naganandini ||* 14

*Yathā Prāṇo Maheśāni Dehe Tiṣṭhati Sundari |*
*Tathā Tvaṃ Jagatāmādye Caraṇe Patito'smyaham ||* 15

*Iti Matvā Mahādevi Rakṣa Māṃ Tava Kiṅkaram |*
*Tato Devī Maheśānī Trailokyamohinī Śivā ||* 16

*Mahādevaṃ Pariṣvajya Prāha Gadgadayā Girā |*
*Sadā Dehasvarūpāhaṃ Dehī Tvaṃ Parameśvara ||* 17

*Tathāpi Vañcanāṃ Kartuṃ Māmitthaṃ Vadasi Priyam |*
*Mahādevaḥ Punaḥ Prāha Bhairavi Prāṇavallabhe ||* 18

*Nāmnāṃ Sahasraṃ Tārāyāḥ Śrotumicchasyaśeṣataḥ |*

*Śrīdevyuvāca |*

*Na Śrutaṃ Parameśāna Tārānāmasahasrakam |*
*Kathayasva Mahābhāga Satyaṃ Paramasundaram ||* 19

*Śrīpārvatyuvāca |*

*Kathamīśāna Sarvajña Labhante Siddhimuttamām |*
*Sādhakāḥ Sarvadā Yena Tanme Kathaya Sundara ||* 20

*Yasmāt Parataraṃ Nāsti Stotraṃ Tantreṣu Niścitam |*
*Sarvapāpaharaṃ Divyaṃ Sarvāpadvinivārakam ||* 21

*Sarvajñānakaraṃ Puṇyaṃ Sarvamaṅgalasaṃyutam |*
*Puraścaryāśataistulyaṃ Stotraṃ Sarvapriyaṅkaram ||* 22

*Vaśyapradaṃ Māraṇadamuccāṭanapradaṃ Mahat |*
*Nāmnāṃ Sahasraṃ Tārāyāḥ Kathayasva Sureśvara ||* 23

*Śrīmahādeva Uvāca |*

*Nāmnāṃ Sahasraṃ Tārāyāḥ Stotrapāṭhād Bhaviṣyati |*
*Nāmnāṃ Sahasraṃ Tārāyāḥ Kathayiṣyāmyaśeṣataḥ ||* 24

*Śṛṇu Devi Sadā Bhaktyā Bhaktānāṃ Paramaṃ Hitam |*
*Vinā Pūjopahāreṇa Vinā Jā(Pyena Yat Phalam ||* 25

*Tat Phalaṃ Sakalaṃ Devi Kathayiṣyāmi Tacchṛṇu* |

*Oṃ Asya Śrītārāsahasranāmastotramahāmantrasya,*
*Akṣobhya Ṛṣiḥ, Bṛhatī-Uṣṇik Chandaḥ,*
*Śrī Ugratārā Śrīmadekajaṭā Śrīnīlasarasvatī Devatā,*
*Puruṣārthacatuṣṭayasiddhyarthe Viniyogaḥ* ||

*Tārā Rātrirmahārātrirkālarātrirmahāmatiḥ* |
*Kālikā Kāmadā Māyā Mahāmāyā Mahāsmṛtiḥ* || 26

*Mahādānaratā Yajñā Yajñotsavavibhūṣitā* |
*Candravvajrā Cakorākṣī Cārunetrā Sulocanā* || 27

*Trinetrā Mahatī Devī Kuraṅgākṣī Manoramā* |
*Brāhmī Nārāyaṇī Jyotsnā Cārukeśī Sumūrdhajā* || 28

*Vārāhī Vāruṇī Vidyā Mahāvidyā Maheśvarī* |
*Siddhā Kuñcitakeśā Ca Mahāyajñasvarūpiṇī* || 29

*Gaurī Campakavarṇā Ca Kṛśāṅgī Śivamohinī* |
*Sarvānandasvarūpā Ca Sarvaśaṅkaikatāriṇī* || 30

*Vidyānandamayī Nandā Bhadrakālīsvarūpiṇī* |
*Gāyatrī Sucaritrā Ca Kaulavrataparāyaṇā* || 31

*Hiraṇyagarbhā Bhūgarbhā Mahāgarbhā Sulocanī* |
*Himavattanayā Divyā Mahāmeghasvarūpiṇī* || 32

*Jaganmātā Jagaddhātrī Jagatāmupakāriṇī* |
*Aindrī Saumyā Tathā Ghorā Vāruṇī Mādhavī Tathā* || 33

*Āgneyī Nairṛtī Caiva Aiśānī Caṇḍikātmikā* |
*Sumerutanayā Nityā Sarveṣāmupakāriṇī* || 34

*Lalajjihvā Sarojākṣī Muṇḍasrakparibhūṣitā* |
*Sarvānandamayī Sarvā Sarvānandasvarūpiṇī* || 35

*Dhṛtirmedhā Tathā Lakṣmīḥ Śraddhā Pannagagāminī* |
*Rukmiṇī Jānakī Durgāmbikā Satyavatī Ratiḥ* || 36

*Kāmākhyā Kāmadā Nandā Nārasiṃhī Sarasvatī* |
*Mahādevaratā Caṇḍī Caṇḍadordaṇḍakhaṇḍinī* || 37

*Dīrghakeśī Sukeśī Ca Piṅgakeśī Mahākacā* |
*Bhavānī Bhavapatnī Ca Bhavabhītiharā Satī* || 38

*Paurandarī Tathā Viṣṇorjāyā Māheśvarī Tathā |*
*Sarveṣāṃ Jananī Vidyā Cārvaṅgī Daityanāśinī ||* 39

*Sarvarūpā Maheśāni Kāminī Varavarṇinī |*
*Mahāvidyā Mahāmāyā Mahāmedhā Mahotsavā ||* 40

*Virūpā Viśvarūpā Ca Mṛḍānī Mṛḍavallabhā |*
*Koṭicandrapratīkāśā Śatasūryaprakāśinī ||* 41

*Jahnukanyā Mahogrā Ca Pārvatī Viśvamohinī |*
*Kāmarūpā Maheśānī Nityotsāhā Manasvinī ||* 42

*Vaikuṇṭhanāthapatnī Ca Tathā Śaṅkaramohinī |*
*Kāśyapī Kamalā Kṛṣṇā Kṛṣṇarūpā Ca Kālinī ||* 43

*Māheśvarī Vṛṣārūḍhā Sarvavismayakāriṇī |*
*Mānyā Mānavatī Śuddhā Kanyā Himagirestathā ||* 44

*Aparṇā Padmapatrākṣī Nāgayajñopavītinī |*
*Mahāśaṅkhadharā Kāntā Kamanīyā Nagātmajā ||* 45

*Brahmāṇī Vaiṣṇavī Śambhorjāyā Gaṅgā Jaleśvarī |*
*Bhāgīrathī Manobuddhirnityā Vidyāmayī Tathā ||* 46

*Harapriyā Girisutā Harapatnī Tapasvinī |*
*Mahāvyādhiharā Devī Mahāghorasvarūpiṇī ||* 47

*Mahāpuṇyaprabhā Bhīmā Madhukaiṭabhanāśinī |*
*Śaṅkhinī Vajriṇī Dhātrī Tathā Pustakadhāriṇī ||* 48

*Cāmuṇḍā Capalā Tuṅgā Śumbadaityanikṛntanī |*
*Śāntirnidrā Mahānidrā Pūrṇanidrā Ca Reṇukā ||* 49

*Kaumārī Kulajā Kāntī Kaulavrataparāyaṇā |*
*Vanadurgā Sadācārā Draupadī Drupadātmajā ||* 50

*Yaśasvinī Yaśasyā Ca Yaśodhātrī Yaśaḥpradā |*
*Sṛṣṭirūpā Mahāgaurī Niśumbaprāṇanāśinī ||* 51

*Padminī Vasudhā Pṛthvī Rohiṇī Vindhyavāsinī |*
*Śivaśaktirmahāśaktiḥ Śaṅkhinī Śaktinirgatā ||* 52

*Daityaprāṇaharā Devī Sarvarakṣaṇakāriṇī |*
*Kṣāntiḥ Kṣemaṅkarī Caiva Buddhirūpā Mahādhanā ||* 53

*Śrīvidyā Bhairavi Bhavyā Bhavānī Bhavanāśinī |*
*Tāpinī Bhāvinī Sītā Tīkṣṇatejaḥsvarūpiṇī ||* 54

*Dātrī Dānaparā Kālī Durgā Daityavibhūṣaṇā* |
*Mahāpuṇyapradā Bhīmā Madhukaiṭabhanāśinī* || 55

*Padmā Padmāvatī Kṛṣṇā Tuṣṭā Puṣṭā Tathorvaśī* |
*Vajriṇī Vajrahastā Ca Tathā Nārāyaṇī Śivā* || 56

*Khaḍginī Khaḍgahastā Ca Khaḍgakharparadhāriṇī* |
*Devāṅganā Devakanyā Devamātā Pulomajā* || 57

*Sukhinī Svargadātrī Ca Sarvasaukhyavivardhinī* |
*Śīlā Śīlāvatī Sūkṣmā Sūkṣmākārā Varapradā* || 58

*Vareṇyā Varadā Vāṇī Jñāninī Jñānadā Sadā* |
*Ugrakālī Mahākālī Bhadrakālī Ca Dakṣiṇā* || 59

*Bhṛguvaṃśasamudbhūtā Bhārgavī Bhṛguvallabhā* |
*Śūlinī Śūlahastā Ca Kartrīkharparadhāriṇī* || 60

*Mahāvaṃśasamudbhūtā Mayūravaravāhanā* |
*Mahāśaṅkharatā Raktā Raktakharparadhāriṇī* || 61

*Raktāmbaradharā Rāmā Ramaṇī Suranāyikā* |
*Mokṣadā Śivadā Śyāmā Madavibhramamantharā* || 62

*Paramānandadā Jyeṣṭhā Yoginī Gaṇasevitā* |
*Sārā Jāmbavatī Caiva Satyabhāmā Nagātmajā* || 63

*Raudrā Raudrabalā Ghorā Rudrasārāruṇātmikā* |
*Rudrarūpā Mahāraudrī Raudradaityavināśinī* || 64

*Kaumārī Kauśikī Caṇḍā Kāladaityavināśinī* |
*Śambhupatnī Śambhuratā Śambujāyā Mahodarī* || 65

*Śivapatnī Śivaratā Śivajāyā Śivapriyā* |
*Harapatnī Hararatā Harajāyā Harapriyā* || 66

*Madanāntakakāntā Ca Madanāntakavallabhā* |
*Girijā Girikanyā Ca Giriśasya Ca Vallabhā* || 67

*Bhūtā Bhavyā Bhavā Spaṣṭā Pāvanī Parapālinī* |
*Adṛśyā Ca Vyaktarūpā Iṣṭāniṣṭapravarddhinī* || 68

*Acyutā Pracyutaprāṇā Pramadā Vāsaveśvarī* |
*Apāṃnidhisamudbhūtā Dhāriṇī Ca Pratiṣṭhitā* || 69

*Udbhavā Kṣobhaṇā Kṣemā Śrīgarbhā Parameśvarī |*
*Kamalā Puṣpadehā Ca Kāminī Kañjalocanā || 70*

*Śaraṇyā Kamalā Prītirvimalānandavardhinī |*
*Kapardinī Karālā Ca Nirmalā Devarūpiṇī || 71*

*Udīrṇabhūṣaṇā Bhavyā Surasenā Mahodarī |*
*Śrīmatī Śiśirā Navyā Śiśirācalakanyakā || 72*

*Suramānyā Suraśreṣṭhā Jyeṣṭhā Prāṇeśvarī Sthirā |*
*Tamoghnī Dhvāntasaṃhantrī Prayatātmā Pativratā || 73*

*Pradyotinī Rathārūḍhā Sarvalokaprakāśinī |*
*Medhāvinī Mahāvīryā Haṃsī Saṃsāratāriṇī || 74*

*Praṇataprāṇināmārtihāriṇī Daityanāśinī |*
*Ḍākinī Śākinīdevī Varakhaṭvāṅgadhāriṇī || 75*

*Kaumudī Kumudā Kundā Kaulikā Kulajāmarā |*
*Garvitā Guṇasampannā Nagajā Khagavāhinī || 76*

*Candrānanā Mahogrā Ca Cārumūrdhajaśobhanā |*
*Manojñā Mādhavī Mānyā Mānanīyā Satāṃ Suhṛt || 77*

*Jyeṣṭhā Śreṣṭhā Maghā Puṣyā Dhaniṣṭhā Pūrvaphālgunī |*
*Raktabījanihantrī Ca Raktabījavināśinī || 78*

*Caṇḍamuṇḍanihantrī Ca Caṇḍamuṇḍavināśinī |*
*Kartrī Hartrī Sukartrī Ca Vimalāmalavāhinī || 79*

*Vimalā Bhāskarī Vīṇā Mahiṣāsuraghātinī |*
*Kālindī Yamunā Vṛddhā Surabhiḥ Bālikā Satī || 80*

*Kauśalyā Kaumudī Maitrīrūpiṇī Cāpyarundhatī |*
*Purārigṛhiṇī Pūrṇā Pūrṇānandasvarūpiṇī || 81*

*Puṇḍarīkākṣapatnī Ca Puṇḍarīkākṣavallabhā |*
*Sampūrṇacandravadanā Bālacandrasamaprabhā || 82*

*Revatī Ramaṇī Citrā Citrāmbaravibhūṣaṇām |*
*Sītā Vīṇāvatī Caiva Yaśodā Vijayā Priyā || 83*

*Navapuṣpasamudbhūtā Navapuṣpotsavotsavā |*
*Navapuṣpasrajāmālā Mālyabhūṣaṇabhūṣitā || 84*

*Navapuṣpasamaprāṇā Navapuṣpotsavapriyā |*
*Pretamaṇḍalamadhyastā Sarvāṅgasundarī Śivā || 85*

*Navapuṣpātmikā Ṣaṣṭhī Puṣpastavakamaṇḍalā* |
*Navapuṣpaguṇopetā Śmaśānabhairavapriyā* || 86

*Kulaśāstrapradīpā Ca Kulamārgapravarddhinī* |
*Śmaśānabhairavī Kālī Bhairavī Bhairavapriyā* || 87

*Ānandabhairavī Dhyeyā Bhairavī Kurubhairavī* |
*Mahābhairavasamprītā Bhairavīkulamohinī* || 88

*Śrīvidyābhairavī Nītibhairavī Guṇabhairavī* |
*Sammohabhairavī Puṣṭibhairavī Tuṣṭibhairavī* || 89

*Saṃhārabhairavī Sṛṣṭibhairavī Sthitibhairavī* |
*Ānandabhairavī Vīrā Sundarī Sthitisundarī* || 90

*Guṇānandasvarūpā Ca Sundarī Kālarūpiṇī* |
*Śrīmāyāsundarī Saumyasundarī Lokasundarī* || 91

*Śrīvidyāmohinī Buddhirmahābuddhisvarūpiṇī* |
*Mallikā Hārarasikā Hārālambanasundarī* || 92

*Nīlapaṅkajavarṇā Ca Nāgakesarabhūṣitā* |
*Japākusumasaṅkāśā Japākusumaśobhitā* || 93

*Priyā Priyaṅkarī Viṣṇordānavendravināśinī* |
*Jñāneśvarī Jñānadātrī Jñānānandapradāyinī* || 94

*Guṇagauravasampannā Guṇaśīlasamanvitā* |
*Rūpayauvanasampannā Rūpayauvanaśobhitā* || 95

*Guṇāśrayā Guṇaratā Guṇagauravasundarī* |
*Madirāmodamattā Ca Tāṭaṅkadvayaśobhitā* || 96

*Vṛkṣamūlasthitā Devī Vṛkṣaśākhoparisthitā* |
*Tālamadhyāgranilayā Vṛkṣamadhyanivāsinī* || 97

*Svayambhūpuṣpasaṃkāśā Svayambhūpuṣpadhāriṇī* |
*Svayambhūkusumaprītā Svayambhūpuṣpaśobhinī* || 98

*Svayambhūpuṣparasikā Nagnā Dhyānavatī Sudhā* |
*Śukrapriyā Śukraratā Śukramajjanatatparā* || 99

*Pūrṇaparṇā Suparṇā Ca Niṣparṇā Pāpanāśinī* |
*Madirāmodasampannā Madirāmodadhāriṇī* || 100

*Sarvāśrayā Sarvaguṇā Nandanandanadhāriṇī* |
*Nārīpuṣpasamudbhūtā Nārīpuṣpotsavotsavā* || 101

*Nārīpuṣpasamaprāṇā Nārīpuṣparatā Mṛgī |*
*Sarvakālodbhavaprītā Sarvakālodbhavotsavā* || 102

*Caturbhujā Daśabhujā Aṣṭādaśabhujā Tathā |*
*Dvibhujā Ṣaḍbhujā Prītā Raktapaṅkajaśobhitā* || 103

*Kauberī Kauravī Kauryā Kurukullā Kapālinī |*
*Sudīrghakadalījaṅghā Rambhorū Rāmavallabhā* || 104

*Niśācarī Niśāmūrtirniśācandrasamaprabhā |*
*Cāndrī Cāndrakalā Candrā Cārucandranibhānanā* || 105

*Srotasvatī Srutimatī Sarvadurgatināśinī |*
*Sarvādhārā Sarvamayī Sarvānandasvarūpiṇī* || 106

*Sarvacakreśvarī Sarvā Sarvamantramayī Śubhā |*
*Sahasranayanaprāṇā Sahasranayanapriyā* || 107

*Sahasraśīrṣā Suṣamā Sadambhā Sarvabhakṣikā |*
*Yaṣṭikā Yaṣṭicakrasthā Ṣadvargaphaladāyinī* || 108

*Ṣaḍviṃśapadmamadhyasthā Ṣaḍviṃśakulamadhyagā |*
*Hūṁkāravarṇanilayā Hūṁkārākṣarabhūṣaṇā* || 109

*Hakāravarṇanilayā Hakārākṣarabhūṣaṇā |*
*Hāriṇī Hāravalitā Hārahīrakabhūṣaṇā* || 110

*Hrīṃkārabījasahitā Hrīṃkārairupaśobhitā |*
*Kandarpasya Kalā Kundā Kaulinī Kuladarpitā* || 111

*Ketakīkusumaprāṇā Ketakīkṛtabhūṣaṇā |*
*Ketakīkusumāsaktā Ketakīparibhūṣitā* || 112

*Karpūrapūrṇavadanā Mahāmāyā Maheśvarī |*
*Kalā Keliḥ Kriyā Kīrṇā Kadambakusumotsukā* || 113

*Kādambinī Kariśuṇḍā Kuñjareśvaragāminī |*
*Kharvā Sukhañjanayanā Khañjanadvandvabhūṣaṇā* || 114

*Khadyota Iva Durlakṣā Khadyota Iva Cañcalā |*
*Mahāmāyā Jgaddhātrī Gītavādyapriyā Ratiḥ* || 115

*Gaṇeśvarī Gaṇejyā Ca Guṇapūjyā Guṇapradā |*
*Guṇāḍhyā Guṇasampannā Guṇadātrī Guṇātmikā* || 116

*Gurvī Gurutarā Gaurī Gāṇapatyaphalapradā |*
*Mahāvidyā Mahāmedhā Tulinī Gaṇamohinī* || 117

*Bhavyā Bhavapriyā Bhāvyā Bhāvanīyā Bhavātmikā |*
*Ghargharā Ghoravadanā Ghoradaityavināśinī* || 118

*Ghorā Ghoravatī Ghoṣā Ghoraputrī Ghanācalā |*
*Carcarī Cārunayanā Cāruvaktrā Caturguṇā* || 119

*Caturvedamayī Caṇḍī Candrāsyā Caturānanā |*
*Calaccakoranayanā Calatkhañjanalocanā* || 120

*Caladambhojanilayā Caladambhojalocanā |*
*Chatrī Chatrapriyā Chatrā Chatracāmaraśobhitā* || 121

*Chinnachadā Chinnaśirāśchinnanāsā Chalātmikā |*
*Chalāḍhyā Chalasaṃtrastā Chalarūpā Chalasthirā* || 122

*Chakāravarṇanilayā Chakārāḍhyā Chalapriyā |*
*Chadminī Chadmaniratā Chadmacchadmanivāsinī* || 123

*Jagannāthapriyā Jīvā Jaganmuktikarī Matā |*
*Jīrṇā Jīmūtavanitā Jīmūtairupaśobhitā* || 124

*Jāmātṛvaradā Jambhā Jamalārjunabhañjinī |*
*Jharjharī Jhākṛtirjhallī Jharī Jharjharikā Tathā* || 125

*Ṭaṅkārakāriṇī Ṭīkā Sarvaṭaṅkārakāriṇī |*
*Ṭhaṃkarāṅgī Ḍamarukā Ḍākārā Ḍamarupriyā* || 126

*Ḍhakkārāvaratā Nityā Tulasī Maṇibhūṣitā |*
*Tulā Ca Tolikā Tīrṇā Tārā Tāraṇikā Tathā* || 127

*Tantravijñā Tantraratā Tantravidyā Ca Tantradā |*
*Tāntrikī Tantrayogyā Ca Tantrasārā Ca Tantrikā* || 128

*Tantradhārī Tantrakarī Sarvatantrasvarūpiṇī |*
*Tuhināṃśusamānāsyā Tuhināṃśusamaprabhā* || 129

*Tuṣārākaratulyāṅgī Tuṣārādhārasundarī |*
*Tantrasārā Tantrakaro Tantrasārasvarūpiṇī* || 130

*Tuṣāradhāmatulyāsyā Tuṣārāṃśusamaprabhā |*
*Tuṣārādrisutā Tārkṣyā Tārāṅgī Tālasundarī* || 131

*Tārasvareṇa Sahitā Tārasvaravibhūṣitā |*
*Thakārakūṭanilayā Thakārākṣaramālinī* || 132

*Dayāvatī Dīnaratā Duḥkhadāridryanāśinī |*
*Daurbhāgyaduḥkhadalinī Daurbhāgyapadanāśinī* || 133

*Duhitā Dīnabandhuśca Dānavendravināśinī* |
*Dānapātrī Dānaratā Dānasammānatoṣitā* || 134

*Dāntyādisevitā Dāntā Dayā Dāmodarapriyā* |
*Dadhīcivaradā Tuṣṭā Dānavendravimardinī* || 135

*Dīrghanetrā Dīrghakacā Dīrghanāsā Ca Dīrghikā* |
*Dāridryaduḥkhasaṃnāśā Dāridryaduḥkhanāśinī* || 136

*Dāmbhikā Danturā Dambhā Dambhāsuravarapradā* |
*Dhanadhānyapradā Dhanyā Dhaneśvaradhanapradā* || 137

*Dharmapatnī Dharmaratā Dharmādharmavivivarddhinī* |
*Dharmiṇī Dharmikā Dharmyā Dharmādharmavivarddhinī* || 138

*Dhaneśvarī Dharmaratā Dharmānandapravarddhinī* |
*Dhanādhyakṣā Dhanaprītā Dhanāḍhyā Dhanatoṣitā* || 139

*Dhīrā Dhairyavatī Dhiṣṇyā Dhavalāmbhojasaṃnibhā* |
*Dhariṇī Dhāriṇī Dhātrī Dhūraṇī Dharaṇī Dharā* || 140

*Dhārmikā Dharmasahitā Dharmanindakavarjitā* |
*Navīnā Nagajā Nimnā Nimnanābhirnageśvarī* || 141

*Nūtanāmbhojanayanā Navīnāmbhojasundarī* |
*Nāgarī Nagarajyeṣṭhā Nagarājasutā Nagā* || 142

*Nāgarājakṛtatoṣā Nāgarājavibhūṣitā* |
*Nāgeśvarī Nāgarūḍhā Nāgarājakuleśvarī* || 143

*Navīnendukalā Nāndī Nandikeśvaravallabhā* |
*Nīrajā Nīrajākṣī Ca Nīrajadvandvalocanā* || 144

*Nīrā Nīrabhavā Vāṇī Nīranirmaladehinī* |
*Nāgayajñopavītāḍhyā Nāgayajñopavītikā* || 145

*Nāgakesarasaṃtuṣṭā Nāgakesaramālinī* |
*Navīnaketakīkunda Mallikāmbhojabhūṣitā* || 146 *

*Nāyikā Nāyakaprītā Nāyakapremabhūṣitā* |
*Nāyakapremasahitā Nāyakapremabhāvitā* || 147

*Nāyakānandanilayā Nāyakānandakāriṇī* |
*Narmakarmaratā Nityaṃ Narmakarmaphalapradā* || 148

*Narmakarmapriyā Narmā Narmakarmakṛtālayā* |
*Narmaprītā Narmaratā Narmadhyānaparāyaṇā* || 149

*Pauṣṇapriyā Ca Pauṣpejyā Puṣpadāmavibhūṣitā |*
*Puṇyadā Pūrṇimā Pūrṇā Koṭipuṇyaphalapradā* || 150

*Purāṇāgamagopyā Ca Purāṇāgamagopitā |*
*Purāṇagocarā Pūrṇā Pūrvā Prauḍhā Vilāsinī* || 151

*Prahlādahṛdayāhlādagehinī Puṇyacāriṇī |*
*Phālgunī Phālgunaprītā Phālgunapredhāriṇī* || 152

*Phālgunapremadā Caiva Phaṇirājavibhūṣitā |*
*Phaṇikāñcī Phaṇiprītā Phaṇihāravibhūṣitā* || 153

*Phaṇīśakṛtasarvāṅgabhūṣaṇā Phaṇihāriṇī |*
*Phaṇiprītā Phaṇiratā Phaṇikaṅkaṇadhāriṇī* || 154

*Phaladā Triphalā Śaktā Phalābharaṇabhūṣitā |*
*Phakārakūṭasarvāṅgī Phālgunānandavarddhinī* || 155

*Vāsudevaratā Vijñā Vijñavijñānakāriṇī |*
*Vīṇāvatī Balākīrṇā Bālapīyūṣarocikā* || 156

*Bālāvasumatī Vidyā Vidyāhāravibhūṣitā |*
*Vidyāvatī Vaidyapadaprītā Vaivasvatī Baliḥ* || 157

*Balividhvaṃsinī Caiva Varāṅgasthā Varānanā |*
*Viṣṇorvakṣaḥsthalasthā Ca Vāgvatī Vindhyavāsinī* || 158

*Bhītidā Bhayadā Bhānoraṃśujālasamaprabhā |*
*Bhārgavejyā Bhṛgoḥ Pūjyā Bharadvāranamaskṛtā* || 159

*Bhītidā Bhayasaṃhantrī Bhīmākārā Ca Sundarī |*
*Māyāvatī Mānaratā Mānasammānatatparā* || 160

*Mādhavānandadā Mādhvī Madirāmuditekṣaṇā |*
*Mahotsavaguṇopetā Mahatī Ca Mahadguṇā* || 161

*Madirāmodaniratā Madirāmajjane Ratā |*
*Yaśodharī Yaśovidyā Yaśodānandavarddhinī* || 162

*Yaśaḥkarpūradhavalā Yaśodāmavibhūṣitā |*
*Yamarājapriyā Yogamārgānandapravarddhinī* || 163

*Yamasvasā Ca Yamunā Yogamārgapravarddhinī |*
*Yādavānandakartrī Ca Yādavānandavarddhinī* || 164

*Yajñaprītā Yajñamayī Yajñakarmavibhūṣitā |*
*Rāmaprītā Rāmaratā Rāmatoṣaṇatatparā* || 165

*Rājñī Rājakulejyā Ca Rājarājeśvarī Ramā |*
*Ramaṇī Rāmaṇī Ramyā Rāmānandapradāyinī || 166*

*Rajanīkarapūrṇāsyā Raktotpalavilocanā |*
*Lāṅgalipremasaṃtuṣṭā Lāṅgalipraṇayapriyā || 167*

*Lākṣāruṇā Ca Lalanā Līlā Līlāvatī Layā |*
*Laṅkeśvaraguṇaprītā Laṅkeśavaradāyinī || 168*

*Lavaṅgīkusumaprītā Lavaṅgakusumasrajā |*
*Dhātā Vivasvadgṛhiṇī Vivasvatpremadhāriṇī || 169*

*Śavoparisamāsīnā Śavavakṣaḥsthalasthitā |*
*Śaraṇāgatarakṣitrī Śaraṇyā Śrīḥ Śaradguṇā || 170*

*Ṣaṭkoṇacakramadhyasthā Sampadārthaniṣevitā |*
*Hūṃkārākāriṇī Devī Hūṃkārarūpaśobhitā || 171*

*Kṣemaṅkarī Tathā Kṣemā Kṣemadhāmavivarddhinī |*
*Kṣemāmnāyā Tathājñā Ca Iḍā Iśvaravallabhā || 172*

*Ugradakṣā Tathā Cograā Akārādisvarodbhavā |*
*Ṛkāravarṇakūṭasthā Ṝkārasvarabhūṣitā || 173*

*Ekārā Ca Tathā Caikā Ekārākṣaravāsitā |*
*Aiṣṭā Caiṣā Tathā Cauṣā Aukārākṣaradhāriṇī || 174*

*Aṃ Aḥkārasvarūpā Ca Sarvāgamasugopitā |*
*Ityetat Kathitaṃ Devi Tārānāmasahasrakam || 175*

*Ya Idaṃ Paṭhati Stotraṃ Pratyahaṃ Bhaktibhāvataḥ |*
*Divā Vā Yadi Vā Rātrau Sandhyayorubhayorapi || 176*

*Stavarājasya Pāṭhena Rājā Bhavati Kiṅkaraḥ |*
*Sarvāgameṣu Pūjyaḥ Syāt Sarvatantre Svayaṃ Haraḥ || 177*

*Śivasthāne Śmaśāne Ca Śūnyāgāre Catuṣpathe |*
*Ya Paṭhecchṛṇuyād Vāpi Sa Yogī Nātra Saṃśayaḥ || 178*

*Yāni Nāmāni Santyasmin Prasaṅgād Muravairiṇaḥ |*
*Grāhyāṇi Tāni Kalyāṇi Nānyānyapi Kadācana || 179*

*Harernāma Na Gṛhṇīyād Na Spṛśet Tulasīdalam |*
*Nānyacintā Prakartavyā Nānyanindā Kadācana || 180*

*Sindūrakaravīrādyaiḥ Puṣpairlohitakaistathā |*
*Yo'rcayed Bhaktibhāvena Tasyāsādhyaṃ Na Kiñcana || 181*

*Vātastambhaṃ Jalastambhaṃ Gatistambhaṃ Vivasvataḥ* |
*Vahneḥ Stambhaṃ Karotyeva Stavasyāsya Prakīrtanāt* || 182

*Śriyamākarṣayet Tūrṇamānṛṇyaṃ Jāyate Haṭhāt* |
*Yathā Tṛṇaṃ Dahed Vahnistathārīn Mardayet Kṣaṇāt* || 183

*Mohayed Rājapatnīśca Devānapi Vaśaṃ Nayet* |
*Yaḥ Paṭhet Śṛṇuyād Vāpi Ekacittena Sarvadā* || 184

*Dīrghāyuśca Sukhī Vāgmī Vāṇī Tasya Vaśaṅkarī* |
*Sarvatīrthābhiṣekeṇa Gayāśrāddhena Yat Phalam* || 185

*Tatphalaṃ Labhate Satyaṃ Yaḥ Paṭhedekacittataḥ* |
*Yeṣāmārādhane Śraddhā Ye Tu Sādhitumudyatāḥ* || 186

*Teṣāṃ Kṛtitvaṃ Sarvaṃ Syād Gatirdevi Parā Ca Sā* |
*Ṛtuyuktalatāgāre Sthitvā Daṇḍena Tāḍayet* || 187

*Japtvā Stutvā Ca Bhaktyā Ca Gacched Vai Tāriṇīpadam* |
*Aṣṭamyāṃ Ca Caturdaśyāṃ Navamyāṃ Śanivāsare* || 188

*Saṃkrāntyāṃ Maṇḍale Rātrau Amāvāsyāṃ Ca Yo'rcayet* |
*Varṣaṃ Vyāpya Ca Deveśi Tasyādhīnāśca Siddhayaḥ* || 189

*Sutahīnā Ca Yā Nārī Daurbhāgyāmayapīḍitā* |
*Vandhyā Vā Kākavandhyā Vā Mṛtagarbhā Ca Yāṅganā* || 190

*Dhanadhānyavihīnā Ca Rogaśokākulā Ca Yā* |
*Sāpi Caitad Mahādevi Bhūrjapatre Likhettataḥ* || 191

*Savye Bhuje Ca Badhnīyāt Sarvasaukhyavatī Bhavet* |
*Evaṃ Pumānapi Prāyo Duḥkhena Paripīḍitaḥ* || 192

*Sabhāyāṃ Vyasane Ghore Vivāde Śatrusaṃkaṭe* |
*Caturaṅge Ca Tathā Yuddhe Sarvatrāriprapīḍite* || 193

*Smaraṇādeva Kalyāṇi Saṃkṣayaṃ Yānti Dūrataḥ* |
*Pūjanīyaṃ Prayatnena Śūnyāgāre Śivālaye* || 194

*Bilvamūle Śmaśāne Ca Taṭe Vā Kulamaṇḍale* |
*Śarkarāsavasaṃyuktairbhaktairdugdhaiḥ Sapāyasaiḥ* || 195

*Apūpāpiṣṭasaṃyuktairnaivedyaiśca Yathocitaiḥ* |
*Niveditaṃ Ca Yaddravyaṃ Bhoktavyaṃ Ca Vidhānataḥ* || 196

*Tanna Ced Bhujyate Mohād Bhoktuṃ Necchanti Devatāḥ* |
*Anenaiva Vidhānena Yo'rcayet Parameśvarīm* || 197

*Sa Bhūmivalaye Devi Sākṣādīśo Na Saṃśayaḥ |*
*Mahāśaṅkhena Deveśi Sarvaṃ Kāryaṃ Japādikam || 198*

*Kulasarvasvakasyaivaṃ Prabhāvo Varṇito Mayā |*
*Na Śakyate Samākhyātuṃ Varṣakoṭiśatairapi || 199*

*Kiñcid Mayā Ca Cāpalyāt Kathitaṃ Parameśvari |*
*Janmāntarasahasreṇa Varṇituṃ Naiva Śakyate || 200*

*Kulīnāya Pradātavyaṃ Tārābhaktiparāya Ca |*
*Anyabhaktāya No Deyaṃ Vaiṣṇavāya Viśeṣataḥ || 201*

*Kulīnāya Mahecchāya Bhaktiśraddhāparāya Ca |*
*Mahātmane Sadā Deyaṃ Parīkṣitaguṇāya Ca || 202*

*Nābhaktāya Pradātavyaṃ Pathyantaraparāya Ca |*
*Na Deyaṃ Devadeveśi Gopyaṃ Sarvāgameṣu Ca || 203*

*Pūjājapavihīnāya Strīsurānindakāya Ca |*
*Na Stavaṃ Darśayet Kvāpi Sandarśya Śivahā Bhavet || 204*

*Paṭhanīyaṃ Sadā Devi Sarvāvasthāsu Sarvadā |*
*Yaḥ Stotraṃ Kulanāyike Pratidinaṃ Bhaktyā Paṭhed Mānavaḥ*
*Sa Syādvittacayairdhaneśvarasamo Vidyāmadairvākpatiḥ |*
*Saundaryeṇa Ca Mūrtimān Manasijaḥ Kīrtyā Ca Nārāyaṇaḥ*
*Śaktyā Śaṅkara Eva Saukhyavibhavairbhūmeḥ Patirnānyathā || 205*

*Iti Te Kathitaṃ Guhyaṃ Tārānāmasahasrakam |*
*Asmāt Parataraṃ Stotraṃ Nāsti Tantreṣu Niścayaḥ || 206*

*Iti Śrībṛhannīlatantre Bhairavabhairavīsaṃvāde*
*Tārāsahasranāmanirūpaṇaṃ Aṣṭādaśaḥ Paṭalaḥ ||*

## तारासहस्रनामस्तोत्रम् बृहन्नीलतन्त्रार्गतम्

श्रीदेव्युवाच ।

देव देव महादेव सृष्टिस्थित्यन्तकारक ।
प्रसङ्गेन महादेव्या विस्तरं कथितं मयि ॥ १

देव्या नीलसरस्वत्याः सहस्रं परमेश्वर ।
नाम्नां श्रोतुं महेशान प्रसादः क्रियतां मयि ।

कथयस्व महादेव यद्यहं तव वल्लभा ॥ २

श्रीभैरव उवाच ।

साधु पृष्टं महादेवि सर्वतन्त्रेषु गोपितम् ।
नाम्नां सहस्रं तारायाः कथितुं नैव शक्यते ॥३

प्रकाशात् सिद्धिहानिः स्यात् श्रिया च परिहीयते ।
प्रकाशयति यो मोहात् षण्मासाद् मृत्युमाप्नुयात् ॥४

अकथ्यं परमेशानि अकथ्यं चैव सुन्दरि ।
क्षमस्व वरदे देवि यदि स्नेहोऽस्ति मां प्रति ॥ ५

सर्वस्वं शृणु हे देवि सर्वागमविदां वरे ।
धनसारं महादेवि गोप्तव्यं परमेश्वरि ॥ ६

आयुर्गोप्यं गृहच्छिद्रं गोप्यं न पापभाग् भवेत् ।
सुगोप्यं परमेशानि गोपनात् सिद्धिमश्नुते ॥७

प्रकाशात् कार्यहानिश्च प्रकाशात् प्रलयं भवेत् ।
तस्माद् भद्रे महेशानि न प्रकाश्यं कदाचन ॥ ८

इति देववचः श्रुत्वा देवी परमसुन्दरी ।
विस्मिता परमेशानी विषणा तत्र जायते ॥ ९

शृणु हे परमेशान कृपासागरपारग ।
तव स्नेहो महादेव मयि नास्त्यत्र निश्चितम् ॥ १०

भद्रं भद्रं महादेव इति कृत्वा महेश्वरी ।
विमुखीभूय देवेशी तत्रास्ते शैलजा शुभा ॥ ११

विलोक्य विमुखीं देवीं महादेवो महेश्वरः ।
प्रहस्य परमेशानीं परिष्वज्य प्रियां कथाम् ॥ १२

कथयामास तत्रैव महादेव्यै महेश्वरि ।
मम सर्वस्वरूपा त्वं जानीहि नगनन्दिनि ॥ १३

त्वां विनाहं महादेवि पूर्वोक्तशवरूपवान् ।
क्षमस्व परमानन्दे क्षमस्व नगनन्दिनि ॥ १४

यथा प्राणो महेशानि देहे तिष्ठति सुन्दरि ।
तथा त्वं जगतामाद्ये चरणे पतितोऽस्म्यहम् ॥ १५

इति मत्वा महादेवि रक्ष मां तव किङ्करम् ।
ततो देवी महेशानी त्रैलोक्यमोहिनी शिवा ॥ १६

महादेवं परिष्वज्य प्राह गद्गदया गिरा ।
सदा देहस्वरूपाहं देही त्वं परमेश्वर ॥ १७

तथापि वञ्चनां कर्तुं मामित्थंवदसि प्रियम् ।
महादेवः पुनः प्राह भैरवि प्राणवल्लभे ॥ १८

नाम्नां सहस्रं तारायाः श्रोतुमिच्छस्यशेषतः ।

श्रीदेव्युवाच ।

न श्रुतं परमेशान तारानामसहस्रकम् ।
कथयस्व महाभाग सत्यं परमसुन्दरम् ॥ १९

श्रीपार्वत्युवाच ।

कथमीशान सर्वज्ञ लभन्ते सिद्धिमुत्तमाम् ।
साधकाः सर्वदा येन तन्मे कथय सुन्दर ॥ २०

यस्मात् परतरं नास्ति स्तोत्रं तन्त्रेषु निश्चितम् ।
सर्वपापहरं दिव्यं सर्वापद्विनिवारकम् ॥ २१

सर्वज्ञानकरं पुण्यं सर्वमङ्गलसंयुतम् ।
पुरश्चर्याशतैस्तुल्यं स्तोत्रं सर्वप्रियङ्करम् ॥ २२

वश्यप्रदं मारणदमुच्चाटनप्रदं महत् ।
नाम्नां सहस्रं तारायाः कथयस्व सुरेश्वर ॥ २३

श्रीमहादेव उवाच ।

नाम्नां सहस्रं तारायाः स्तोत्रपाठाद् भविष्यति ।
नाम्नां सहस्रं तारायाः कथयिष्याम्यशेषतः ॥ २४

शृणु देवि सदा भक्त्या भक्तानां परमं हितम् ।
विना पूजोपहारेण विना जा(प्येन यत् फलम् ॥ २५

तत् फलं सकलं देवि कथयिष्यामि तच्छृणु ।

ॐ अस्य श्रीतारासहस्रनामस्तोत्रमहामन्त्रस्य,
अक्षोभ्य ऋषिः, बृहती-उष्णिक् छन्दः,
श्री उग्रतारा श्रीमदेकजटा श्रीनीलसरस्वती देवता,
पुरुषार्थचतुष्टयसिद्ध्यर्थे विनियोगः ॥

तारा रात्रिर्महारात्रिर्कालरात्रिर्महामतिः ।
कालिका कामदा माया महामाया महास्मृतिः ॥ २६

महादानरता यज्ञा यज्ञोत्सवविभूषिता ।
चन्द्रव्वज्रा चकोराक्षी चारुनेत्रा सुलोचना ॥ २७

त्रिनेत्रा महती देवी कुरङ्गाक्षी मनोरमा ।
ब्राह्मी नारायणी ज्योत्स्ना चारुकेशी सुमूर्धजा ॥ २८

वाराही वारुणी विद्या महाविद्या महेश्वरी ।
सिद्धा कुञ्चितकेशा च महायज्ञस्वरूपिणी ॥ २९

गौरी चम्पकवर्णा च कृशाङ्गी शिवमोहिनी ।
सर्वानन्दस्वरूपा च सर्वशङ्कैकतारिणी ॥ ३०

विद्यानन्दमयी नन्दा भद्रकालीस्वरूपिणी ।
गायत्री सुचरित्रा च कौलव्रतपरायणा ॥ ३१

हिरण्यगर्भा भूगर्भा महागर्भा सुलोचनी ।
हिमवत्तनया दिव्या महामेघस्वरूपिणी ॥ ३२

जगन्माता जगद्धात्री जगतामुपकारिणी ।
ऐन्द्री सौम्या तथा घोरा वारुणी माधवी तथा ॥ ३३

आग्नेयी नैरृती चैव ऐशानी चण्डिकात्मिका ।
सुमेरुतनया नित्या सर्वेषामुपकारिणी ॥ ३४

ललज्जिह्वा सरोजाक्षी मुण्डस्रक्परिभूषिता ।
सर्वानन्दमयी सर्वा सर्वानन्दस्वरूपिणी ॥ ३५

धृतिर्मेधा तथा लक्ष्मीः श्रद्धा पन्नगगामिनी ।
रुक्मिणी जानकी दुर्गाम्बिका सत्यवती रतिः ॥ ३६

कामाख्या कामदा नन्दा नारसिंही सरस्वती ।
महादेवरता चण्डी चण्डदोर्दण्डखण्डिनी ॥ ३७

दीर्घकेशी सुकेशी च पिङ्गकेशी महाकचा ।
भवानी भवपत्नी च भवभीतिहरा सती ॥ ३८

पौरन्दरी तथा विष्णोर्जाया माहेश्वरी तथा ।
सर्वेषां जननी विद्या चार्वङ्गी दैत्यनाशिनी ॥ ३९

सर्वरूपा महेशानि कामिनी वरवर्णिनी ।
महाविद्या महामाया महामेधा महोत्सवा ॥ ४०

विरूपा विश्वरूपा च मृडानी मृडवल्लभा ।
कोटिचन्द्रप्रतीकाशा शतसूर्यप्रकाशिनी ॥ ४१

जह्नुकन्या महोग्रा च पार्वती विश्वमोहिनी ।
कामरूपा महेशानी नित्योत्साहा मनस्विनी ॥ ४२

वैकुण्ठनाथपत्नी च तथा शङ्करमोहिनी ।
काश्यपी कमला कृष्णा कृष्णरूपा च कालिनी ॥ ४३

माहेश्वरी वृषारूढा सर्वविस्मयकारिणी ।
मान्या मानवती शुद्धा कन्या हिमगिरेस्तथा ॥ ४४

अपर्णा पद्मपत्राक्षी नागयज्ञोपवीतिनी ।
महाशङ्खधरा कान्ता कमनीया नगात्मजा ॥ ४५

ब्रह्माणी वैष्णवी शम्भोर्जाया गङ्गा जलेश्वरी ।
भागीरथी मनोबुद्धिर्नित्या विद्यामयी तथा ॥ ४६

हरप्रिया गिरिसुता हरपत्नी तपस्विनी ।
महाव्याधिहरा देवी महाघोरस्वरूपिणी ॥ ४७

महापुण्यप्रभा भीमा मधुकैटभनाशिनी ।
शङ्खिनी वज्रिणी धात्री तथा पुस्तकधारिणी ॥ ४८

चामुण्डा चपला तुङ्गा शुम्बदैत्यनिकृन्तनी ।
शान्तिर्निद्रा महानिद्रा पूर्णनिद्रा च रेणुका ॥ ४९

कौमारी कुलजा कान्ती कौलव्रतपरायणा ।
वनदुर्गा सदाचारा द्रौपदी द्रुपदात्मजा ॥ ५०

यशस्विनी यशस्या च यशोधात्री यशःप्रदा ।
सृष्टिरूपा महागौरी निशुम्बप्राणनाशिनी ॥ ५१

पद्मिनी वसुधा पृथ्वी रोहिणी विन्ध्यवासिनी ।
शिवशक्तिर्महाशक्तिः शङ्खिनी शक्तिनिर्गता ॥ ५२

दैत्यप्राणहरा देवी सर्वरक्षणकारिणी ।
क्षान्तिः क्षेमङ्करी चैव बुद्धिरूपा महाधना ॥ ५३

श्रीविद्या भैरवि भव्या भवानी भवनाशिनी ।
तापिनी भाविनी सीता तीक्ष्णतेजःस्वरूपिणी ॥ ५४

दात्री दानपरा काली दुर्गा दैत्यविभूषणा ।
महापुण्यप्रदा भीमा मधुकैटभनाशिनी ॥ ५५

पद्मा पद्मावती कृष्णा तुष्टा पुष्टा तथोर्वशी ।
वज्रिणी वज्रहस्ता च तथा नारायणी शिवा ॥ ५६

खड्गिनी खड्गहस्ता च खड्गखर्परधारिणी ।
देवाङ्गना देवकन्या देवमाता पुलोमजा ॥ ५७

सुखिनी स्वर्गदात्री च सर्वसौख्यविवर्धिनी ।
शीला शीलावती सूक्ष्मा सूक्ष्माकारा वरप्रदा ॥ ५८

वरेण्या वरदा वाणी ज्ञानिनी ज्ञानदा सदा ।
उग्रकाली महाकाली भद्रकाली च दक्षिणा ॥ ५९

भृगुवंशसमुद्भूता भार्गवी भृगुवल्लभा ।
शूलिनी शूलहस्ता च कर्त्रीखर्परधारिणी ॥ ६०

महावंशसमुद्भूता मयूरवरवाहना ।
महाशङ्खरता रक्ता रक्तखर्परधारिणी ॥ ६१

रक्ताम्बरधरा रामा रमणी सुरनायिका ।
मोक्षदा शिवदा श्यामा मदविभ्रममन्थरा ॥ ६२

परमानन्ददा ज्येष्ठा योगिनी गणसेविता ।
सारा जाम्बवती चैव सत्यभामा नगात्मजा ॥ ६३

रौद्रा रौद्रबला घोरा रुद्रसारारुणात्मिका ।
रुद्ररूपा महारौद्री रौद्रदैत्यविनाशिनी ॥ ६४

कौमारी कौशिकी चण्डा कालदैत्यविनाशिनी ।
शम्भुपत्नी शम्भुरता शम्बुजाया महोदरी ॥ ६५

शिवपत्नी शिवरता शिवजाया शिवप्रिया ।
हरपत्नी हररता हरजाया हरप्रिया ॥ ६६

मदनान्तककान्ता च मदनान्तकवल्लभा ।
गिरिजा गिरिकन्या च गिरीशस्य च वल्लभा ॥ ६७

भूता भव्या भवा स्पष्टा पावनी परपालिनी ।
अदृश्या च व्यक्तरूपा इष्टानिष्टप्रवर्द्धिनी ॥ ६८

अच्युता प्रच्युतप्राणा प्रमदा वासवेश्वरी ।
अपांनिधिसमुद्भूता धारिणी च प्रतिष्ठिता ॥ ६९

उद्भवा क्षोभणा क्षेमा श्रीगर्भा परमेश्वरी ।
कमला पुष्पदेहा च कामिनी कञ्जलोचना ॥ ७०

शरण्या कमला प्रीतिर्विमलानन्दवर्धिनी ।
कपर्दिनी कराला च निर्मला देवरूपिणी ॥ ७१

उदीर्णभूषणा भव्या सुरसेना महोदरी ।
श्रीमती शिशिरा नव्या शिशिराचलकन्यका ॥ ७२

सुरमान्या सुरश्रेष्ठा ज्येष्ठा प्राणेश्वरी स्थिरा ।
तमोघ्नी ध्वान्तसंहन्त्री प्रयतात्मा पतिव्रता ॥ ७३

प्रद्योतिनी रथारूढा सर्वलोकप्रकाशिनी ।
मेधाविनी महावीर्या हंसी संसारतारिणी ॥ ७४

प्रणतप्राणिनामार्तिहारिणी दैत्यनाशिनी ।
डाकिनी शाकिनीदेवी वरखट्वाङ्गधारिणी ॥ ७५

कौमुदी कुमुदा कुन्दा कौलिका कुलजामरा ।
गर्विता गुणसम्पन्ना नगजा खगवाहिनी ॥ ७६

चन्द्रानना महोग्रा च चारुमूर्धजशोभना ।
मनोज्ञा माधवी मान्या माननीया सतां सुहृत् ॥ ७७

ज्येष्ठा श्रेष्ठा मघा पुष्या धनिष्ठा पूर्वफाल्गुनी ।
रक्तबीजनिहन्त्री च रक्तबीजविनाशिनी ॥ ७८

चण्डमुण्डनिहन्त्री च चण्डमुण्डविनाशिनी ।
कर्त्री हर्त्री सुकर्त्री च विमलामलवाहिनी ॥ ७९

विमला भास्करी वीणा महिषासुरघातिनी ।
कालिन्दी यमुना वृद्धा सुरभिः बालिका सती ॥ ८०

कौशल्या कौमुदी मैत्रीरूपिणी चाप्यरुन्धती ।
पुरारिगृहिणी पूर्णा पूर्णानन्दस्वरूपिणी ॥ ८१

पुण्डरीकाक्षपत्नी च पुण्डरीकाक्षवल्लभा ।
सम्पूर्णचन्द्रवदना बालचन्द्रसमप्रभा ॥ ८२

रेवती रमणी चित्रा चित्राम्बरविभूषणां ।
सीता वीणावती चैव यशोदा विजया प्रिया ॥ ८३

नवपुष्पसमुद्भूता नवपुष्पोत्सवोत्सवा ।
नवपुष्पस्रजामाला माल्यभूषणभूषिता ॥ ८४

नवपुष्पसमप्राणा नवपुष्पोत्सवप्रिया ।
प्रेतमण्डलमध्यस्ता सर्वाङ्गसुन्दरी शिवा ॥ ८५

नवपुष्पात्मिका षष्ठी पुष्पस्तवकमण्डला ।
नवपुष्पगुणोपेता श्मशानभैरवप्रिया ॥ ८६

कुलशास्त्रप्रदीपा च कुलमार्गप्रवर्द्धिनी ।
श्मशानभैरवी काली भैरवी भैरवप्रिया ॥ ८७

आनन्दभैरवी ध्येया भैरवी कुरुभैरवी ।
महाभैरवसम्प्रीता भैरवीकुलमोहिनी ॥ ८८

श्रीविद्याभैरवी नीतिभैरवी गुणभैरवी ।
सम्मोहभैरवी पुष्टिभैरवी तुष्टिभैरवी ॥ ८९

संहारभैरवी सृष्टिभैरवी स्थितिभैरवी ।
आनन्दभैरवी वीरा सुन्दरी स्थितिसुन्दरी ॥ ९०

गुणानन्दस्वरूपा च सुन्दरी कालरूपिणी ।
श्रीमायासुन्दरी सौम्यसुन्दरी लोकसुन्दरी ॥ ९१

श्रीविद्यामोहिनी बुद्धिर्महाबुद्धिस्वरूपिणी ।
मल्लिका हाररसिका हारालम्बनसुन्दरी ॥ ९२

नीलपङ्कजवर्णा च नागकेसरभूषिता ।
जपाकुसुमसङ्काशा जपाकुसुमशोभिता ॥ ९३

प्रिया प्रियङ्करी विष्णोर्दानवेन्द्रविनाशिनी ।
ज्ञानेश्वरी ज्ञानदात्री ज्ञानानन्दप्रदायिनी ॥ ९४

गुणगौरवसम्पन्ना गुणशीलसमन्विता ।
रूपयौवनसम्पन्ना रूपयौवनशोभिता ॥ ९५

गुणाश्रया गुणरता गुणगौरवसुन्दरी ।
मदिरामोदमत्ता च ताटङ्कद्वयशोभिता ॥ ९६

वृक्षमूलस्थिता देवी वृक्षशाखोपरिस्थिता ।
तालमध्याग्रनिलया वृक्षमध्यनिवासिनी ॥ ९७

स्वयम्भूपुष्पसंकाशा स्वयम्भूपुष्पधारिणी ।
स्वयम्भूकुसुमप्रीता स्वयम्भूपुष्पशोभिनी ॥ ९८

स्वयम्भूपुष्परसिका नग्ना ध्यानवती सुधा ।
शुक्रप्रिया शुक्ररता शुक्रमज्जनतत्परा ॥ ९९

पूर्णपर्णा सुपर्णा च निष्पर्णा पापनाशिनी ।
मदिरामोदसम्पन्ना मदिरामोदधारिणी ॥ १००

सर्वाश्रया सर्वगुणा नन्दनन्दनधारिणी ।
नारीपुष्पसमुद्भूता नारीपुष्पोत्सवोत्सवा ॥ १०१

नारीपुष्पसमप्राणा नारीपुष्परता मृगी ।
सर्वकालोद्भवप्रीता सर्वकालोद्भवोत्सवा ॥ १०२

चतुर्भुजा दशभुजा अष्टादशभुजा तथा ।
द्विभुजा षड्भुजा प्रीतारक्तपङ्कजशोभिता ॥ १०३

कौबेरी कौरवी कौर्या कुरुकुल्ला कपालिनी ।
सुदीर्घकदलीजङ्घा रम्भोरू रामवल्लभा ॥ १०४

निशाचरी निशामूर्तिर्निशाचन्द्रसमप्रभा ।
चान्द्री चान्द्रकला चन्द्रा चारुचन्द्रनिभानना ॥ १०५

स्रोतस्वती स्रुतिमती सर्वदुर्गतिनाशिनी ।
सर्वाधारा सर्वमयी सर्वानन्दस्वरूपिणी ॥ १०६

सर्वचक्रेश्वरी सर्वा सर्वमन्त्रमयी शुभा ।
सहस्रनयनप्राणा सहस्रनयनप्रिया ॥ १०७

सहस्रशीर्षा सुषमा सदम्भा सर्वभक्षिका ।
यष्टिका यष्टिचक्रस्था षड्वर्गफलदायिनी ॥ १०८

षड्विंशपद्ममध्यस्था षड्विंशकुलमध्यगा ।
हूँकारवर्णनिलया हूँकाराक्षरभूषणा ॥ १०९

हकारवर्णनिलया हकाराक्षरभूषणा ।
हारिणी हारवलिता हारहीरकभूषणा ॥ ११०

ह्रींकारबीजसहिता ह्रींकारैरुपशोभिता ।
कन्दर्पस्य कला कुन्दा कौलिनी कुलदर्पिता ॥ १११

केतकीकुसुमप्राणा केतकीकृतभूषणा ।
केतकीकुसुमासक्ता केतकीपरिभूषिता ॥ ११२

कर्पूरपूर्णवदना महामाया महेश्वरी ।
कला केलिः क्रिया कीर्णा कदम्बकुसुमोत्सुका ॥ ११३

कादम्बिनी करिशुण्डा कुञ्जरेश्वरगामिनी ।
खर्वा सुखञ्जनयना खञ्जनद्वन्द्वभूषणा ॥ ११४

खद्योत इव दुर्लक्षा खद्योत इव चञ्चला ।
महामाया ज्गद्धात्री गीतवाद्यप्रिया रतिः ॥ ११५

गणेश्वरी गणेज्या च गुणपूज्या गुणप्रदा ।
गुणाढ्या गुणसम्पन्ना गुणदात्री गुणात्मिका ॥ ११६

गुर्वी गुरुतरा गौरी गाणपत्यफलप्रदा ।
महाविद्या महामेधा तुलिनी गणमोहिनी ॥ ११७

भव्या भवप्रिया भाव्या भावनीया भवात्मिका ।
घर्घरा घोरवदना घोरदैत्यविनाशिनी ॥ ११८

घोरा घोरवती घोषा घोरपुत्री घनाचला ।
चर्चरी चारुनयना चारुवक्त्रा चतुर्गुणा ॥ ११९

चतुर्वेदमयी चण्डी चन्द्रास्या चतुरानना ।
चलच्चकोरनयना चलत्खञ्जनलोचना ॥ १२०

चलदम्भोजनिलया चलदम्भोजलोचना ।
छत्री छत्रप्रिया छत्रा छत्रचामरशोभिता ॥ १२१

छिन्नछदा छिन्नशिराश्छिन्ननासा छलात्मिका ।
छलाढ्या छलसंत्रस्ता छलरूपा छलस्थिरा ॥ १२२

छकारवर्णनिलया छकाराढ्या छलप्रिया ।
छद्मिनी छद्मनिरता छद्मच्छद्मनिवासिनी ॥ १२३

जगन्नाथप्रिया जीवा जगन्मुक्तिकरी मता ।
जीर्णा जीमूतवनिता जीमूतैरुपशोभिता ॥ १२४

जामातृवरदा जम्भा जमलार्जुनभञ्जिनी ।
झर्झरी झाकृतिर्झल्ली झरी झर्झरिका तथा ॥ १२५

टङ्कारकारिणी टीका सर्वटङ्कारकारिणी ।
ठंकराङ्गी डमरुका डाकारा डमरुप्रिया ॥ १२६

ढक्कारावरता नित्या तुलसी मणिभूषिता ।
तुला च तोलिका तीर्णा तारा तारणिका तथा ॥ १२७

तन्त्रविज्ञा तन्त्ररता तन्त्रविद्या च तन्त्रदा ।
तान्त्रिकी तन्त्रयोग्या च तन्त्रसारा च तन्त्रिका ॥ १२८

तन्त्रधारी तन्त्रकरी सर्वतन्त्रस्वरूपिणी ।
तुहिनांशुसमानास्या तुहिनांशुसमप्रभा ॥ १२९

तुषाराकरतुल्याङ्गी तुषाराधारसुन्दरी ।
तन्त्रसारा तन्त्रकरो तन्त्रसारस्वरूपिणी ॥ १३०

तुषारधामतुल्यास्या तुषारांशुसमप्रभा ।
तुषाराद्रिसुता ताक्ष्या ताराङ्गी तालसुन्दरी ॥ १३१

तारस्वरेण सहिता तारस्वरविभूषिता ।
थकारकूटनिलया थकाराक्षरमालिनी ॥ १३२

दयावती दीनरता दुःखदारिद्र्यनाशिनी ।
दौर्भाग्यदुःखदलिनी दौर्भाग्यपदनाशिनी ॥ १३३

दुहिता दीनबन्धुश्च दानवेन्द्रविनाशिनी ।
दानपात्री दानरता दानसम्मानतोषिता ॥ १३४

दान्त्यादिसेविता दान्ता दया दामोदरप्रिया ।
दधीचिवरदा तुष्टा दानवेन्द्रविमर्दिनी ॥ १३५

दीर्घनेत्रा दीर्घकचा दीर्घनासा च दीर्घिका ।
दारिद्र्यदुःखसंनाशा दारिद्र्यदुःखनाशिनी ॥ १३६

दाम्भिका दन्तुरा दम्भा दम्भासुरवरप्रदा ।
धनधान्यप्रदा धन्या धनेश्वरधनप्रदा ॥ १३७

धर्मपत्नी धर्मरता धर्माधर्मविविवर्द्धिनी ।
धर्मिणी धर्मिका धर्म्या धर्माधर्मविवर्द्धिनी ॥ १३८

धनेश्वरी धर्मरता धर्मानन्दप्रवर्द्धिनी ।
धनाध्यक्षा धनप्रीता धनाढ्या धनतोषिता ॥ १३९

धीरा धैर्यवती धिष्ण्या धवलाम्भोजसंनिभा ।
धरिणी धारिणी धात्री धूरणी धरणी धरा ॥ १४०

धार्मिका धर्मसहिता धर्मनिन्दकवर्जिता ।
नवीना नगजा निम्ना निम्ननाभिर्नगेश्वरी ॥ १४१

नूतनाम्भोजनयना नवीनाम्भोजसुन्दरी ।
नागरी नगरज्येष्ठा नगराजसुता नगा ॥ १४२

नागराजकृततोषा नागराजविभूषिता ।
नागेश्वरी नागरूढा नागराजकुलेश्वरी ॥ १४३

नवीनेन्दुकला नान्दी नन्दिकेश्वरवल्लभा ।
नीरजा नीरजाक्षी च नीरजद्वन्द्वलोचना ॥ १४४

नीरा नीरभवा वाणी नीरनिर्मलदेहिनी ।
नागयज्ञोपवीताढ्या नागयज्ञोपवीतिका ॥ १४५

नागकेसरसंतुष्टा नागकेसरमालिनी ।
नवीनकेतकीकुन्द मल्लिकाम्भोजभूषिता ॥ १४६ *

नायिका नायकप्रीता नायकप्रेमभूषिता ।
नायकप्रेमसहिता नायकप्रेमभाविता ॥ १४७

नायकानन्दनिलया नायकानन्दकारिणी ।
नर्मकर्मरता नित्यं नर्मकर्मफलप्रदा ॥ १४८

नर्मकर्मप्रिया नर्मा नर्मकर्मकृतालया ।
नर्मप्रीता नर्मरता नर्मध्यानपरायणा ॥ १४९

पौष्णप्रिया च पौष्पेज्या पुष्पदामविभूषिता ।
पुण्यदा पूर्णिमा पूर्णा कोटिपुण्यफलप्रदा ॥ १५०

पुराणागमगोप्या च पुराणागमगोपिता ।
पुराणगोचरा पूर्णा पूर्वा प्रौढा विलासिनी ॥ १५१

प्रह्लादहृदयाह्लादगेहिनी पुण्यचारिणी ।
फाल्गुनी फाल्गुनप्रीता फाल्गुनप्रेधारिणी ॥ १५२

फाल्गुनप्रेमदा चैव फणिराजविभूषिता ।
फणिकाञ्ची फणिप्रीता फणिहारविभूषिता ॥ १५३

फणीशकृतसर्वाङ्गभूषणा फणिहारिणी ।
फणिप्रीता फणिरता फणिकङ्कणधारिणी ॥ १५४

फलदा त्रिफला शक्ता फलाभरणभूषिता ।
फकारकूटसर्वाङ्गी फाल्गुनानन्दवर्द्धिनी ॥ १५५

वासुदेवरता विज्ञा विज्ञविज्ञानकारिणी ।
वीणावती बलाकीर्णा बालपीयूषरोचिका ॥ १५६

बालावसुमती विद्या विद्याहारविभूषिता ।
विद्यावती वैद्यपदप्रीता वैवस्वती बलिः ॥ १५७

बलिविध्वंसिनी चैव वराङ्गस्था वरानना ।
विष्णोर्वक्षःस्थलस्था च वाग्वती विन्ध्यवासिनी ॥ १५८

भीतिदा भयदा भानोरंशुजालसमप्रभा ।
भार्गवेज्या भृगोः पूज्या भरद्वारनमस्कृता ॥ १५९

भीतिदा भयसंहन्त्री भीमाकारा च सुन्दरी ।
मायावती मानरता मानसम्मानतत्परा ॥ १६०

माधवानन्ददा माध्वी मदिरामुदितेक्षणा ।
महोत्सवगुणोपेता महती च महद्गुणा ॥ १६१

मदिरामोदनिरता मदिरामज्जने रता ।
यशोधरी यशोविद्या यशोदानन्दवर्द्धिनी ॥ १६२

यशःकर्पूरधवला यशोदामविभूषिता ।
यमराजप्रिया योगमार्गानन्दप्रवर्द्धिनी ॥ १६३

यमस्वसा च यमुना योगमार्गप्रवर्द्धिनी ।
यादवानन्दकर्त्री च यादवानन्दवर्द्धिनी ॥ १६४

यज्ञप्रीता यज्ञमयी यज्ञकर्मविभूषिता ।
रामप्रीता रामरता रामतोषणतत्परा ॥ १६५

राज्ञी राजकुलेज्या च राजराजेश्वरी रमा ।
रमणी रामणी रम्या रामानन्दप्रदायिनी ॥ १६६

रजनीकरपूर्णास्या रक्तोत्पलविलोचना ।
लाङ्गलिप्रेमसंतुष्टा लाङ्गलिप्रणयप्रिया ॥ १६७

लाक्षारुणा च ललना लीला लीलावती लया ।
लङ्केश्वरगुणप्रीता लङ्केशवरदायिनी ॥ १६८

लवङ्गीकुसुमप्रीता लवङ्गकुसुमस्रजा ।
धाता विवस्वद्द्रुहिणी विवस्वत्प्रेमधारिणी ॥ १६९

शवोपरिसमासीना शववक्षःस्थलस्थिता ।
शरणागतरक्षित्री शरण्या श्रीः शरद्गुणा ॥ १७०

षट्कोणचक्रमध्यस्था सम्पदार्थनिषेविता ।
हूंकाराकारिणी देवी हूंकाररूपशोभिता ॥ १७१

क्षेमङ्करी तथा क्षेमा क्षेमधामविवर्द्धिनी ।
क्षेमाम्नाया तथाज्ञा च इडा इश्वरवल्लभा ॥ १७२

उग्रदक्षा तथा चोग्रा अकारादिस्वरोद्भवा ।
ऋकारवर्णकूटस्था ऋकारस्वरभूषिता ॥ १७३

एकारा च तथा चैका एकाराक्षरवासिता ।
ऐष्टा चैषा तथा चौषा औकाराक्षरधारिणी ॥ १७४

अं अःकारस्वरूपा च सर्वागमसुगोपिता ।
इत्येतत् कथितं देवि तारानामसहस्रकम् ॥ १७५

य इदं पठति स्तोत्रं प्रत्यहं भक्तिभावतः ।
दिवा वा यदि वा रात्रौ सन्ध्ययोरुभयोरपि ॥ १७६

स्तवराजस्य पाठेन राजा भवति किङ्करः ।
सर्वागमेषु पूज्यः स्यात् सर्वतन्त्रे स्वयं हरः ॥ १७७

शिवस्थाने श्मशाने च शून्यागारे चतुष्पथे ।
य पठेच्छृणुयाद् वापि स योगी नात्र संशयः ॥ १७८

यानि नामानि सन्त्यस्मिन् प्रसङ्गाद् मुरवैरिणः ।
ग्राह्याणि तानि कल्याणि नान्यान्यपि कदाचन ॥ १७९

हरेर्नाम न गृह्णीयाद् न स्पृशेत् तुलसीदलम् ।
नान्यचिन्ता प्रकर्तव्या नान्यनिन्दा कदाचन ॥ १८०

सिन्दूरकरवीराद्यैः पुष्पैर्लोहितकैस्तथा ।
योऽर्चयेद् भक्तिभावेन तस्यासाध्यं न किञ्चन ॥ १८१

वातस्तम्भं जलस्तम्भं गतिस्तम्भं विवस्वतः ।
वह्नेः स्तम्भं करोत्येव स्तवस्यास्य प्रकीर्तनात् ॥ १८२

श्रियमाकर्षयेत् तूर्णमानृण्यं जायते हठात् ।
यथा तृणं दहेद् वह्निस्तथारीन् मर्दयेत् क्षणात् ॥ १८३

मोहयेद् राजपत्नीश्च देवानपि वशं नयेत् ।
यः पठेत् शृणुयाद् वापि एकचित्तेन सर्वदा ॥ १८४

दीर्घायुश्च सुखी वाग्मी वाणी तस्य वशङ्करी ।
सर्वतीर्थाभिषेकेण गयाश्राद्धेन यत् फलम् ॥ १८५

तत्फलं लभते सत्यं यः पठेदेकचित्ततः ।
येषामाराधने श्रद्धा ये तु साधितुमुद्यताः ॥ १८६

तेषां कृतित्वं सर्वं स्याद् गतिर्देवि परा च सा ।
ऋतुयुक्तलतागारे स्थित्वा दण्डेन ताडयेत् ॥ १८७

जप्त्वा स्तुत्वा च भक्त्या च गच्छेद् वै तारिणीपदम् ।
अष्टम्यां च चतुर्दश्यां नवम्यां शनिवासरे ॥ १८८

संक्रान्त्यां मण्डले रात्रौ अमावास्यां च योऽर्चयेत् ।
वर्षं व्याप्य च देवेशि तस्याधीनाश्च सिद्धयः ॥ १८९

सुतहीना च या नारी दौर्भाग्यामयपीडिता ।
वन्ध्या वा काकवन्ध्या वा मृतगर्भा च याङ्गना ॥ १९०

धनधान्यविहीना च रोगशोकाकुला च या ।
सापि चैतद् महादेवि भूर्जपत्रे लिखेत्ततः ॥ १९१

सव्ये भुजे च बध्नीयात् सर्वसौख्यवती भवेत् ।
एवं पुमानपि प्रायो दुःखेन परिपीडितः ॥ १९२

सभायां व्यसने घोरे विवादे शत्रुसंकटे ।
चतुरङ्गे च तथा युद्धे सर्वत्रारिप्रपीडिते ॥ १९३

स्मरणादेव कल्याणि संक्षयं यान्ति दूरतः ।
पूजनीयं प्रयत्नेन शून्यागारे शिवालये ॥ १९४

बिल्वमूले श्मशाने च तटे वा कुलमण्डले ।
शर्करासवसंयुक्तैर्भक्तैर्दुग्धैः सपायसैः ॥ १९५

अपूपापिष्टसंयुक्तैर्नैवेद्यैश्च यथोचितैः ।
निवेदितं च यद्द्रव्यं भोक्तव्यं च विधानतः ॥ १९६

तन्न चेद् भुज्यते मोहाद् भोक्तुं नेच्छन्ति देवताः ।
अनेनैव विधानेन योऽर्चयेत् परमेश्वरीम् ॥ १९७

स भूमिवलये देवि साक्षादीशो न संशयः ।
महाशङ्खेन देवेशि सर्वं कार्यं जपादिकम् ॥ १९८

कुलसर्वस्वकस्यैवं प्रभावो वर्णितो मया ।
न शक्यते समाख्यातुं वर्षकोटिशतैरपि ॥ १९९

किञ्चिद् मया च चापल्यात् कथितं परमेश्वरि ।
जन्मान्तरसहस्रेण वर्णितुं नैव शक्यते ॥ २००

कुलीनाय प्रदातव्यं ताराभक्तिपराय च ।
अन्यभक्ताय नो देयं वैष्णवाय विशेषतः ॥ २०१

कुलीनाय महेच्छाय भक्तिश्रद्धापराय च ।
महात्मने सदा देयं परीक्षितगुणाय च ॥ २०२

नाभक्ताय प्रदातव्यं पथ्यन्तरपराय च ।
न देयं देवदेवेशि गोप्यं सर्वागमेषु च ॥ २०३

पूजाजपविहीनाय स्त्रीसुरानिन्दकाय च ।
न स्तवं दर्शयेत् क्वापि सन्दर्श्य शिवहा भवेत् ॥ २०४

पठनीयं सदा देवि सर्वावस्थासु सर्वदा ।
यः स्तोत्रं कुलनायिके प्रतिदिनं भक्त्या पठेद् मानवः
स स्याद्वित्तचयैर्धनेश्वरसमो विद्यामदैर्वाक्पतिः ।

सौन्दर्येण च मूर्तिमान् मनसिजः कीर्त्या च नारायणः
शक्त्या शङ्कर एव सौख्यविभवैर्भूमेः पतिर्नान्यथा ॥ २०५

इति ते कथितं गुह्यं तारानामसहस्रकम् ।
अस्मात् परतरं स्तोत्रं नास्ति तन्त्रेषु निश्चयः ॥ २०६

इति श्रीबृहन्नीलतन्त्रे भैरवभैरवीसंवादे तारासहस्रनामनिरूपणं अष्टादशः पटलः ॥

*****

## *Śrī Tārā Sahasra Nāmāvaliḥ*

*Oṃ Asya Śrīmahogratārā Divya Sāmrājya Medhā Nāma Sahasrakasya Akṣobhyarṣiḥ Bṛhati Chandaḥ* |
*Ugratārāditriśakti Devatā Haṃ Bījaṃ Phaṭ Śaktiḥ Haṃ Kīlakaṃ Śrīmahogratārā Pratyakṣa Darśanādyarthe Viniyogaḥ* ||

*Oṃ Krāṃ Tārāyai Namaḥ* |

*Oṃ Strīhṛdayamahātārāyai Namaḥ* |

*Oṃ Kramugratārāyai Namaḥ* |

*Oṃ Tāriṇyai Namaḥ* |

*Oṃ Taryai Namaḥ* |

*Oṃ Mahogratārāyai Namaḥ* |

*Oṃ Strītārāyai Namaḥ* |

*Oṃ Trikaṭaikajaṭādharāyai Namaḥ* |

*Oṃ Tatathaiyyāyai Namaḥ* |

*Oṃ Bhinapagāyai Namaḥ* |

*Oṃ Tālatāṇḍavarūpiṇyai Namaḥ* |

*Oṃ Tāṇḍavāhlādaniratatahaṇyai Namaḥ* |

*Oṃ Tahaṇākṛtyai Namaḥ* |

*Oṃ Tantryai Namaḥ* |

*Oṃ Vādyaratāyai Namaḥ* |

*Oṃ Tantrāyai Namaḥ* |

*Oṃ Tantraśāstraparāyaṇāyai Namaḥ* |

*Oṃ Tārūṇyāmṛtakallolāyai Namaḥ* |

*Oṃ Tārūṇyāmṛtakanyakāyai Namaḥ* |

*Oṃ Tārūṇyāmṛtacāndryai Namaḥ* | 20

*Oṃ Tattvadarśanatatparāyai Namaḥ* |

*Oṃ Tīrthasevāparātuṣṭāyai Namaḥ* |

*Oṃ Trāṃ Trīṃ Trūṃ Traiṃ Svarūpiṇyai Namaḥ* |

*Oṃ Oṅkārātraḥsvarūpāyai Namaḥ* |

*Oṃ Trasāyai Namaḥ* |

*Oṃ Trastagatīsthāyai Namaḥ* |

*Oṃ Tanimrālālavṛkṣasthāyai Namaḥ* | *

*Oṃ Tālīpānaparāyaṇāyai Namaḥ* |

*Oṃ Taruṇīkuṇḍaniratāyai Namaḥ* |

*Oṃ Taruṇīkuṇḍarūpiṇyai Namaḥ* |

*Oṃ Taruṇīkusumāhlādāyai Namaḥ* |

*Oṃ Taruṇībījarūpiṇyai Namaḥ* |

*Oṃ Taruṇīgarbhasambhūtāyai Namaḥ* |

*Oṃ Taruṇīdhyānatatparāyai Namaḥ* |

*Oṃ Taruṇīpūjāniratāyai Namaḥ* |

*Oṃ Taruṇībhaktatatparāyai Namaḥ* |

*Oṃ Taruṇīlocanānandalaharyai Namaḥ* |

*Oṃ Tārkṣyavāhanāyai Namaḥ* |

*Oṃ Tārarūpāyai Namaḥ* |

*Oṃ Tāmraparṇyai Namaḥ* | 40

*Oṃ Tāmrapatrasamasthitāyai Namaḥ* |

*Oṃ Taruṇīkusumāmohāyai Namaḥ* |

*Oṃ Taruṇīpuṣparūpiṇyai Namaḥ* |

*Oṃ Taruṇītāḍikānnāthāyai Namaḥ* |

*Oṃ Taruṇīmukhagocarāyai Namaḥ* |

*Oṃ Taruṇīkeśasaṃsthāyai Namaḥ* |

*Oṃ Taruṇīmukhamadhyagāyai Namaḥ* |

*Oṃ Taruṇīvākyamadhyāyai Namaḥ* |

*Oṃ Taruṇītāṇḍavarṇavāyai Namaḥ* |

*Oṃ Taruṇīgānasantuṣṭāyai Namaḥ* |

*Oṃ Taruṇībhaktatatparāyai Namaḥ* ǀ

*Oṃ Taruṇīmuktīmālāyai Namaḥ* ǀ

*Oṃ Taruṇībhaktarūpiṇyai Namaḥ* ǀ

*Oṃ Taruṇīgamanaprītyāyai Namaḥ* ǀ

*Oṃ Taruṇīhāsyatatparāyai Namaḥ* ǀ

*Oṃ Taruṇīnāmikānantāyai Namaḥ* ǀ

*Oṃ Taruṇīratnarūpiṇyai Namaḥ* ǀ

*Oṃ Taruṇīgamanaprītyāyai Namaḥ* ǀ

*Oṃ Taruṇīyogarūpiṇyai Namaḥ* ǀ

*Oṃ Taruṇīcumbanaratāyai Namaḥ* ǀ 60

*Oṃ Taruṇīliṅgarūpiṇyai Namaḥ* ǀ

*Oṃ Tulāyai Namaḥ* ǀ

*Oṃ Tulātalpāyai Namaḥ* ǀ

*Oṃ Tulajāpuravāsinyai Namaḥ* ǀ

*Oṃ Tanāna Nāsvarūpāyai Namaḥ* ǀ *

*Oṃ Tathairūpapradhāriṇyai Namaḥ* ǀ

*Oṃ Totalāyai Namaḥ* ǀ

*Oṃ Tailasaṃprītāyai Namaḥ* ǀ

*Oṃ Tṛpyatimārgaparāyaṇāyai Namaḥ* ǀ

*Oṃ Tṛsitāyai Namaḥ* ǀ

*Oṃ Tṛṇarūpāyai Namaḥ* ǀ

*Oṃ Tārtīyaguṇabhūṣitāyai Namaḥ* ǀ

*Oṃ Tārtīyabījarūpāyai Namaḥ* ǀ

*Oṃ Tārtīyākṣararūpiṇyai Namaḥ* ǀ

*Oṃ Tattvajñānāyai Namaḥ* ǀ

*Oṃ Tattvabuddhyai Namaḥ* ǀ

*Oṃ Tattvanāthāyai Namaḥ* ǀ

*Oṃ Tathāmatyai Namaḥ* ǀ

*Oṃ Taulityai Namaḥ* I

*Oṃ Tvavāpyai Namaḥ* I 80 *

*Oṃ Tarasthārūpiṇyai Namaḥ* I

*Oṃ Tamātaramadhyasvarūpāyai Namaḥ* I

*Oṃ Taradannara Namaḥ* I *

*Oṃ Tāmatyai Namaḥ* I *

*Oṃ Tarumūlasthitāyai Namaḥ* I

*Oṃ Tandrāyai Namaḥ* I

*Oṃ Tuṣṭistraikālyarūpiṇyai Namaḥ* I

*Oṃ Trikālyadāyai Namaḥ* I

*Oṃ Trairpakṣa Tārāṇāpaka Bhūṣaṇāyai Namaḥ* I *

*Oṃ Tvaritāyai Namaḥ* I

*Oṃ Tvaritaprītāyai Namaḥ* I

*Oṃ Tattvadarśyai Namaḥ* I

*Oṃ Tamasvinyai Namaḥ* I

*Oṃ Tārākṣahāriṇyai Namaḥ* I

*Oṃ Tīrṇāyai Namaḥ* I

*Oṃ Tārūṇyakuṇḍabhoginyai Namaḥ* I

*Oṃ Thakāravarṇanilayāyai Namaḥ* I

*Oṃ Thakārākṣararūpiṇyai Namaḥ* I

*Oṃ Thaithairūpāyai Namaḥ* I

*Oṃ Tharigrūpāyai Namaḥ* I

*Oṃ Thauṅgadādikarūpiṇyai Namaḥ* I 100

*Oṃ Sthūlavudhnyai Namaḥ* I

*Oṃ Sthūlatanusthātadhyānaparāyaṇāyai Namaḥ* I

*Oṃ Thethakuṭākṣaraupyāṃ Thīnthū Ṅkārākṣaramālinyai Namaḥ* I*

*Oṃ Thara Rūpādakṣaṇāyai Namaḥ* I *

*Oṃ Dānasanmānadāyinyai Namaḥ* I

*Oṃ Dakṣaputryai Namaḥ* I

*Oṃ Dakṣayajñanāśinyai Namaḥ* I

*Oṃ Dānavyai Namaḥ* I

*Oṃ Dayāyai Namaḥ* I

*Oṃ Dayāhṛdayādāntāyai Namaḥ* I

*Oṃ Daityanāśanakāriṇyai Namaḥ* I

*Oṃ Dayāle Namaḥ* I

*Oṃ Daityaśamanyai Namaḥ* I

*Oṃ Dravyaghne Namaḥ* I

*Oṃ Dravyavatsālyai Namaḥ* I

*Oṃ Dravyagītāyai Namaḥ* I

*Oṃ Dravyamātre Namaḥ* I

*Oṃ Dāntāyai Namaḥ* I

*Oṃ Dāridryanāśinyai Namaḥ* I

*Oṃ Dayārtāyai Namaḥ* I 120

*Oṃ Dīpinyai Namaḥ* I

*Oṃ Diśāyai Namaḥ* I

*Oṃ Dīpamārgaparāyaṇāyai Namaḥ* I

*Oṃ Dīnaprītāyai Namaḥ* I

*Oṃ Dīrghajivhāyai Namaḥ* I

*Oṃ Dāridryanāśinyai Namaḥ* I

*Oṃ Dittyai Namaḥ* I

*Oṃ Duḥkhasaṃhāriṇyai Namaḥ* I

*Oṃ Duṣṭadaityavidhvaṃsanakṣamāyai Namaḥ* I

*Oṃ Dāḍimīpuṣparūpāyai Namaḥ* I

*Oṃ Dāḍimīpuṣpapūjitāyai Namaḥ* I

*Oṃ Dāḍimīvājadattāyai Namaḥ* I

*Oṃ Dāḍīrūpāyai Namaḥ* I

*Oṃ Darasthitāyai Namaḥ* I

*Oṃ Dīrghākṣyai Namaḥ* I

*Oṃ Dīrghanāsāyai Namaḥ* I

*Oṃ Dīkṣitāyai Namaḥ* I

*Oṃ Dīkṣiteśvaryai Namaḥ* I

*Oṃ Durgāyai Namaḥ* I

*Oṃ Durgavihantryai Namaḥ* I 140

*Oṃ Duḥkhapraṇāśinyai Namaḥ* I

*Oṃ Daryai Namaḥ* I

*Oṃ Daurgāsuravihantryai Namaḥ* I

*Oṃ Durgadāraṇatatparāyai Namaḥ* I

*Oṃ Dānadakṣāyai Namaḥ* I

*Oṃ Dānapūjāyai Namaḥ* I

*Oṃ Dānatuṣṭāyai Namaḥ* I

*Oṃ Dayātatyai Namaḥ* I

*Oṃ Dāsyai Namaḥ* I

*Oṃ Dāsīkuṇḍaratyai Namaḥ* I

*Oṃ Dāsīpuṣpaparāyaṇāyai Namaḥ* I

*Oṃ Dāsībījaratāyai Namaḥ* I

*Oṃ Dānāyai Namaḥ* I

*Oṃ Dīnāradāyinyai Namaḥ* I

*Oṃ Drutyai Namaḥ* I

*Oṃ Drutasiddhakaryai Namaḥ* I

*Oṃ Dīrghāyai Namaḥ* I

*Oṃ Dīrghākāyai Namaḥ* I *

*Oṃ Dīkṣitapriyāyai Namaḥ* I

*Oṃ Dāsīcumbanasantuṣṭāyai Namaḥ* I 160

*Oṃ Dāsīmathanatatparāyai Namaḥ* I

*Oṃ Dāsīkuṇḍaprītaprāṇāyai Namaḥ* I

*Oṃ Dāndīndūndaiṃ Svarūpiṇyai Namaḥ* I

*Oṃ Dūṃ Bījajapasantuṣṭāyai Namaḥ* I

*Oṃ Dūṃvusvāhāsvarūpiṇyai Namaḥ* I *

*Oṃ Dhanadāyai Namaḥ* I

*Oṃ Dhananāthāyai Namaḥ* I

*Oṃ Dhanadhānyavivardhinyai Namaḥ* I

*Oṃ Dhūṃ Bījanilayāyai Namaḥ* I

*Oṃ Dhūmrāyai Namaḥ* I 170

*Oṃ Dhūdhūndhūmāvatyai Namaḥ* I

*Oṃ Dhṛtyai Namaḥ* I

*Oṃ Dhairyadāyai Namaḥ* I

*Oṃ Dhāriṇyai Namaḥ* I

*Oṃ Dhairyāyai Namaḥ* I

*Oṃ Dharitryai Namaḥ* I

*Oṃ Dharādharāyai Namaḥ* I

*Oṃ Dharmiṣṭhāyai Namaḥ* I

*Oṃ Dharmaniratāyai Namaḥ* I

*Oṃ Dharmamārgaparāyaṇāyai Namaḥ* I 180

*Oṃ Dharmaprāṇāyai Namaḥ* I

*Oṃ Dharmagatyai Namaḥ* I

*Oṃ Dhārāsampātarūpiṇyai Namaḥ* I

*Oṃ Dhimitharihavarūpāyai Namaḥ* I

*Oṃ Dharmatārāyai Namaḥ* I

*Oṃ Dhanārcitāyai Namaḥ* I

*Oṃ Dhyai Namaḥ* I *

*Oṃ Dhiṣaṇāyai Namaḥ* ।

*Oṃ Dhīragatyai Namaḥ* ।

*Oṃ Dhīrādhīrasvarūpiṇyai Namaḥ* । 190

*Oṃ Dhātrīprasūnasantuṣṭāyai Namaḥ* ।

*Oṃ Dhātrīphalakucadvayāyai Namaḥ* ।

*Oṃ Dhātrīdhyānaratāyai Namaḥ* ।

*Oṃ Dhyānāyai Namaḥ* ।

*Oṃ Dhyānatattvaparāyaṇāyai Namaḥ* ।

*Oṃ Dhyānadātryai Namaḥ* ।

*Oṃ Dhyānagātrāyai Namaḥ* ।

*Oṃ Dhyānasthāyai Namaḥ* ।

*Oṃ Dhyānarūpiṇyai Namaḥ* ।

*Oṃ Dhyeyarūpāyai Namaḥ* । 200

*Oṃ Dhyeyagamyāyai Namaḥ* ।

*Oṃ Dhyeyacakrasamasthitāyai Namaḥ* ।

*Oṃ Dhyānaparāyaṇaprītāyai Namaḥ* ।

*Oṃ Dhyānadhyeyasvarūpiṇyai Namaḥ* ।

*Oṃ Dhyānagamyāyai Namaḥ* ।

*Oṃ Dhyānatuṣṭāyai Namaḥ* ।

*Oṃ Dhyānagānaparāyaṇāyai Namaḥ* ।

*Oṃ Dhikatāndhisvarūpāyai Namaḥ* ।

*Oṃ Dhaidhaiśabdaparāyaṇāyai Namaḥ* ।

*Oṃ Dharmiṇyai Namaḥ* ।

*Oṃ Dharmapakṣāṅgāyai Namaḥ* ।

*Oṃ Dharmakarmaparāyaṇāyai Namaḥ* ।

*Oṃ Dharmagrāmaratāṅghriṃ Dhrīndhrīndhūndhauṃ Svarūpiṇyai Namaḥ* । *

*Oṃ Nararūpāyai Namaḥ* ।

*Oṃ Naraprītāyai Namaḥ* ।

*Oṃ Naranāthāyai Namaḥ* ।

*Oṃ Narātmikāyai Namaḥ* ।

*Oṃ Nārasiṃhyai Namaḥ* ।

*Oṃ Natyai Namaḥ* ।

*Oṃ Nāryai Namaḥ* । 220

*Oṃ Narapuṣpasvarūpiṇyai Namaḥ* ।

*Oṃ Narapuṣpapriyaprāṇāyai Namaḥ* ।

*Oṃ Narapuṣpapratarpitāyai Namaḥ* ।

*Oṃ Narapuṣpārcanapuṣpāyai Namaḥ* ।

*Oṃ Narapuṣpakriyāmatyai Namaḥ* ।

*Oṃ Narapuṣpārcanānandāyai Namaḥ* ।

*Oṃ Narapuṣpāmbarāyai Namaḥ* ।

*Oṃ Nadyai Namaḥ* ।

*Oṃ Narayajñāyai Namaḥ* ।

*Oṃ Narānandāyai Namaḥ* ।

*Oṃ Narayajñaparāyaṇāyai Namaḥ* ।

*Oṃ Naranāpūratānāyai Namaḥ* ।

*Oṃ Natanānāsvarūpiṇyai Namaḥ* ।

*Oṃ Nānāmānāyai Namaḥ* ।

*Oṃ Nanananāsvarūpāyai Namaḥ* ।

*Oṃ Nāprarvitāyai Namaḥ* । *

*Oṃ Nāprītāyai Namaḥ* ।

*Oṃ Nāpraśālāyai Namaḥ* ।

*Oṃ Nāṭikānandatoṣitāyai Namaḥ* ।

*Oṃ Nānābhāṣāprarūḍhāyai Namaḥ* । 240

*Oṃ Nānāvarṇasvarūpiṇyai Namaḥ* I

*Oṃ Nāginyai Namaḥ* I

*Oṃ Nāgabhūṣāyai Namaḥ* I

*Oṃ Nāgārhārnāgarūpiṇyai Namaḥ* I

*Oṃ Nagajvānagasambhūtāyai Namaḥ* I

*Oṃ Nagavaṃśa Pratoṣitāyai Namaḥ* I

*Oṃ Nādarūpāyai Namaḥ* I

*Oṃ Nādagatyai Namaḥ* I

*Oṃ Nādabrahmaparāyaṇāyai Namaḥ* I

*Oṃ Nāradapriyasantuṣṭāyai Namaḥ* I

*Oṃ Nāradapriyamānasāyai Namaḥ* I

*Oṃ Nāradāyai Namaḥ* I *

*Oṃ Nāradeśyai Namaḥ* I

*Oṃ Nadīnimnasvarūpiṇyai Namaḥ* I

*Oṃ Nimnanābhyai Namaḥ* I

*Oṃ Nyai Namaḥ* I *

*Oṃ Yonyai Namaḥ* I

*Oṃ Nimnanetrāyai Namaḥ* I

*Oṃ Narottamāyai Namaḥ* I

*Oṃ Naravāhanasantuṣṭāyai Namaḥ* I 260

*Oṃ Naravāhanatatparāyai Namaḥ* I

*Oṃ Nānnīnnūnnainnauṃ Svarūpāyai Namaḥ* I

*Oṃ Namorūpāyai Namo Namaḥ* I

*Oṃ Namaskārapriyāyai Namaḥ* I

*Oṃ Nityāyai Namaḥ* I

*Oṃ Nityānandasvarūpiṇyai Namaḥ* I

*Oṃ Nityapūjārcanaprītāyai Namaḥ* I

*Oṃ Nityapūjāparāyaṇāyai Namaḥ* I

*Oṃ Nityotsavaparānandāyai Namaḥ* |

*Oṃ Nīrarūpāyai Namaḥ* |

*Oṃ Nīrākṛtyai Namaḥ* |

*Oṃ Narmadāyai Namaḥ* |

*Oṃ Narmarūpāyai Namaḥ* |

*Oṃ Narmakuṇḍavīkānyai Namaḥ* | *

*Oṃ Narmakuṇḍalelihānāyai Namaḥ* |

*Oṃ Narmanaṭapriyāyai Namaḥ* |

*Oṃ Naimittikārcanaprītāyai Namaḥ* |

*Oṃ Naimittikaparāyaṇāyai Namaḥ* |

*Oṃ Narmadāyai Namaḥ* |

*Oṃ Narmadātryai Namaḥ* | 280

*Oṃ Narmakarmaparāyaṇāyai Namaḥ* |

*Oṃ Nīvīmocanasantuṣṭāyai Namaḥ* |

*Oṃ Nīvīmocanatatparāyai Namaḥ* |

*Oṃ Nārīpuṣpapriyāprāṇāyai Namaḥ* |

*Oṃ Nārīpuṣpaparāyaṇāyai Namaḥ* |

*Oṃ Nārīpuṣpamatīprītāyai Namaḥ* |

*Oṃ Nārīpuṣpasvarūpiṇyai Namaḥ* |

*Oṃ Nairyāpikāyai Namaḥ* |

*Oṃ Navavīṇāyai Namaḥ* |

*Oṃ Nāḍīnādaparāyaṇāyai Namaḥ* |

*Oṃ Nāḍīnādaparānandāyai Namaḥ* |

*Oṃ Nāḍīnādaparāgatyai Namaḥ* |

*Oṃ Nāḍīnādātmikāyai Namaḥ* |

*Oṃ Naukāyai Namaḥ* |

*Oṃ Naukākrīḍāparāyaṇāyai Namaḥ* |

*Oṃ Padmapūjanasantuṣṭāyai Namaḥ* |

*Oṃ Padmahomaparāyaṇāyai Namaḥ* I

*Oṃ Paramānandasandohāyai Namaḥ* I

*Oṃ Paramākāśarūpiṇyai Namaḥ* I

*Oṃ Parātītāyai Namaḥ* I 300

*Oṃ Parāgamyāyai Namaḥ* I

*Oṃ Paramātmane Namaḥ* I

*Oṃ Parāgatyai Namaḥ* I

*Oṃ Pampātīranivāsāyai Namaḥ* I

*Oṃ Pradyumnaprītirūpiṇyai Namaḥ* I

*Oṃ PrāṇaVāyai Namaḥ* I *

*Oṃ Prāṇavejyāyai Namaḥ* I

*Oṃ Paratattvāyai Namaḥ* I

*Oṃ Parāyaṇāyai Namaḥ* I

*Oṃ Padmapatrāyai Namaḥ* I

*Oṃ Padmatuṣṭāyai Namaḥ* I

*Oṃ Tuṣṭīpāvanarūpiṇyai Namaḥ* I

*Oṃ Pāpasaṃhāriṇyai Namaḥ* I

*Oṃ Tuṣṭāyai Namaḥ* I

*Oṃ Puṇyadātryai Namaḥ* I

*Oṃ Parātaryai Namaḥ* I *

*Oṃ Puryai Namaḥ* I

*Oṃ Purāryai Namaḥ* I

*Oṃ Gṛhiṇyai Namaḥ* I

*Oṃ Purāṇāgamarūpiṇyai Namaḥ* I 320

*Oṃ Purāṇagamyāyai Namaḥ* I

*Oṃ Pānāṭyāyai Namaḥ* I *

*Oṃ Pānatoṣaṇatatparāyai Namaḥ* I

*Oṃ Pānānandāyai Namaḥ* |

*Oṃ Pītatanusthāyai Namaḥ* |

*Oṃ Taivapyai Namaḥ* | *

*Oṃ Rasasvanyai Namaḥ* |

*Oṃ Pīnayonyai Namaḥ* |

*Oṃ Pītajaṅghāyai Namaḥ* |

*Oṃ Pītāmbaradharāvatyai Namaḥ* |

*Oṃ Pītāmbarāyai Namaḥ* |

*Oṃ Pītagarbhāyai Namaḥ* |

*Oṃ Pītapuṣpārcanapriyāyai Namaḥ* |

*Oṃ Pītapuṣpāñjaliratāyai Namaḥ* |

*Oṃ Pītadrada Nivāsinyai Namaḥ* | *

*Oṃ Pīṭhasthāyai Namaḥ* |

*Oṃ Pīṭharūpāyai Namaḥ* |

*Oṃ Pīṭhavāsaparāyaṇāyai Namaḥ* |

*Oṃ Paradārapriyāyai Namaḥ* |

*Oṃ Patrādharadhāra Praharṣiṇyai Namaḥ* | 340

*Oṃ Paradārapraharasyai Namaḥ* | *

*Oṃ Paradāravirodhinyai Namaḥ* |

*Oṃ Paradārapriyāpātrāyai Namaḥ* |

*Oṃ Pātratoṣaṇatatparāyai Namaḥ* |

*Oṃ Pātrarūpāyai Namaḥ* |

*Oṃ Pātratuṣṭyai Namaḥ* |

*Oṃ Pātradānaparāyaṇāyai Namaḥ* |

*Oṃ Pātrapuṣpapriyāyai Namaḥ* |

*Oṃ Pātrakuṇḍānandapareśvaryai Namaḥ* |

*Oṃ Pātrārādhanasantuṣṭāyai Namaḥ* |

*Oṃ Pātraprāsādarūpiṇyai Namaḥ* |

*Oṃ Pavitrāyai Namaḥ* I

*Oṃ Puṇyacāritrāyai Namaḥ* I

*Oṃ Pavitrāropaṇātmikāyai Namaḥ* I

*Oṃ Pavitraropaṇaratāyai Namaḥ* I

*Oṃ Pātragānaparāyaṇāyai Namaḥ* I

*Oṃ Pātragīta Pātranapāyai Namaḥ* I *

*Oṃ Pātrasaṃyogarūpiṇyai Namaḥ* I

*Oṃ Pātrakuṇḍavikasatāyai Namaḥ* I

*Oṃ Pātrakuṇḍavilohinyai Namaḥ* I 360

*Oṃ Pātrakuṇḍadhvaniratāyai Namaḥ* I

*Oṃ Pātrakuṇḍadhvanipriyāyai Namaḥ* I

*Oṃ Paranidrāvinirmuktāyai Namaḥ* I

*Oṃ Paradravyavimocanyai Namaḥ* I

*Oṃ Parasvanāśinīprītāyai Namaḥ* I

*Oṃ Pārvatyai Namaḥ* I

*Oṃ Parvatātmajāyai Namaḥ* I

*Oṃ Parvatejyāyai Namaḥ* I

*Oṃ Parvaratāyai Namaḥ* I

*Oṃ Parvatapriyarūpiṇyai Namaḥ* I

*Oṃ Parāyaṇāyai Namaḥ* I

*Oṃ Pāracyai Namaḥ* I

*Oṃ Patidharmavidhāriṇyai Namaḥ* I

*Oṃ Patipriyāyai Namaḥ* I

*Oṃ Prītiratāyai Namaḥ* I

*Oṃ Patigamyāyai Namaḥ* I

*Oṃ Pativratāyai Namaḥ* I

*Oṃ Pativratadharāyai Namaḥ* I

*Oṃ Pīnavakṣojadvayadhāriṇyai Namaḥ* I

*Oṃ Piśācapremasantuṣṭāyai Namaḥ* I 380

*Oṃ Pretakoṭisamākulāyai Namaḥ* I

*Oṃ Pretagarbhāyai Namaḥ* I

*Oṃ Pretarūpāyai Namaḥ* I

*Oṃ Pretabhūṣaṇabhūṣaṇyai Namaḥ* I

*Oṃ Pretamālākaṇṭhabhūṣāyai Namaḥ* I

*Oṃ Pretalehanatatparāyai Namaḥ* I

*Oṃ Pretāśyai Namaḥ* I

*Oṃ Pretarājñyai Namaḥ* I

*Oṃ Pretavrataparāyaṇāyai Namaḥ* I

*Oṃ Piśācānandasantoṣāyai Namaḥ* I

*Oṃ Pārthaprītiparāyaṇāyai Namaḥ* I

*Oṃ Pārthivāyai Namaḥ* I

*Oṃ Pārthavejyāyai Namaḥ* I

*Oṃ Pṛthulāyai Namaḥ* I

*Oṃ Pṛthurūpiṇyai Namaḥ* I

*Oṃ Pṛthvyai Namaḥ* I

*Oṃ Pṛthivyai Namaḥ* I

*Oṃ Piṅgāyai Namaḥ* I

*Oṃ Piṅganetrāyai Namaḥ* I 400

*Oṃ Piṅkaṭāyai Namaḥ* I *

*Oṃ Pāpān Vināśinyai Namaḥ* I

*Oṃ Padyāyai Namaḥ* I

*Oṃ Gadyapadyaparāyaṇāyai Namaḥ* I

*Oṃ Padyātmikāyai Namaḥ* I

*Oṃ Padyaratāyai Namaḥ* I

*Oṃ Pāmpīmpūmpauṃ*

*Svarūpiṇyai Namaḥ* ।

*Oṃ Pāmpīṅkārāratāyai Namaḥ* ।

*Oṃ Prāṇāyai Namaḥ* ।

*Oṃ Prāṇadātryai Namaḥ* ।

*Oṃ Pratāpinyai Namaḥ* ।

*Oṃ Prabhāvatyai Namaḥ* ।

*Oṃ Prabhāpremāyai Namaḥ* ।

*Oṃ Premayogaparāyaṇāyai Namaḥ* ।

*Oṃ Prajñāyai Namaḥ* ।

*Oṃ Prajñāvatīprajñāyai Namaḥ* ।

*Oṃ Prajñānapratibhāvatyai Namaḥ* ।

*Oṃ Pratibhāyai Namaḥ* ।

*Oṃ Praṇatīprāṇāyai Namaḥ* ।

*Oṃ Prajñāpatigrahasthitāyai Namaḥ* । 420

*Oṃ Prajāpatyai Namaḥ* ।

*Oṃ Priyāpārāyai Namaḥ* । *

*Oṃ Purīndradhvajaśobhitāyai Namaḥ* ।

*Oṃ Pramatīprāṇadhartryai Namaḥ* ।

*Oṃ Pratijñāpāragāminyai Namaḥ* ।

*Oṃ Phumphuṅkārāyai Namaḥ* ।

*Oṃ Phaṭkārāyai Namaḥ* ।

*Oṃ Phaṭkārarūpadhāriṇyai Namaḥ* ।

*Oṃ Phrīṅkāraphūtkṛtyai Namaḥ* ।

*Oṃ Phrūṃ Sphaṅkārārūpadhāriṇyai Namaḥ* ।

*Oṃ Phroṅkārāpheravyai Namaḥ* ।

*Oṃ Phrāmphrūmphetkāryai Namaḥ* ।

*Oṃ Phaṇadhāriṇyai Namaḥ* ।

*Oṃ Pheṇiprītāyai Namaḥ* ।

*Oṃ Phaṇeratāyai Namaḥ* |

*Oṃ Phaṇadarśanatoṣiṇyai Namaḥ* |

*Oṃ Phaṇibhūṣaṇasambhūṣāyai Namaḥ* |

*Oṃ Phaṇināthapriyārcitāyai Namaḥ* |

*Oṃ Phaṇibandhasamudbhūtāyai Namaḥ* |

*Oṃ Phaṇivaṃśasuśobhinyai Namaḥ* | 440

*Oṃ Paśuhastāyai Namaḥ* |

*Oṃ Paśumatyai Namaḥ* |

*Oṃ Paraśurāmaprasādinyai Namaḥ* |

*Oṃ Phetkārabhairavyai Namaḥ* |

*Oṃ Phrauṇṭāyai Namaḥ* |

*Oṃ Phretkārāravabhāṣiṇyai Namaḥ* |

*Oṃ Phretkārāyai Namaḥ* |

*Oṃ Phālgunānandāyai Namaḥ* |

*Oṃ Phalyai Namaḥ* |

*Oṃ Phullapriyāyai Namaḥ* |

*Oṃ Phulāyai Namaḥ* |

*Oṃ Phaladātryai Namaḥ* |

*Oṃ Phalaratāyai Namaḥ* |

*Oṃ Phalarūpāyai Namaḥ* |

*Oṃ Phalātmikāyai Namaḥ* |

*Oṃ Phalahomapriyasphālāyai Namaḥ* |

*Oṃ Phalanāmaparāyaṇāyai Namaḥ* |

*Oṃ Bṛhaspatimukhasthāyai Namaḥ* |

*Oṃ Bṛhatīchandarūpiṇyai Namaḥ* |

*Oṃ Bṛhatsevāyai Namaḥ* | 460

*Oṃ Bṛhatbrahmyai Namaḥ* |

*Oṃ Brahmībrahmaprapūjitāyai Namaḥ* I

*Oṃ Brahmavṛttadharāvīṇāyai Namaḥ* I

*Oṃ Bāṇasandhānakāriṇyai Namaḥ* I

*Oṃ Bāṇāsurārcitāyai Namaḥ* I

*Oṃ Brūṃ Brāmbrīmbraimbrauṃ Svarūpiṇyai Namaḥ* I

*Oṃ Barhipichumiyāyai Namaḥ* I *

*Oṃ Barhāyai Namaḥ* I

*Oṃ Barhapichavibhūṣaṇāyai Namaḥ* I

*Oṃ Baṭukāyai Namaḥ* I

*Oṃ Baṭukejyāyai Namaḥ* I

*Oṃ Baṭukaprāṇamānasāyai Namaḥ* I

*Oṃ Baṭūkābhairavaratāyai Namaḥ* I

*Oṃ Baṭukārcanatoṣiṇyai Namaḥ* I

*Oṃ Baṭukārcanasantuṣṭāyai Namaḥ* I

*Oṃ Balīdānapriyāvalyai Namaḥ* I

*Oṃ Balipūjyāyai Namaḥ* I

*Oṃ Baliratāyai Namaḥ* I

*Oṃ Balidānanivāsinyai Namaḥ* I

*Oṃ Balidvārasthitāyai Namaḥ* I 480

*Oṃ Bālāyai Namaḥ* I

*Oṃ Bālāmbāyai Namaḥ* I

*Oṃ Bālabhairavyai Namaḥ* I

*Oṃ Bālakrīḍāmayaprāṇāyai Namaḥ* I

*Oṃ Bālakapriyakāriṇyai Namaḥ* I

*Oṃ Balituṣṭāyai Namaḥ* I

*Oṃ Baliratāyai Namaḥ* I

*Oṃ Balitoṣaṇakāriṇyai Namaḥ* I

*Oṃ Balimātre Namaḥ* I

*Oṃ Balimayyai Namaḥ* I

*Oṃ Balitattvātmikāvalyai Namaḥ* I

*Oṃ Balāyai Namaḥ* I

*Oṃ Balārcanaprītāyai Namaḥ* I

*Oṃ Baladhāraṇatatparāyai Namaḥ* I

*Oṃ Baṭukārādhanaratāyai Namaḥ* I

*Oṃ Baṭukejyāyai Namaḥ* I

*Oṃ Baṭupriyāyai Namaḥ* I

*Oṃ Baṭukārādhanaprītāyai Namaḥ* I

*Oṃ Baṭukāryavatāriṇyai Namaḥ* I

*Oṃ Baṭutārāyai Namaḥ* I 500

*Oṃ Baṭuchinnāyai Namaḥ* I

*Oṃ Baṭukālyai Namaḥ* I

*Oṃ Bṛhanmayyai Namaḥ* I

*Oṃ Bṛhatkukṣyai Namaḥ* I

*Oṃ Bṛhattārāyai Namaḥ* I

*Oṃ Bṛhattantrāgameśvaryai Namaḥ* I

*Oṃ Bṛhadruṇāyai Namaḥ* I *

*Oṃ Bṛhadyantrāyai Namaḥ* I

*Oṃ Bṛhattantrāyai Namaḥ* I

*Oṃ Bṛhatkalāyai Namaḥ* I

*Oṃ Bṛhanmātre Namaḥ* I

*Oṃ Bṛhajjvālāyai Namaḥ* I

*Oṃ Bṛhanmānamayyai Namaḥ* I

*Oṃ Bṛhate Namaḥ* I

*Oṃ Bṛhattāṇḍavarūpāyai Namaḥ* I

*Oṃ Bṛhattāruṇyarūpiṇyai Namaḥ* I

*Oṃ Bṛhadāraṇyasaṃsevyāyai Namaḥ* I

*Oṃ Bālacandrakirīṭinyai Namaḥ* ।

*Oṃ Baladāyai Namaḥ* ।

*Oṃ Bāhubhūṣāyai Namaḥ* । 520

*Oṃ Bāhumālāvibhūṣaṇāyai Namaḥ* ।

*Oṃ Bāhulāyai Namaḥ* ।

*Oṃ Bāhuleyesyai Namaḥ* । *

*Oṃ Bāhuleyasvarūpiṇyai Namaḥ* ।

*Oṃ Bahubhāṣāmayyai Namaḥ* ।

*Oṃ Buddhyāyai Namaḥ* । *

*Oṃ Buddhidāyai Namaḥ* ।

*Oṃ Buddhidāyinyai Namaḥ* ।

*Oṃ Buddhyai Namaḥ* ।

*Oṃ Buddhimatāyai Namaḥ* ।

*Oṃ Bauddhāyai Namaḥ* ।

*Oṃ Bauddhācāraparāyaṇāyai Namaḥ* ।

*Oṃ Bauddhamārgapriyāprītāyai Namaḥ* ।

*Oṃ Bauddhamārgapravartinyai Namaḥ* ।

*Oṃ Bṛhaspatisutārādhyāyai Namaḥ* ।

*Oṃ Buddhimātre Namaḥ* ।

*Oṃ Budheśvaryai Namaḥ* ।

*Oṃ Bauddhāvārūpiṇyai Namaḥ* ।

*Oṃ Bhāryāyai Namaḥ* ।

*Oṃ Bhānavyai Namaḥ* । 540

*Oṃ Bhānurūpiṇyai Namaḥ* ।

*Oṃ Bhānumattāyai Namaḥ* ।

*Oṃ Bhānumayyai Namaḥ* ।

*Oṃ Bhānubhāryāyai Namaḥ* ।

*Oṃ Bhaveśvaryai Namaḥ* I

*Oṃ Bhavapatnyai Namaḥ* I

*Oṃ Bhayaharāyai Namaḥ* I

*Oṃ Bhavadānavanāśinyai Namaḥ* I

*Oṃ Bhavamātre Namaḥ* I

*Oṃ Bhavaratāśrava Tāraṇatāriṇyai Namaḥ* I *

*Oṃ Bhartṛpriyāyai Namaḥ* I

*Oṃ Bhartṛratāyai Namaḥ* I

*Oṃ Bhartṛbhāvaprakāśinyai Namaḥ* I

*Oṃ Bhartṛnītikaryai Namaḥ* I

*Oṃ Bhāryāyai Namaḥ* I

*Oṃ Bharatṛdāyai Namaḥ* I

*Oṃ Bhīmabhīṣaṇyai Namaḥ* I

*Oṃ Bhikṣupūjyāyai Namaḥ* I

*Oṃ Bhikṣumātre Namaḥ* I

*Oṃ Bhikṣumānasatoṣiṇyai Namaḥ* I 560

*Oṃ Bhīmasenapriyāyai Namaḥ* I

*Oṃ Bhīmāyai Namaḥ* I

*Oṃ Bhīmākṣyai Namaḥ* I

*Oṃ Bhīmabhītidāyai Namaḥ* I

*Oṃ Bhrāntahantryai Namaḥ* I

*Oṃ Bhayaharāyai Namaḥ* I

*Oṃ Bhavapāśavimocinyai Namaḥ* I

*Oṃ Bhavadāvānalaghnyai Namaḥ* I

*Oṃ Bhaktapūjyāyai Namaḥ* I

*Oṃ Bhavārtighne Namaḥ* I

*Oṃ Bhaktatuṣṭāyai Namaḥ* I

*Oṃ Bhaumamātre Namaḥ* I

*Oṃ Bhopāyai Namaḥ* I

*Oṃ Bhopapratāśinyai Namaḥ* I *

*Oṃ Bhṛgarūpāyai Namaḥ* I *

*Oṃ Bhṛgupatnyai Namaḥ* I

*Oṃ Bhṛgutāṇḍavakāriṇyai Namaḥ* I

*Oṃ Bhṛgusevāratāyai Namaḥ* I

*Oṃ Bhrāntihāriṇyai Namaḥ* I

*Oṃ Bhāratapriyāyai Namaḥ* I 580

*Oṃ Bhāratyai Namaḥ* I

*Oṃ Bhānaveśyāyai Namaḥ* I

*Oṃ Bhāṣāyai Namaḥ* I

*Oṃ Bhīmāmayyai Namaḥ* I

*Oṃ Bhavāyai Namaḥ* I

*Oṃ Bhānumatyai Namaḥ* I

*Oṃ Bhuktimayyai Namaḥ* I

*Oṃ Bhrūṃ Bījākṣararūpiṇyai Namaḥ* I

*Oṃ Bhrāmbhrīmbhrūmbhraiṃ Svarūpiṇyai Namaḥ* I

*Oṃ Bhramatīvavināśinyai Namaḥ* I

*Oṃ Bhaṅgāyai Namaḥ* I

*Oṃ Bhaṅgāpriyāyai Namaḥ* I

*Oṃ Bhṛṅgyai Namaḥ* I

*Oṃ Bhṛṅgadhvaniparāyaṇāyai Namaḥ* I

*Oṃ Bhrātṛjāyāyai Namaḥ* I

*Oṃ Bhagavatyai Namaḥ* I

*Oṃ Bhavānyai Namaḥ* I

*Oṃ Bhaktavatsalāyai Namaḥ* I

*Oṃ Bhavasiddhāyai Namaḥ* I

*Oṃ Bhagejyāyai Namaḥ* I 600

*Oṃ Bhagamālāyai Namaḥ* I

*Oṃ Bhaveśvaryai Namaḥ* I

*Oṃ Bhrāntāyai Namaḥ* I

*Oṃ Bhramarikāyai Namaḥ* I

*Oṃ Bhītyai Namaḥ* I

*Oṃ Bhrājiṣṇave Namaḥ* I

*Oṃ Bhaktarūpiṇyai Namaḥ* I

*Oṃ Bhaktamānasasantuṣṭāyai Namaḥ* I

*Oṃ Bhavatyai Namaḥ* I

*Oṃ Bhramarāmbikāyai Namaḥ* I

*Oṃ Bhrāmaryai Namaḥ* I

*Oṃ Bhrāntamālāyai Namaḥ* I

*Oṃ Bhavejyāyai Namaḥ* I

*Oṃ Bhavasiddhidāyai Namaḥ* I

*Oṃ Bhagarūpāyai Namaḥ* I

*Oṃ Bhagaratāyai Namaḥ* I

*Oṃ Bhagagītīmayyai Namaḥ* I

*Oṃ Bhagāyai Namaḥ* I

*Oṃ Bhaṅkārarūpiṇyai Namaḥ* I

*Oṃ Bhrāmāyai Namaḥ* I 620

*Oṃ Bhagamālāvibhūṣaṇāyai Namaḥ* I

*Oṃ Bhagaliṅgasvarūpāyai Namaḥ* I

*Oṃ Bhagaliṅgaparāyaṇāyai Namaḥ* I

*Oṃ Bhagaliṅgāmṛtāndolāyai Namaḥ* I

*Oṃ Bhagāvilolupāyai Namaḥ* I

*Oṃ Bhagārcanaratānandyai Namaḥ* I

*Oṃ Bhagabhāgyaparāyaṇāyai Namaḥ* I

*Oṃ Bhagatattvāyai Namaḥ* I

*Oṃ Bhagāvhāyai Namaḥ* I *

*Oṃ Bhagaliṅgadhvanyai Namaḥ* I

*Oṃ Bhagāyai Namaḥ* I

*Oṃ Bhaganyai Namaḥ* I *

*Oṃ Bhārgavejyāyai Namaḥ* I

*Oṃ Bhagamālāyai Namaḥ* I

*Oṃ Bhagāṅkurāyai Namaḥ* I

*Oṃ Bhagakuṇḍāhlādaratāyai Namaḥ* I

*Oṃ Bhagakuṇḍavikāsinyai Namaḥ* I

*Oṃ Bhavitryai Namaḥ* I

*Oṃ Bhavitāyai Namaḥ* I

*Oṃ Bhūtāyai Namaḥ* I 640

*Oṃ Bhūtamātre Namaḥ* I

*Oṃ Bhūpatyai Namaḥ* I

*Oṃ Bhūpejyāyai Namaḥ* I

*Oṃ Bhūpasantuṣṭāyai Namaḥ* I

*Oṃ Bhaikṣyacarvaṇatatparāyai Namaḥ* I

*Oṃ Bhaganāmasmṛtiparāyai Namaḥ* I

*Oṃ Bhagajāpaparāyaṇāyai Namaḥ* I

*Oṃ Bhagatantrāyai Namaḥ* I

*Oṃ Bhagāmohāyai Namaḥ* I

*Oṃ Bhagagandhaparāyaṇāyai Namaḥ* I

*Oṃ Bhagavāpīsnānaratāyai Namaḥ* I

*Oṃ Bhagatīrthanivāsinyai Namaḥ* I

*Oṃ Bhagadarśanasantuṣṭāyai Namaḥ* I

*Oṃ Bhagacumbanatoṣiṇyai Namaḥ* I

*Oṃ Bhagajihvāyai Namaḥ* I

*Oṃ Bhagamukhāyai Namaḥ* I

*Oṃ Bhagacakṣuṣe Namaḥ* I

*Oṃ Bhagāmbujāyai Namaḥ* I

*Oṃ Bhūteśyai Namaḥ* I

*Oṃ Bhūtadurgasthāyai Namaḥ* I 660

*Oṃ Bhūpatitvapradāyinyai Namaḥ* I

*Oṃ Bhūmbhūṅkārasvarūpāyai Namaḥ* I

*Oṃ Bhadraśabdaparāyaṇāyai Namaḥ* I

*Oṃ Bhahabhahārakāmahāyai Namaḥ* I *

*Oṃ Bhāṣyakartre Namaḥ* I

*Oṃ Bhayāpahāyai Namaḥ* I

*Oṃ Bharatāyai Namaḥ* I

*Oṃ Bharateśyai Namaḥ* I

*Oṃ Bharatāprāṇadāyinyai Namaḥ* I

*Oṃ Bharatāpremasantuṣṭāyai Namaḥ* I

*Oṃ Bharatādhārarūpiṇyai Namaḥ* I

*Oṃ Bhūbhārāyai Namaḥ* I

*Oṃ Bhūdharādhīśāyai Namaḥ* I

*Oṃ Bhūdharāyai Namaḥ* I

*Oṃ Bhūdharapriyāyai Namaḥ* I

*Oṃ Māmīpānandanāyai Namaḥ* I *

*Oṃ Māyāyai Namaḥ* I

*Oṃ Madyapānaparāyaṇāyai Namaḥ* I

*Oṃ Madhuprītāyai Namaḥ* I

*Oṃ Madhuratāyai Namaḥ* I 680

*Oṃ Madhurāyai Namaḥ* I

*Oṃ Madhurāmadhave Namaḥ* I

*Oṃ Madirāyai Namaḥ* I

*Oṃ Madironmattāyai Namaḥ* |

*Oṃ Mānanīyāyai Namaḥ* |

*Oṃ Madoddhatāyai Namaḥ* |

*Oṃ Mādhvīpānaratāyai Namaḥ* |

*Oṃ Mātre Namaḥ* |

*Oṃ Māyābījahvayāmatyai Namaḥ* |

*Oṃ Nimātre Namaḥ* |

*Oṃ Mālinyai Namaḥ* |

*Oṃ Mātrāyai Namaḥ* |

*Oṃ Madanīmṛtadarpikāyai Namaḥ* |

*Oṃ Mānākṣyai Namaḥ* |

*Oṃ Mātulānyai Namaḥ* |

*Oṃ Modinyai Namaḥ* |

*Oṃ Madanāturāyai Namaḥ* |

*Oṃ Mrāmmrīmmrūmraiṃ Svarūpāyai Namaḥ* |

*Oṃ Mraummraḥ Sarvasvarūpiṇyai Namaḥ* |

*Oṃ Mitākṣarāyai Namaḥ* | 700

*Oṃ Mitāhārāyai Namaḥ* |

*Oṃ Mitācāramanomayyai Namaḥ* |

*Oṃ Malināyai Namaḥ* |

*Oṃ Malinyai Namaḥ* |

*Oṃ Maitrāyai Namaḥ* |

*Oṃ Maitravāruṇatāruṇyai Namaḥ* |

*Oṃ Māyāvatyai Namaḥ* |

*Oṃ Mānavatyai Namaḥ* |

*Oṃ Mahāmadhumatimayyai Namaḥ* |

*Oṃ Mahīdharasaktāyai Namaḥ* |

*Oṃ Mātrāyai Namaḥ* |

*Oṃ Mātrāsvaravibhedinyai Namaḥ* |

*Oṃ Mīnarūpāyai Namaḥ* |

*Oṃ Mīnanāthāyai Namaḥ* |

*Oṃ Mālatyai Namaḥ* |

*Oṃ Madhulolupāyai Namaḥ* |

*Oṃ Madhupānaratāyai Namaḥ* |

*Oṃ Māryai Namaḥ* |

*Oṃ Mahāmāryai Namaḥ* |

*Oṃ Mahīpatyai Namaḥ* | 720

*Oṃ Mahākālyai Namaḥ* |

*Oṃ Mahātārāyai Namaḥ* |

*Oṃ Mahāchinnāyai Namaḥ* |

*Oṃ Maheśvaryai Namaḥ* |

*Oṃ Māheśyai Namaḥ* |

*Oṃ Madasthāyai Namaḥ* |

*Oṃ Madanasthānarūpiṇyai Namaḥ* |

*Oṃ Madanapriyakāntāyai Namaḥ* |

*Oṃ Mahāyogeśvaryai Namaḥ* |

*Oṃ Makhyai Namaḥ* | *

*Oṃ Mahāmadanasantuṣṭāyai Namaḥ* |

*Oṃ Mahāmadanabhūṣitāyai Namaḥ* |

*Oṃ Mahitāyai Namaḥ* |

*Oṃ Mahilāyai Namaḥ* |

*Oṃ Māyāyai Namaḥ* |

*Oṃ Makārākṣararūpiṇyai Namaḥ* |

*Oṃ Makārarūpiṇyai Namaḥ* |

*Oṃ Mudrāyai Namaḥ* |

*Oṃ Mudrāmodaparāyaṇāyai Namaḥ* |

*Oṃ Mehasthāyai Namaḥ* । 740

*Oṃ Mehamātre Namaḥ* ।

*Oṃ Mehamitrāyai Namaḥ* ।

*Oṃ Mahatpriyāyai Namaḥ* ।

*Oṃ Mahatāyai Namaḥ* ।

*Oṃ Mojasākārāyai Namaḥ* ।

*Oṃ Mahatānandadāyinyai Namaḥ* ।

*Oṃ Madhumāṃsāyai Namaḥ* ।

*Oṃ Mehatārāyai Namaḥ* ।

*Oṃ Mehaprastārarūpiṇyai Namaḥ* ।

*Oṃ Mehaputryai Namaḥ* ।

*Oṃ Mīnākṣyai Namaḥ* ।

*Oṃ Mitabhāṣāyai Namaḥ* ।

*Oṃ Mitārthavite Namaḥ* ।

*Oṃ Madanāntakakāntāyai Namaḥ* ।

*Oṃ Madanāntakarūpiṇyai Namaḥ* ।

*Oṃ Mahoragāyai Namaḥ* ।

*Oṃ Mahośuṣāyai Namaḥ* ।

*Oṃ Mahatyai Namaḥ* ।

*Oṃ Mahiṣāpahāyai Namaḥ* ।

*Oṃ Mahiṣāsuranirnāśyai Namaḥ* । 760

*Oṃ Muṇḍamālāvibhūṣaṇāyai Namaḥ* ।

*Oṃ Muṇḍaprākārasaṃrūpāyai Namaḥ* ।

*Oṃ Muṇḍāsuravimardinyai Namaḥ* ।

*Oṃ Mānasāyai Namaḥ* ।

*Oṃ Mānaseśyai Namaḥ* ।

*Oṃ Mudriṇyambāsvarūpiṇyai Namaḥ* ।

*Oṃ Mudriṇyai Namaḥ* I

*Oṃ Mantriṇyai Namaḥ* I

*Oṃ Mantrāyai Namaḥ* I

*Oṃ Mahāmantrāyai Namaḥ* I

*Oṃ Mahārṇavāyai Namaḥ* I

*Oṃ Mahārṇavasthitāyai Namaḥ* I

*Oṃ Mohāyai Namaḥ* I

*Oṃ Mohinīnāśinyai Namaḥ* I

*Oṃ Marute Namaḥ* I

*Oṃ Manave Namaḥ* I

*Oṃ Manumayyai Namaḥ* I

*Oṃ Mādryai Namaḥ* I

*Oṃ Madrakuñjaravāsinyai Namaḥ* I

*Oṃ Madrakumbhasthalārūḍhāyai Namaḥ* I 780

*Oṃ Madmuktāvibhūṣaṇāyai Namaḥ* I *

*Oṃ Muktāhāravibhūṣāḍhyāyai Namaḥ* I

*Oṃ Muktakeśyai Namaḥ* I

*Oṃ Mahūrtadāyai Namaḥ* I

*Oṃ Mohakartryai Namaḥ* I

*Oṃ Mohahīnāyai Namaḥ* I

*Oṃ Mahāmohaparāyaṇāyai Namaḥ* I

*Oṃ Mantraprāṇārpaṇaprītāyai Namaḥ* I

*Oṃ Mantraprāṇārpaṇārcitāyai Namaḥ* I

*Oṃ Mahaughānandāyai Namaḥ* I

*Oṃ Mandagandhāyai Namaḥ* I

*Oṃ Madyapūjanatatparāyai Namaḥ* I

*Oṃ Makāravarṇasarvāṅgyai Namaḥ* I

*Oṃ Mitabhogāyai Namaḥ* I

*Oṃ Mitānmitāyai Namaḥ* I

*Oṃ Mahādhūmrāvatyai Namaḥ* I

*Oṃ Muktāyai Namaḥ* I

*Oṃ Mahāmuktāvibhūṣaṇāyai Namaḥ* I

*Oṃ Muktārajatanāsāyai Namaḥ* I

*Oṃ Muktāchatravibhūṣaṇāyai Namaḥ* I 800

*Oṃ Muktadānaratāyai Namaḥ* I

*Oṃ Madhyāyai Namaḥ* I

*Oṃ Madhyamāyai Namaḥ* I

*Oṃ Madhyameśvaryai Namaḥ* I

*Oṃ Mitīrmītīmatyai Namaḥ* I

*Oṃ Mīnaketave Namaḥ* I

*Oṃ Makararūpiṇyai Namaḥ* I

*Oṃ Makarasthāyai Namaḥ* I

*Oṃ Mahādevyai Namaḥ* I

*Oṃ Mahādevamanomayyai Namaḥ* I

*Oṃ Mahotsavāyai Namaḥ* I

*Oṃ Durgāyai Namaḥ* I

*Oṃ Māyāyai Namaḥ* I

*Oṃ Mahāpūjārametyadāyai Namaḥ* I *

*Oṃ Mahāgrahasvarūpāyai Namaḥ* I

*Oṃ Maghānakṣatrarūpiṇyai Namaḥ* I

*Oṃ Madyamāṃsāvṛtaratāyai Namaḥ* I

*Oṃ Māghasnānaparāyaṇāyai Namaḥ* I

*Oṃ Mārgaśīrṣapriyānandāyai Namaḥ* I

*Oṃ Mārgadarśanatatparāyai Namaḥ* I 820

*Oṃ Mārgamārgāmātrakāyai Namaḥ* I

*Oṃ Mātṛkālipirūpiṇyai Namaḥ* ।

*Oṃ Mātṛkānyāsasantuṣṭāyai Namaḥ* ।

*Oṃ Mātṛkānyāsarūpiṇyai Namaḥ* ।

*Oṃ Mālinīnyāsasantuṣṭāyai Namaḥ* ।

*Oṃ Mālinīmokṣadāyinyai Namaḥ* ।

*Oṃ Mokṣadātryai Namaḥ* ।

*Oṃ Mokṣagatyai Namaḥ* ।

*Oṃ Mokṣamārgaparāyaṇāyai Namaḥ* ।

*Oṃ Muktāyai Namaḥ* ।

*Oṃ Muktipriyakaryai Namaḥ* ।

*Oṃ Muktisthāyai Namaḥ* ।

*Oṃ Muktitāṇḍavāyai Namaḥ* ।

*Oṃ Mahānandāyai Namaḥ* ।

*Oṃ Mahākālyai Namaḥ* ।

*Oṃ Mahābhuvanatāriṇyai Namaḥ* ।

*Oṃ Mahendrapūjyāyai Namaḥ* ।

*Oṃ Māheśyai Namaḥ* ।

*Oṃ Matisāgaradāyinyai Namaḥ* ।

*Oṃ Yakṣāyai Namaḥ* । 840

*Oṃ Yakṣasvarūpāyai Namaḥ* ।

*Oṃ Yakṣiṇyai Namaḥ* ।

*Oṃ Yakṣapūjitāyai Namaḥ* ।

*Oṃ Yādevyai Namaḥ* ।

*Oṃ Yādavārādhyāyai Namaḥ* ।

*Oṃ Yaduvaṃśasamudbhavāyai Namaḥ* ।

*Oṃ Yamunāyai Namaḥ* ।

*Oṃ Yajurvedāyai Namaḥ* ।

*Oṃ Yajurvedaparāyaṇāyai Namaḥ* ।

*Oṃ Yāminyai Namaḥ* ǀ

*Oṃ Yamapūjyāyai Namaḥ* ǀ

*Oṃ Yamamātāpatipriyāyai Namaḥ* ǀ

*Oṃ Yātrāyai Namaḥ* ǀ

*Oṃ Yātrayaśodāyai Namaḥ* ǀ *

*Oṃ Yaśovardhanatatparāyai Namaḥ* ǀ

*Oṃ Yaśakarpūradhavalāyai Namaḥ* ǀ *

*Oṃ Yoginyai Namaḥ* ǀ

*Oṃ Yaśasvinyai Namaḥ* ǀ

*Oṃ Yāṃyīṃyūṃ*
*Yākinīrūpāyai Namaḥ* ǀ

*Oṃ Yaiṃyauṃ Yaṅkārarūpiṇyai Namaḥ* ǀ 860

*Oṃ Yogamātre Namaḥ* ǀ

*Oṃ Yogagamyāyai Namaḥ* ǀ

*Oṃ Yogamārgaparāyaṇāyai Namaḥ* ǀ

*Oṃ Yogīśāyai Namaḥ* ǀ

*Oṃ Yojanāyai Namaḥ* ǀ

*Oṃ Yāmāyai Namaḥ* ǀ

*Oṃ Yojanāyutavistarāyai Namaḥ* ǀ

*Oṃ Yathoktācāraniratāyai Namaḥ* ǀ

*Oṃ Yathoktaphaladāyinyai Namaḥ* ǀ

*Oṃ Yakṣakardamasambhūṣāyai Namaḥ* ǀ

*Oṃ Yavargarūpiṇīpatyai Namaḥ* ǀ

*Oṃ Ramaṇyai Namaḥ* ǀ

*Oṃ Ramaṇīprītāyai Namaḥ* ǀ

*Oṃ Ramāyai Namaḥ* ǀ

*Oṃ Ratneśvaryai Namaḥ* ǀ

*Oṃ Ratyai Namaḥ* ǀ

*Oṃ Ratipriyāyai Namaḥ* I

*Oṃ Ratiratāyai Namaḥ* I

*Oṃ Ratitoṣaṇatatparāyai Namaḥ* I

*Oṃ Ratnagarbhāyai Namaḥ* I 880

*Oṃ Ratnabījāyai Namaḥ* I

*Oṃ Rājīvalocanāyai Namaḥ* I

*Oṃ Ramāyai Namaḥ* I

*Oṃ Rāmbījāyai Namaḥ* I

*Oṃ Rīṃsvarūpāyai Namaḥ* I

*Oṃ Rāṃrīṃrūṃraiṃ Svarūpiṇyai Namaḥ* I

*Oṃ Rauṃraḥ*
*Varṇasvarūpāyai Namaḥ* I

*Oṃ Rājyadātryai Namaḥ* I

*Oṃ Rasātulāyai Namaḥ* I

*Oṃ Rasatuṣṭāyai Namaḥ* I

*Oṃ Rasagatyai Namaḥ* I

*Oṃ Raghuvaṃśasamudbhavāyai Namaḥ* I

*Oṃ Ratirūpāyai Namaḥ* I

*Oṃ Ratāntāyai Namaḥ* I

*Oṃ Ratigarbhaparāyaṇāyai Namaḥ* I

*Oṃ Rājīvanetrāyai Namaḥ* I

*Oṃ Rājñyai Namaḥ* I

*Oṃ Ramaṇāsurakanyakāyai Namaḥ* I

*Oṃ Rājarājeśvarīdraṣṭāyai Namaḥ* I

*Oṃ Raudryai Namaḥ* I 900

*Oṃ Rudrapriyāyai Namaḥ* I

*Oṃ Haṭe Namaḥ* I

*Oṃ Hadrakanyāyai Namaḥ* ।

*Oṃ Hadrajāyāyai Namaḥ* ।

*Oṃ Hadramātāratānandāyai Namaḥ* ।

*Oṃ Hadrejyāyai Namaḥ* ।

*Oṃ Trirūpāyai Namaḥ* ।

*Oṃ Rātriñcaravibhedinyai Namaḥ* ।

*Oṃ Rākṣasaghnyai Namaḥ* ।

*Oṃ Rakṣaṇāyai Namaḥ* ।

*Oṃ Rakṣovidrāviṇyai Namaḥ* ।

*Oṃ Ratāyai Namaḥ* ।

*Oṃ Hacirāyai Namaḥ* । *

*Oṃ Hacirūpāyai Namaḥ* ।

*Oṃ Rociṣāyai Namaḥ* ।

*Oṃ Romarūpiṇyai Namaḥ* ।

*Oṃ Romagarbhāyai Namaḥ* ।

*Oṃ Romadehāyai Namaḥ* ।

*Oṃ Romabhūṣaṇatatparāyai Namaḥ* ।

*Oṃ Rasāyai Namaḥ* ।  920

*Oṃ Rasavatyai Namaḥ* ।

*Oṃ Rājyalakṣmyai Namaḥ* ।

*Oṃ Rāvaṇanāśinyai Namaḥ* ।

*Oṃ Rāvaṇejyāyai Namaḥ* ।

*Oṃ Ravadatāyai Namaḥ* । *

*Oṃ Rāvaṇapriyadāyinyai Namaḥ* ।

*Oṃ Rajovatyai Namaḥ* ।

*Oṃ Rajaḥprāṇāyai Namaḥ* ।

*Oṃ Rajoguṇamayyai Namaḥ* ।

*Oṃ Ravāyai Namaḥ* ।

*Oṃ Ratipuṣpapriyāyai Namaḥ* I

*Oṃ Rūṃrūṃ Rākiṇyai Namaḥ* I

*Oṃ Reṇukāyai Namaḥ* I

*Oṃ Rayāyai Namaḥ* I

*Oṃ Raiṃ Bījanilayāyai Namaḥ* I

*Oṃ Raiṇṇāyai Namaḥ* I

*Oṃ Reṇurūpāyai Namaḥ* I

*Oṃ Hākinyai Namaḥ* I

*Oṃ Hakvāṅgadasya Bhaginyai Namaḥ* I

*Oṃ Hakyarūpāyai Namaḥ* I 940

*Oṃ Rūpabhuve Namaḥ* I

*Oṃ Raupyaparāyai Namaḥ* I

*Oṃ Raupyaraupyāyai Namaḥ* I

*Oṃ Raupyagehavibhūṣaṇāyai Namaḥ* I

*Oṃ Raupyasiṃhāsanaratāyai Namaḥ* I

*Oṃ Raupyadānaparāyaṇāyai Namaḥ* I 946

*Iti Śrīmahogrātārākṣobhyasaṃvāde Akṣobhyasaṃhitāyāṃ Śatārdhasahasrāṃ Namaḥ* I

*Oṃ Tārāviracitaṃ Divyasāmrājyamedhākhyaṃ Nāmasahasraṃ Viṃśati Paṭalaḥ Namaḥ* I

There are 946 names corresponding to the *Tārā Sahasranāma Stotram*. Remaining doubtful names are marked with * mark.

*****

श्रीतारासहस्रनामावलिः

ॐ अस्य श्रीमहोग्रतारा दिव्य साम्राज्य मेधा नाम सहस्रकस्य अक्षोभ्यऋषिः बृहति छन्दः । उग्रतारादित्रिशक्ति देवता हं बीजं फट् शक्तिःहं कीलकं श्री महोग्रतारा प्रत्यक्ष दर्शनाद्यर्थे विनियोगः ॥

ॐ क्रां तारायै नमः ।
ॐ स्त्रीहृदयमहातारायै नमः ।
ॐ क्रमुग्रतारायै नमः ।
ॐ तारिण्यै नमः ।
ॐ तर्यै नमः ।
ॐ महोग्रतारायै नमः ।
ॐ स्त्रीतारायै नमः ।
ॐ त्रिकटैकजटाधरायै नमः ।
ॐ ततथैय्यायै नमः ।
ॐ भिनपगायै नमः ।
ॐ तालताण्डवरूपिण्यै नमः ।
ॐ ताण्डवाह्लादनिरततहण्यै नमः ।
ॐ तहणाकृत्यै नमः ।
ॐ तन्त्र्यै नमः ।
ॐ वाद्यरतायै नमः ।
ॐ तन्त्रायै नमः ।
ॐ तन्त्रशास्त्रपरायणायै नमः ।
ॐ तारूण्यामृतकल्लोलायै नमः ।
ॐ तारूण्यामृतकन्यकायै नमः ।
ॐ तारूण्यामृतचान्द्र्यै नमः । २०

ॐ तत्त्वदर्शनतत्परायै नमः ।
ॐ तीर्थसेवापरातुष्टायै नमः ।
ॐ त्रां त्रीं त्रूं त्रैं स्वरूपिण्यै नमः ।
ॐ ओङ्कारात्रःस्वरूपायै नमः ।
ॐ त्रसायै नमः ।
ॐ त्रस्तगतीस्थायै नमः ।

ॐ तनिम्रालाल वृक्षस्थायै नमः। *
ॐ तालीपानपरायणायै नमः।
ॐ तरुणीकुण्डनिरतायै नमः।
ॐ तरुणीकुण्डरूपिण्यै नमः।
ॐ तरुणीकुसुमाह्लादायै नमः।
ॐ तरुणीबीजरूपिण्यै नमः।
ॐ तरुणीगर्भसम्भूतायै नमः।
ॐ तरुणीध्यानतत्परायै नमः।
ॐ तरुणीपूजानिरतायै नमः।
ॐ तरुणीभक्ततत्परायै नमः।
ॐ तरुणीलोचनानन्दलहर्यै नमः।
ॐ तार्क्ष्यवाहनायै नमः।
ॐताररूपायै नमः।
ॐ ताम्रपर्ण्यै नमः। ४०

ॐ ताम्रपत्रसमस्थितायै नमः।
ॐ तरुणीकुसुमामोहायै नमः।
ॐ तरुणीपुष्परूपिण्यै नमः।
ॐ तरुणीताडिकान्नाथायै नमः।
ॐ तरुणीमुखगोचरायै नमः।
ॐ तरुणीकेशसंस्थायै नमः।
ॐ तरुणीमुखमध्यगायै नमः।
ॐ तरुणीवाक्यमध्यायै नमः।
ॐ तरुणीताण्डवर्णवायै नमः।
ॐ तरुणीगानसन्तुष्टायै नमः।
ॐ तरुणीभक्ततत्परायै नमः।
ॐ तरुणीमुक्तीमालायै नमः।
ॐ तरुणीभक्तरूपिण्यै नमः।
ॐ तरुणीगमनप्रीत्यायै नमः।
ॐ तरुणीहास्यतत्परायै नमः।
ॐ तरुणीनामिकानन्तायै नमः।
ॐ तरुणीरत्नरूपिण्यै नमः।

ॐ तरुणीगमनप्रीत्यायै नमः ।
ॐ तरुणीयोगरूपिण्यै नमः ।
ॐ तरुणीचुम्बनरतायै नमः । ६०

ॐ तरुणीलिङ्गरूपिण्यै नमः ।
ॐ तुलायै नमः ।
ॐ तुलातल्पायै नमः ।
ॐ तुलजापुरवासिन्यै नमः ।
ॐ तनान नास्वरूपायै नमः । *
ॐ तथैरूपप्रधारिण्यै नमः ।
ॐ तोतलायै नमः ।
ॐ तैलसंप्रीतायै नमः ।
ॐ तृप्यतिमार्गपरायणायै नमः ।
ॐ तृसितायै नमः ।
ॐ तृणरूपायै नमः ।
ॐ तार्तीयगुणभूषितायै नमः ।
ॐ तार्तीयबीजरूपायै नमः ।
ॐ तार्तीयाक्षररूपिण्यै नमः ।
ॐ तत्त्वज्ञानायै नमः ।
ॐ तत्त्वबुद्ध्यै नमः ।
ॐ तत्त्वनाथायै नमः ।
ॐ तथामत्यै नमः ।
ॐ तौलित्यै नमः ।
ॐ त्ववाप्यै नमः । ८० *

ॐ तरस्थारूपिण्यै नमः ।
ॐ तमातरमध्यस्वरूपायै नमः ।
ॐ तरदन्नर नमः । *
ॐ तामत्यै नमः । *
ॐ तरुमूलस्थितायै नमः ।
ॐ तन्द्रायै नमः ।
ॐ तुष्टिस्त्रैकाल्यरूपिण्यै नमः ।

ॐ त्रिकाल्यदायै नमः ।

ॐ त्रैर्पक्ष ताराणापकभूषणायै नमः ।*

ॐ त्वरितायै नमः ।

ॐ त्वरितप्रीतायै नमः ।

ॐ तत्त्वदर्श्यै नमः ।

ॐ तमस्विन्यै नमः ।

ॐ ताराक्षहारिण्यै नमः ।

ॐ तीर्णायै नमः ।

ॐ तारूण्यकुण्डभोगिन्यै नमः ।

ॐ थकारवर्णनिलयायै नमः ।

ॐ थकाराक्षररूपिण्यै नमः ।

ॐ थैथैरूपायै नमः ।

ॐ थरिग्रूपायै नमः ।

ॐ थौङ्गदादिकरूपिण्यै नमः । १००

ॐ स्थूलवुध्न्यै नमः ।

ॐ स्थूलतनुस्थातध्यानपरायणायै नमः ।

ॐ थेथकुटाक्षरौप्यां थीन्थूङ्काराक्षरमालिन्यै नमः ।*

ॐ थररूपादक्षणायै नमः । *

ॐ दानसन्मानदायिन्यै नमः ।

ॐ दक्षपुत्र्यै नमः ।

ॐ दक्षयज्ञनाशिन्यै नमः ।

ॐ दानव्यै नमः ।

ॐ दयायै नमः ।

ॐ दयाहृदयादान्तायै नमः ।

ॐ दैत्यनाशनकारिण्यै नमः ।

ॐ दयाले नमः ।

ॐ दैत्यशमन्यै नमः ।

ॐ द्रव्यघ्ने नमः ।

ॐ द्रव्यवत्साल्यै नमः ।

ॐ द्रव्यगीतायै नमः ।

ॐ द्रव्यमात्रे नमः ।

ॐ दान्तायै नमः ।

ॐ दारिद्र्यनाशिन्यै नमः ।

ॐ दयार्तायै नमः । १२०

ॐ दीपिन्यै नमः ।

ॐ दिशायै नमः ।

ॐ दीपमार्गपरायणायै नमः ।

ॐ दीनप्रीतायै नमः ।

ॐ दीर्घजिव्हायै नमः ।

ॐ दारिद्र्यनाशिन्यै नमः ।

ॐ दित्यै नमः ।

ॐ दुःखसंहारिण्यै नमः ।

ॐ दुष्टदैत्यविध्वंसनक्षमायै नमः ।

ॐ दाडिमीपुष्परूपायै नमः ।

ॐ दाडिमीपुष्पपूजितायै नमः ।

ॐ दाडिमीवाजदत्तायै नमः ।

ॐ दाडीरूपायै नमः ।

ॐ दरस्थितायै नमः ।

ॐ दीर्घाक्ष्यै नमः ।

ॐ दीर्घनासायै नमः ।

ॐ दीक्षितायै नमः ।

ॐ दीक्षितेश्वर्यै नमः ।

ॐ दुर्गायै नमः ।

ॐ दुर्गविहन्त्र्यै नमः । १४०

ॐ दुःखप्रणाशिन्यै नमः ।

ॐ दर्यै नमः ।

ॐ दौर्गासुरविहन्त्र्यै नमः ।

ॐ दुर्गदारणतत्परायै नमः ।

ॐ दानदक्षायै नमः ।

ॐ दानपूजायै नमः ।

ॐ दानतुष्टायै नमः ।

ॐ दयातत्यै नमः ।

ॐ दास्यै नमः ।

ॐ दासीकुण्डरत्यै नमः ।

ॐ दासीपुष्पपरायणायै नमः ।

ॐ दासीबीजरतायै नमः ।

ॐ दानायै नमः ।

ॐ दीनारदायिन्यै नमः ।

ॐ द्रुत्यै नमः ।

ॐ द्रुतसिद्धकर्यै नमः ।

ॐ दीर्घायै नमः ।

ॐ दीर्घाकायै नमः । *

ॐ दीक्षितप्रियायै नमः ।

ॐ दासीचुम्बनसन्तुष्टायै नमः ।१६०

ॐ दासीमथनतत्परायै नमः ।

ॐ दासीकुण्डप्रीतप्राणायै नमः ।

ॐ दान्दीन्दून्दैं स्वरूपिण्यै नमः ।

ॐ दूं बीजजपसन्तुष्टायै नमः ।

ॐ दूंवुस्वाहास्वरूपिण्यै नमः । *

ॐ धनदायै नमः ।

ॐ धननाथायै नमः ।

ॐ धनधान्यविवर्धिन्यै नमः ।

ॐ धूं बीजनिलयायै नमः ।

ॐ धूम्रायै नमः ।

ॐ धूधून्धूमावत्यै नमः ।

ॐ धृत्यै नमः ।

ॐ धैर्यदायै नमः ।

ॐ धारिण्यै नमः ।

ॐ धैर्यायै नमः ।

ॐ धरित्र्यै नमः ।

ॐ धराधरायै नमः ।

ॐ धर्मिष्ठायै नमः ।

ॐ धर्मनिरतायै नमः ।

ॐ धर्ममार्गपरायणायै नमः । १८०

ॐ धर्मप्राणायै नमः ।

ॐ धर्मगत्यै नमः ।

ॐ धारासम्पातरूपिण्यै नमः ।

ॐ धिमिथरिहवरूपायै नमः ।

ॐ धर्मतारायै नमः ।

ॐ धनार्चितायै नमः ।

ॐ ध्यै नमः । *

ॐ धिषणायै नमः ।

ॐ धीरगत्यै नमः ।

ॐ धीराधीरस्वरूपिण्यै नमः ।

ॐ धात्रीप्रसूनसन्तुष्टायै नमः ।

ॐ धात्रीफलकुचद्वयायै नमः ।

ॐ धात्रीध्यानरतायै नमः ।

ॐ ध्यानायै नमः ।

ॐ ध्यानतत्त्वपरायणायै नमः ।

ॐ ध्यानदात्र्यै नमः ।

ॐ ध्यानगात्रायै नमः ।

ॐ ध्यानस्थायै नमः ।

ॐ ध्यानरूपिण्यै नमः ।

ॐ ध्येयरूपायै नमः । २००

ॐ ध्येयगम्यायै नमः ।

ॐ ध्येयचक्रसमस्थितायै नमः ।

ॐ ध्यानपरायणप्रीतायै नमः ।

ॐ ध्यानध्येयस्वरूपिण्यै नमः ।

ॐ ध्यानगम्यायै नमः ।

ॐ ध्यानतुष्टायै नमः ।

ॐ ध्यानगानपरायणायै नमः ।

ॐ धिकतान्धिस्वरूपायै नमः ।

ॐ धैधैशब्दपरायणायै नमः ।

ॐ धर्मिण्यै नमः ।

ॐ धर्मपक्षाङ्गायै नमः ।

ॐ धर्मकर्मपरायणायै नमः ।

ॐ धर्मग्रामरताङ्घ्रिं ध्रीन्ध्रीन्धून्धौंस्वरूपिण्यै नमः । *

ॐ नररूपायै नमः ।

ॐ नरप्रीतायै नमः ।

ॐ नरनाथायै नमः ।

ॐ नरात्मिकायै नमः ।

ॐ नारसिंह्यै नमः ।

ॐ नत्यै नमः ।

ॐ नार्यै नमः । २२०

ॐ नरपुष्पस्वरूपिण्यै नमः ।

ॐ नरपुष्पप्रियप्राणायै नमः ।

ॐ नरपुष्पप्रतर्पितायै नमः ।

ॐ नरपुष्पार्चनपुष्पायै नमः ।

ॐ नरपुष्पक्रियामत्यै नमः ।

ॐ नरपुष्पार्चनानन्दायै नमः ।

ॐ नरपुष्पाम्बरायै नमः ।

ॐ नद्यै नमः ।

ॐ नरयज्ञायै नमः ।

ॐ नरानन्दायै नमः ।

ॐ नरयज्ञपरायणायै नमः ।

ॐ नरनापूरतानानायै नमः ।

ॐ नतनानास्वरूपिण्यै नमः ।

ॐ नानामानायै नमः ।

ॐ नननानास्वरूपायै नमः ।

ॐ नाप्रर्वितायै नमः । *

ॐ नाप्रीतायै नमः ।

ॐ नाप्रशालायै नमः ।

ॐ नाटिकानन्दतोषितायै नमः ।

ॐ नानाभाषाप्ररूढायै नमः। २४०

ॐ नानावर्णस्वरूपिण्यै नमः।

ॐ नागिन्यै नमः।

ॐ नागभूषायै नमः।

ॐ नागार्हार्नागरूपिण्यै नमः।

ॐ नगज्वानगसम्भूतायै नमः।

ॐ नगवंश प्रतोषितायै नमः।

ॐ नादरूपायै नमः।

ॐ नादगत्यै नमः।

ॐ नादब्रह्मपरायणायै नमः।

ॐ नारदप्रियसन्तुष्टायै नमः।

ॐ नारदप्रियमानसायै नमः।

ॐ नारदायै नमः। *

ॐ नारदेश्यै नमः।

ॐ नदीनिम्नस्वरूपिण्यै नमः।

ॐ निम्ननाभ्यै नमः।

ॐ न्यै नमः। *

ॐ योन्यै नमः।

ॐ निम्ननेत्रायै नमः।

ॐ नरोत्तमायै नमः।

ॐ नरवाहनसन्तुष्टायै नमः। २६०

ॐ नरवाहनतत्परायै नमः।

ॐ नान्नीन्नून्नैन्नौं स्वरूपायै नमः।

ॐ नमोरूपायै नमो नमः।

ॐ नमस्कारप्रियायै नमः।

ॐ नित्यायै नमः।

ॐ नित्यानन्दस्वरूपिण्यै नमः।

ॐ नित्यपूजार्चनप्रीतायै नमः।

ॐ नित्यपूजापरायणायै नमः।

ॐ नित्योत्सवपरानन्दायै नमः।

ॐ नीररूपायै नमः ।
ॐ नीराकृत्यै नमः ।
ॐ नर्मदायै नमः ।
ॐ नर्मरूपायै नमः ।
ॐ नर्मकुण्डवीकान्यै नमः । *
ॐ नर्मकुण्डलेलिहानायै नमः ।
ॐ नर्मनटप्रियायै नमः ।
ॐ नैमित्तिकार्चनप्रीतायै नमः ।
ॐ नैमित्तिकपरायणायै नमः ।
ॐ नर्मदायै नमः ।
ॐ नर्मदात्र्यै नमः । २८०

ॐ नर्मकर्मपरायणायै नमः ।
ॐ नीवीमोचनसन्तुष्टायै नमः ।
ॐ नीवीमोचनतत्परायै नमः ।
ॐ नारीपुष्पप्रियाप्राणायै नमः ।
ॐ नारीपुष्पपरायणायै नमः ।
ॐ नारीपुष्पमतीप्रीतायै नमः ।
ॐ नारीपुष्पस्वरूपिण्यै नमः ।
ॐ नैर्यापिकायै नमः ।
ॐ नववीणायै नमः ।
ॐ नाडीनादपरायणायै नमः ।
ॐ नाडीनादपरानन्दायै नमः ।
ॐ नाडीनादपरागत्यै नमः ।
ॐ नाडीनादात्मिकायै नमः ।
ॐ नौकायै नमः ।
ॐ नौकाक्रीडापरायणायै नमः ।
ॐ पद्मपूजनसन्तुष्टायै नमः ।
ॐ पद्महोमपरायणायै नमः ।
ॐ परमानन्दसन्दोहायै नमः ।
ॐ परमाकाशरूपिण्यै नमः ।
ॐ परातीतायै नमः । ३००

ॐ परागम्यायै नमः ।

ॐ परमात्मने नमः ।

ॐ परागत्यै नमः ।

ॐ पम्पातीरनिवासायै नमः ।

ॐ प्रद्युम्नप्रीतिरूपिण्यै नमः ।

ॐ प्राणवायै नमः । *

ॐ प्राणवेज्यायै नमः ।

ॐ परतत्त्वायै नमः ।

ॐ परायणायै नमः ।

ॐ पद्मपत्रायै नमः ।

ॐ पद्मतुष्टायै नमः ।

ॐ तुष्टीपावनरूपिण्यै नमः ।

ॐ पापसंहारिण्यै नमः ।

ॐ तुष्टायै नमः ।

ॐ पुण्यदात्र्यै नमः ।

ॐ परातर्यै नमः । *

ॐ पुर्यै नमः ।

ॐ पुरार्यै नमः ।

ॐ गृहिण्यै नमः ।

ॐ पुराणागमरूपिण्यै नमः । ३२०

ॐ पुराणगम्यायै नमः ।

ॐ पानाट्यायै नमः । *

ॐ पानतोषणतत्परायै नमः ।

ॐ पानानन्दायै नमः ।

ॐ पीततनुस्थायै नमः ।

ॐ तैवप्यै नमः । *

ॐ रसस्वन्यै नमः ।

ॐ पीनयोन्यै नमः ।

ॐ पीतजङ्घायै नमः ।

ॐ पीताम्बरधरावत्यै नमः ।

ॐ पीताम्बरायै नमः ।

ॐ पीतगर्भायै नमः ।
ॐ पीतपुष्पार्चनप्रियायै नमः ।
ॐ पीतपुष्पाञ्जलिरतायै नमः ।
ॐ पीतद्रद निवासिन्यै नमः । *
ॐ पीठस्थायै नमः ।
ॐ पीठरूपायै नमः ।
ॐ पीठवासपरायणायै नमः ।
ॐ परदारप्रियायै नमः ।
ॐ पत्राधरधार प्रहर्षिण्यै नमः । ३४०

ॐ परदारप्रहरस्यै नमः । *
ॐ परदारविरोधिन्यै नमः ।
ॐ परदारप्रियापात्रायै नमः ।
ॐ पात्रतोषणतत्परायै नमः ।
ॐ पात्ररूपायै नमः ।
ॐ पात्रतुष्ट्यै नमः ।
ॐ पात्रदानपरायणायै नमः ।
ॐ पात्रपुष्पप्रियायै नमः ।
ॐ पात्रकुण्डानन्दपरेश्वर्यै नमः ।
ॐ पात्राराधनसन्तुष्टायै नमः ।
ॐ पात्रप्रासादरूपिण्यै नमः ।
ॐ पवित्रायै नमः ।
ॐ पुण्यचारित्रायै नमः ।
ॐ पवित्रारोपणात्मिकायै नमः ।
ॐ पवित्ररोपणरतायै नमः ।
ॐ पात्रगानपरायणायै नमः ।
ॐ पात्रगीत पात्रनपायै नमः । *
ॐ पात्रसंयोगरूपिण्यै नमः ।
ॐ पात्रकुण्डविकसतायै नमः ।
ॐ पात्रकुण्डविलोहिन्यै नमः । ३६०

ॐ पात्रकुण्डध्वनिरतायै नमः ।

ॐ पात्रकुण्डध्वनिप्रियायै नमः ।
ॐ परनिद्राविनिर्मुक्तायै नमः ।
ॐ परद्रव्यविमोचन्यै नमः ।
ॐ परस्वनाशिनीप्रीतायै नमः ।
ॐ पार्वत्यै नमः ।
ॐ पर्वतात्मजायै नमः ।
ॐ पर्वतेज्यायै नमः ।
ॐ पर्वरतायै नमः ।
ॐ पर्वतप्रियरूपिण्यै नमः ।
ॐ परायणायै नमः ।
ॐ पारच्यै नमः ।
ॐ पतिधर्मविधारिण्यै नमः ।
ॐ पतिप्रियायै नमः ।
ॐ प्रीतिरतायै नमः ।
ॐ पतिगम्यायै नमः ।
ॐ पतिव्रतायै नमः ।
ॐ पतिव्रतधरायै नमः ।
ॐ पीनवक्षोजद्वयधारिण्यै नमः ।
ॐ पिशाचप्रेमसन्तुष्टायै नमः । ३८०

ॐ प्रेतकोटिसमाकुलायै नमः ।
ॐ प्रेतगर्भायै नमः ।
ॐ प्रेतरूपायै नमः ।
ॐ प्रेतभूषणभूषण्यै नमः ।
ॐ प्रेतमालाकण्ठभूषायै नमः ।
ॐ प्रेतलेहनतत्परायै नमः ।
ॐ प्रेताश्यै नमः ।
ॐ प्रेतराज्यै नमः ।
ॐ प्रेतव्रतपरायणायै नमः ।
ॐ पिशाचानन्दसन्तोषायै नमः ।
ॐ पार्थप्रीतिपरायणायै नमः ।
ॐ पार्थिवायै नमः ।

ॐ पार्थवेज्यायै नमः ।

ॐ पृथुलायै नमः ।

ॐ पृथुरूपिण्यै नमः ।

ॐ पृथ्व्यै नमः ।

ॐ पृथिव्यै नमः ।

ॐ पिङ्गायै नमः ।

ॐ पिङ्गनेत्रायै नमः । ४००

ॐ पिङ्कटायै नमः । *

ॐ पापान् विनाशिन्यै नमः ।

ॐ पद्यायै नमः ।

ॐ गद्यपद्यपरायणायै नमः ।

ॐ पद्यात्मिकायै नमः ।

ॐ पद्यरतायै नमः ।

ॐ पाम्पीम्पूम्पौं स्वरूपिण्यै नमः ।

ॐ पाम्पीङ्काररतायै नमः ।

ॐ प्राणायै नमः ।

ॐ प्राणदात्र्यै नमः ।

ॐ प्रतापिन्यै नमः ।

ॐ प्रभावत्यै नमः ।

ॐ प्रभाप्रेमायै नमः ।

ॐ प्रेमयोगपरायणायै नमः ।

ॐ प्रज्ञायै नमः ।

ॐ प्रज्ञावतीप्रज्ञायै नमः ।

ॐ प्रज्ञानप्रतिभावत्यै नमः ।

ॐ प्रतिभायै नमः ।

ॐ प्रणतीप्राणायै नमः ।

ॐ प्रज्ञापतिग्रहस्थितायै नमः । ४२०

ॐ प्रजापत्यै नमः ।

ॐ प्रियापारायै नमः । *

ॐ पुरीन्द्रध्वजशोभितायै नमः ।

ॐ प्रमतीप्राणधर्त्र्यै नमः ।

ॐ प्रतिज्ञापारगामिन्यै नमः ।

ॐ फुम्फुङ्कारायै नमः ।

ॐ फट्कारायै नमः ।

ॐ फट्काररूपधारिण्यै नमः ।

ॐ फ्रीङ्कारफूत्कृत्यै नमः ।

ॐ फ्रूं स्फङ्कारारूपधारिण्यै नमः ।

ॐ फ्रोङ्कारफेरव्यै नमः ।

ॐ फ्राम्फ्रूम्फेत्कार्यै नमः ।

ॐ फणधारिण्यै नमः ।

ॐ फेणिप्रीतायै नमः ।

ॐ फणेरतायै नमः ।

ॐ फणदर्शनतोषिण्यै नमः ।

ॐ फणिभूषणसम्भूषायै नमः ।

ॐ फणिनाथप्रियार्चितायै नमः ।

ॐ फणिबन्धसमुद्धूतायै नमः ।

ॐ फणिवंशसुशोभिन्यै नमः । ४४०

ॐ पशुहस्तायै नमः ।

ॐ पशुमत्यै नमः ।

ॐ परशुरामप्रसादिन्यै नमः ।

ॐ फेत्कारभैरव्यै नमः ।

ॐ फ्रौण्टायै नमः ।

ॐ फ्रेत्काररवभाषिण्यै नमः ।

ॐ फ्रेत्कारायै नमः ।

ॐ फाल्गुनानन्दायै नमः ।

ॐ फल्यै नमः ।

ॐ फुल्लप्रियायै नमः ।

ॐ फुलायै नमः ।

ॐ फलदात्र्यै नमः ।

ॐ फलरतायै नमः ।

ॐ फलरूपायै नमः ।

ॐ फलात्मिकायै नमः ।
ॐ फलहोमप्रियस्फालायै नमः ।
ॐ फलनामपरायणायै नमः ।
ॐ बृहस्पतिमुखस्थायै नमः ।
ॐ बृहतीछन्दरूपिण्यै नमः ।
ॐ बृहत्सेवायै नमः । ४६०

ॐ बृहत्ब्रह्म्यै नमः ।
ॐ ब्रह्मीब्रह्मप्रपूजितायै नमः ।
ॐ ब्रह्मवृत्तधरावीणायै नमः ।
ॐ बाणसन्धानकारिण्यै नमः ।
ॐ बाणासुरार्चितायै नमः ।
ॐ ब्रूं ब्राम्ब्रीम्ब्रैम्ब्रौं स्वरूपिण्यै नमः ।
ॐ बर्हिपिछुमियायै नमः । *
ॐ बर्हायै नमः ।
ॐ बर्हपिछविभूषणायै नमः ।
ॐ बटुकायै नमः ।
ॐ बटुकेज्यायै नमः ।
ॐ बटुकप्राणमानसायै नमः ।
ॐ बटूकाभैरवरतायै नमः ।
ॐ बटुकार्चनतोषिण्यै नमः ।
ॐ बटुकार्चनसन्तुष्टायै नमः ।
ॐ बलीदानप्रियावल्यै नमः ।
ॐ बलिपूज्यायै नमः ।
ॐ बलिरतायै नमः ।
ॐ बलिदाननिवासिन्यै नमः ।
ॐ बलिद्वारस्थितायै नमः । ४८०

ॐ बालायै नमः ।
ॐ बालाम्बायै नमः ।
ॐ बालभैरव्यै नमः ।
ॐ बालक्रीडामयप्राणायै नमः ।

ॐ बालकप्रियकारिण्यै नमः ।
ॐ बलितुष्टायै नमः ।
ॐ बलिरतायै नमः ।
ॐ बलितोषणकारिण्यै नमः ।
ॐ बलिमात्रे नमः ।
ॐ बलिमय्यै नमः ।
ॐ बलितत्त्वात्मिकावल्यै नमः ।
ॐ बलायै नमः ।
ॐ बलार्चनप्रीतायै नमः ।
ॐ बलधारणतत्परायै नमः ।
ॐ बटुकाराधनरतायै नमः ।
ॐ बटुकेज्यायै नमः ।
ॐ बटुप्रियायै नमः ।
ॐ बटुकाराधनप्रीतायै नमः ।
ॐ बटुकार्यवतारिण्यै नमः ।
ॐ बटुतारायै नमः । ५००

ॐ बटुछिन्नायै नमः ।
ॐ बटुकाल्यै नमः ।
ॐ बृहन्मय्यै नमः ।
ॐ बृहत्कुक्ष्यै नमः ।
ॐ बृहत्तारायै नमः ।
ॐ बृहत्तन्त्रागमेश्वर्यै नमः ।
ॐ बृहद्गुणायै नमः ।*
ॐ बृहद्यन्त्रायै नमः ।
ॐ बृहत्तन्त्रायै नमः ।
ॐ बृहत्कलायै नमः ।
ॐ बृहन्मात्रे नमः ।
ॐ बृहज्ज्वालायै नमः ।
ॐ बृहन्मानमय्यै नमः ।
ॐ बृहते नमः ।
ॐ बृहत्ताण्डवरूपायै नमः ।

ॐ बृहत्तारुण्यरूपिण्यै नमः ।
ॐ बृहदारण्यसंसेव्यायै नमः ।
ॐ बालचन्द्रकिरीटिन्यै नमः ।
ॐ बलदायै नमः ।
ॐ बाहुभूषायै नमः । ५२०

ॐ बाहुमालाविभूषणायै नमः ।
ॐ बाहुलायै नमः ।
ॐ बाहुलेयेस्यै नमः । *
ॐ बाहुलेयस्वरूपिण्यै नमः ।
ॐ बहुभाषामय्यै नमः ।
ॐ बुद्ध्यायै नमः । *
ॐ बुद्धिदायै नमः ।
ॐ बुद्धिदायिन्यै नमः ।
ॐ बुद्ध्यै नमः ।
ॐ बुद्धिमतायै नमः ।
ॐ बौद्धायै नमः ।
ॐ बौद्धाचारपरायणायै नमः ।
ॐ बौद्धमार्गप्रियाप्रीतायै नमः ।
ॐ बौद्धमार्गप्रवर्तिन्यै नमः ।
ॐ बृहस्पतिसुताराध्यायै नमः ।
ॐ बुद्धिमात्रे नमः ।
ॐ बुधेश्वर्यै नमः ।
ॐ बौद्धावारूपिण्यै नमः ।
ॐ भार्यायै नमः ।
ॐ भानव्यै नमः । ५४०

ॐ भानुरूपिण्यै नमः ।
ॐ भानुमत्तायै नमः ।
ॐ भानुमय्यै नमः ।
ॐ भानुभार्यायै नमः ।
ॐ भवेश्वर्यै नमः ।

ॐ भवपत्न्यै नमः ।

ॐ भयहरायै नमः ।

ॐ भवदानवनाशिन्यै नमः ।

ॐ भवमात्रे नमः ।

ॐ भवरताश्रवतारणतारिण्यै नमः । *

ॐ भर्तृप्रियायै नमः ।

ॐ भर्तृरतायै नमः ।

ॐ भर्तृभावप्रकाशिन्यै नमः ।

ॐ भर्तृनीतिकर्यै नमः ।

ॐ भार्यायै नमः ।

ॐ भरतृदायै नमः ।

ॐ भीमभीषण्यै नमः ।

ॐ भिक्षुपूज्यायै नमः ।

ॐ भिक्षु मात्रे नमः ।

ॐ भिक्षु मानसतोषिण्यै नमः । ५६०

ॐ भीमसेनप्रियायै नमः ।

ॐ भीमायै नमः ।

ॐ भीमाक्ष्यै नमः ।

ॐ भीमभीतिदायै नमः ।

ॐ भ्रान्तहन्त्र्यै नमः ।

ॐ भयहरायै नमः ।

ॐ भवपाशविमोचिन्यै नमः ।

ॐ भवदावानलघ्न्यै नमः ।

ॐ भक्तपूज्यायै नमः ।

ॐ भवार्तिघ्ने नमः ।

ॐ भक्ततुष्टायै नमः ।

ॐ भौममात्रे नमः ।

ॐ भोपायै नमः ।

ॐ भोपप्रताशिन्यै नमः । *

ॐ भृगरूपायै नमः । *

ॐ भृगुपत्न्यै नमः ।

ॐ भृगुताण्डवकारिण्यै नमः ।
ॐ भृगुसेवारतायै नमः ।
ॐ भ्रान्तिहारिण्यै नमः ।
ॐ भारतप्रियायै नमः । ५८०

ॐ भारत्यै नमः ।
ॐ भानवेश्यायै नमः ।
ॐ भाषायै नमः ।
ॐ भीमामय्यै नमः ।
ॐ भवायै नमः ।
ॐ भानुमत्यै नमः ।
ॐ भुक्तिमय्यै नमः ।
ॐ भ्रूं बीजाक्षररूपिण्यै नमः ।
ॐ भ्राम्भ्रीम्भ्रूम्भ्रैं स्वरूपिण्यै नमः ।
ॐ भ्रमतीवविनाशिन्यै नमः ।
ॐ भङ्गायै नमः ।
ॐ भङ्गाप्रियायै नमः ।
ॐ भृङ्ग्यै नमः ।
ॐ भृङ्गध्वनिपरायणायै नमः ।
ॐ भ्रातृजायायै नमः ।
ॐ भगवत्यै नमः ।
ॐ भवान्यै नमः ।
ॐ भक्तवत्सलायै नमः ।
ॐ भवसिद्धायै नमः ।
ॐ भगेज्यायै नमः । ६००

ॐ भगमालायै नमः ।
ॐ भवेश्वर्यै नमः ।
ॐ भ्रान्तायै नमः ।
ॐ भ्रमरिकायै नमः ।
ॐ भीत्यै नमः ।
ॐ भ्राजिष्णवे नमः ।

ॐ भक्तरूपिण्यै नमः ।

ॐ भक्तमानससन्तुष्टायै नमः ।

ॐ भवत्यै नमः ।

ॐ भ्रमराम्बिकायै नमः ।

ॐ भ्रामर्यै नमः ।

ॐ भ्रान्तमालायै नमः ।

ॐ भवेज्यायै नमः ।

ॐ भवसिद्धिदायै नमः ।

ॐ भगरूपायै नमः ।

ॐ भगरतायै नमः ।

ॐ भगगीतीमय्यै नमः ।

ॐ भगायै नमः ।

ॐ भङ्काररूपिण्यै नमः ।

ॐ भ्रामायै नमः । ६२०

ॐ भगमालाविभूषणायै नमः ।

ॐ भगलिङ्गस्वरूपायै नमः ।

ॐ भगलिङ्गपरायणायै नमः ।

ॐ भगलिङ्गामृतान्दोलायै नमः ।

ॐ भगाविलोलुपायै नमः ।

ॐ भगार्चनरतानन्द्यै नमः ।

ॐ भगभाग्यपरायणायै नमः ।

ॐ भगतत्त्वायै नमः ।

ॐ भगाव्हायै नमः । *

ॐ भगलिङ्गध्वन्यै नमः ।

ॐ भगायै नमः ।

ॐ भगन्यै नमः । *

ॐ भार्गवेज्यायै नमः ।

ॐ भगमालायै नमः ।

ॐ भगाङ्कुरायै नमः ।

ॐ भगकुण्डाह्लादरतायै नमः ।

ॐ भगकुण्डविकासिन्यै नमः ।

ॐ भवित्र्यै नमः ।

ॐ भवितायै नमः ।

ॐ भूतायै नमः । ६४०

ॐ भूतमात्रे नमः ।

ॐ भूपत्यै नमः ।

ॐ भूपेज्यायै नमः ।

ॐ भूपसन्तुष्टायै नमः ।

ॐ भैक्ष्यचर्वणतत्परायै नमः ।

ॐ भगनामस्मृतिपरायै नमः ।

ॐ भगजापपरायणायै नमः ।

ॐ भगतन्त्रायै नमः ।

ॐ भगामोहायै नमः ।

ॐ भगगन्धपरायणायै नमः ।

ॐ भगवापीस्नानरतायै नमः ।

ॐ भगतीर्थनिवासिन्यै नमः ।

ॐ भगदर्शनसन्तुष्टायै नमः ।

ॐ भगचुम्बनतोषिण्यै नमः ।

ॐ भगजिह्वायै नमः ।

ॐ भगमुखायै नमः ।

ॐ भगचक्षुषे नमः ।

ॐ भगाम्बुजायै नमः ।

ॐ भूतेश्यै नमः ।

ॐ भूतदुर्गस्थायै नमः । ६६०

ॐ भूपतित्वप्रदायिन्यै नमः ।

ॐ भूम्भूङ्कारस्वरूपायै नमः ।

ॐ भद्रशब्दपरायणायै नमः ।

ॐ भहभहारकामहायै नमः । *

ॐ भाष्यकर्त्रे नमः ।

ॐ भयापहायै नमः ।

ॐ भरतायै नमः ।

ॐ भरतेश्यै नमः ।
ॐ भरताप्राणदायिन्यै नमः ।
ॐ भरताप्रेमसन्तुष्टायै नमः ।
ॐ भरताधाररूपिण्यै नमः ।
ॐ भूभारायै नमः ।
ॐ भूधराधीशायै नमः ।
ॐ भूधरायै नमः ।
ॐ भूधरप्रियायै नमः ।
ॐ मामीपानन्दनायै नमः । *
ॐ मायायै नमः ।
ॐ मद्यपानपरायणायै नमः ।
ॐ मधुप्रीतायै नमः ।
ॐ मधुरतायै नमः । ६८०

ॐ मधुरायै नमः ।
ॐ मधुरामधवे नमः ।
ॐ मदिरायै नमः ।
ॐ मदिरोन्मत्तायै नमः ।
ॐ माननीयायै नमः ।
ॐ मदोद्धतायै नमः ।
ॐ माध्वीपानरतायै नमः ।
ॐ मात्रे नमः ।
ॐ मायाबीजद्वयामत्यै नमः ।
ॐ निमात्रे नमः ।
ॐ मालिन्यै नमः ।
ॐ मात्रायै नमः ।
ॐ मदनीमृतदर्पिकायै नमः ।
ॐ मानाक्ष्यै नमः ।
ॐ मातुलान्यै नमः ।
ॐ मोदिन्यै नमः ।
ॐ मदनातुरायै नमः ।
ॐ म्राम्म्रीम्म्रूम्रैं स्वरूपायै नमः ।

ॐ म्रौम्म्रः सर्वस्वरूपिण्यै नमः ।
ॐ मिताक्षरायै नमः । ७००

ॐ मिताहारायै नमः ।
ॐ मिताचारमनोमय्यै नमः ।
ॐ मलिनायै नमः ।
ॐ मलिन्यै नमः ।
ॐ मैत्रायै नमः ।
ॐ मैत्रवारुणतारुण्यै नमः ।
ॐ मायावत्यै नमः ।
ॐ मानवत्यै नमः ।
ॐ महामधुमतिमय्यै नमः ।
ॐ महीधरसक्तायै नमः ।
ॐ मात्रायै नमः ।
ॐ मात्रास्वरविभेदिन्यै नमः ।
ॐ मीनरूपायै नमः ।
ॐ मीननाथायै नमः ।
ॐ मालत्यै नमः ।
ॐ मधुलोलुपायै नमः ।
ॐ मधुपानरतायै नमः ।
ॐ मार्यै नमः ।
ॐ महामार्यै नमः ।
ॐ महीपत्यै नमः । ७२०

ॐ महाकाल्यै नमः ।
ॐ महातारायै नमः ।
ॐ महाछिन्नायै नमः ।
ॐ महेश्वर्यै नमः ।
ॐ माहेश्यै नमः ।
ॐ मदस्थायै नमः ।
ॐ मदनस्थानरूपिण्यै नमः ।
ॐ मदनप्रियकान्तायै नमः ।

ॐ महायोगेश्वर्यै नमः ।

ॐ मख्यै नमः । *

ॐ महामदनसन्तुष्टायै नमः ।

ॐ महामदनभूषितायै नमः ।

ॐ महितायै नमः ।

ॐ महिलायै नमः ।

ॐ मायायै नमः ।

ॐ मकाराक्षररूपिण्यै नमः ।

ॐ मकाररूपिण्यै नमः ।

ॐ मुद्रायै नमः ।

ॐ मुद्रामोदपरायणायै नमः ।

ॐ मेहस्थायै नमः । ७४०

ॐ मेहमात्रे नमः ।

ॐ मेहमित्रायै नमः ।

ॐ महत्प्रियायै नमः ।

ॐ महतायै नमः ।

ॐ मोजसाकारायै नमः ।

ॐ महतानन्ददायिन्यै नमः ।

ॐ मधुमांसायै नमः ।

ॐ मेहतारायै नमः ।

ॐ मेहप्रस्ताररूपिण्यै नमः ।

ॐ मेहपुत्र्यै नमः ।

ॐ मीनाक्ष्यै नमः ।

ॐ मितभाषायै नमः ।

ॐ मितार्थविते नमः ।

ॐ मदनान्तककान्तायै नमः ।

ॐ मदनान्तकरूपिण्यै नमः ।

ॐ महोरगायै नमः ।

ॐ महोशुषायै नमः ।

ॐ महत्यै नमः ।

ॐ महिषापहायै नमः ।

ॐ महिषासुरनिर्नाश्यै नमः । ७६०

ॐ मुण्डमालाविभूषणायै नमः ।

ॐ मुण्डप्राकारसंरूपायै नमः ।

ॐ मुण्डासुरविमर्दिन्यै नमः ।

ॐ मानसायै नमः ।

ॐ मानसेश्यै नमः ।

ॐ मुद्रिण्यम्बास्वरूपिण्यै नमः ।

ॐ मुद्रिण्यै नमः ।

ॐ मन्त्रिण्यै नमः ।

ॐ मन्त्रायै नमः ।

ॐ महामन्त्रायै नमः ।

ॐ महार्णवायै नमः ।

ॐ महार्णवस्थितायै नमः ।

ॐ मोहायै नमः ।

ॐ मोहिनीनाशिन्यै नमः ।

ॐ मरुते नमः ।

ॐ मनवे नमः ।

ॐ मनुमय्यै नमः ।

ॐ माद्र्यै नमः ।

ॐ मद्रकुञ्जरवासिन्यै नमः ।

ॐ मद्रकुम्भस्थलारूढायै नमः । ७८०

ॐ मद्मुक्ताविभूषणायै नमः ।*

ॐ मुक्ताहारविभूषाढ्यायै नमः ।

ॐ मुक्तकेश्यै नमः ।

ॐ महूर्तदायै नमः ।

ॐ मोहकर्त्र्यै नमः ।

ॐ मोहहीनायै नमः ।

ॐ महामोहपरायणायै नमः ।

ॐ मन्त्रप्राणार्पणप्रीतायै नमः ।

ॐ मन्त्रप्राणार्पणार्चितायै नमः ।

ॐ महौघानन्दायै नमः ।
ॐ मन्दगन्धायै नमः ।
ॐ मद्यपूजनतत्परायै नमः ।
ॐ मकारवर्णसर्वाङ्ग्यै नमः ।
ॐ मितभोगायै नमः ।
ॐ मितान्मितायै नमः ।
ॐ महाधूम्रावत्यै नमः ।
ॐ मुक्तायै नमः ।
ॐ महामुक्ताविभूषणायै नमः ।
ॐ मुक्तारजतनासायै नमः ।
ॐ मुक्ताछत्रविभूषणायै नमः । ८००

ॐ मुक्तदानरतायै नमः ।
ॐ मध्यायै नमः ।
ॐ मध्यमायै नमः ।
ॐ मध्यमेश्वर्यै नमः ।
ॐ मितीर्मीतीमत्यै नमः ।
ॐ मीनकेतवे नमः ।
ॐ मकररूपिण्यै नमः ।
ॐ मकरस्थायै नमः ।
ॐ महादेव्यै नमः ।
ॐ महादेवमनोमय्यै नमः ।
ॐ महोत्सवायै नमः ।
ॐ दुर्गायै नमः ।
ॐ मायायै नमः ।
ॐ महापूजारमेत्यदायै नमः । *
ॐ महाग्रहस्वरूपायै नमः ।
ॐ मघानक्षत्ररूपिण्यै नमः ।
ॐ मद्यमांसावृतरतायै नमः ।
ॐ माघस्नानपरायणायै नमः ।
ॐ मार्गशीर्षप्रियानन्दायै नमः ।
ॐ मार्गदर्शनतत्परायै नमः । ८२०

ॐ मार्गमार्गामात्रकायै नमः ।
ॐ मातृकालिपिरूपिण्यै नमः ।
ॐ मातृकान्याससन्तुष्टायै नमः ।
ॐ मातृकान्यासरूपिण्यै नमः ।
ॐ मालिनीन्याससन्तुष्टायै नमः ।
ॐ मालिनीमोक्षदायिन्यै नमः ।
ॐ मोक्षदात्र्यै नमः ।
ॐ मोक्षगत्यै नमः ।
ॐ मोक्षमार्गपरायणायै नमः ।
ॐ मुक्तायै नमः ।
ॐ मुक्तिप्रियकर्यै नमः ।
ॐ मुक्तिस्थायै नमः ।
ॐ मुक्तिताण्डवायै नमः ।
ॐ महानन्दायै नमः ।
ॐ महाकाल्यै नमः ।
ॐ महाभुवनतारिण्यै नमः ।
ॐ महेन्द्रपूज्यायै नमः ।
ॐ माहेश्यै नमः ।
ॐ मतिसागरदायिन्यै नमः ।
ॐ यक्षायै नमः । ८४०

ॐ यक्षस्वरूपायै नमः ।
ॐ यक्षिण्यै नमः ।
ॐ यक्षपूजितायै नमः ।
ॐ यादेव्यै नमः ।
ॐ यादवाराध्यायै नमः ।
ॐ यदुवंशसमुद्भवायै नमः ।
ॐ यमुनायै नमः ।
ॐ यजुर्वेदायै नमः ।
ॐ यजुर्वेदपरायणायै नमः ।
ॐ यामिन्यै नमः ।
ॐ यमपूज्यायै नमः ।

ॐ यममातापतिप्रियायै नमः ।

ॐ यात्रायै नमः ।

ॐ यात्रयशोदायै नमः । *

ॐ यशोवर्धनतत्परायै नमः ।

ॐ यशकर्पूरधवलायै नमः । *

ॐ योगिन्यै नमः ।

ॐ यशस्विन्यै नमः ।

ॐ यांयींयूं याकिनीरूपायै नमः ।

ॐ यैंयौं यङ्कारारूपिण्यै नमः । ८६०

ॐ योगमात्रे नमः ।

ॐ योगगम्यायै नमः ।

ॐ योगमार्गपरायणायै नमः ।

ॐ योगीशायै नमः ।

ॐ योजनायै नमः ।

ॐ यामायै नमः ।

ॐ योजनायुतविस्तरायै नमः ।

ॐ यथोक्ताचारनिरतायै नमः ।

ॐ यथोक्तफलदायिन्यै नमः ।

ॐ यक्षकर्दमसम्भूषायै नमः ।

ॐ यवर्गरूपिणीपत्यै नमः ।

ॐ रमण्यै नमः ।

ॐ रमणीप्रीतायै नमः ।

ॐ रमायै नमः ।

ॐ रत्नेश्वर्यै नमः ।

ॐ रत्यै नमः ।

ॐ रतिप्रियायै नमः ।

ॐ रतिरतायै नमः ।

ॐ रतितोषणतत्परायै नमः ।

ॐ रत्नगर्भायै नमः । ८८०

ॐ रत्नबीजायै नमः ।

ॐ राजीवलोचनायै नमः ।

ॐ रमायै नमः ।

ॐ राम्बीजायै नमः ।

ॐ रींस्वरूपायै नमः ।

ॐ रांरींरूंरैं स्वरूपिण्यै नमः ।

ॐ रौंरः वर्णस्वरूपायै नमः ।

ॐ राज्यदात्र्यै नमः ।

ॐ रसातुलायै नमः ।

ॐ रसतुष्टायै नमः ।

ॐ रसगत्यै नमः ।

ॐ रघुवंशसमुद्भवायै नमः ।

ॐ रतिरूपायै नमः ।

ॐ रतान्तायै नमः ।

ॐ रतिगर्भपरायणायै नमः ।

ॐ राजीवनेत्रायै नमः ।

ॐ राज्ञ्यै नमः ।

ॐ रमणासुरकन्यकायै नमः ।

ॐ राजराजेश्वरीद्रष्टायै नमः ।

ॐ रौद्र्यै नमः । ९००

ॐ रुद्रप्रियायै नमः ।

ॐ रुटे नमः ।

ॐ रुद्रकन्यायै नमः ।

ॐ रुद्रजायायै नमः ।

ॐ रुद्रमातारतानन्दायै नमः ।

ॐ रुद्रेज्यायै नमः ।

ॐ त्रिरूपायै नमः ।

ॐ रात्रिञ्चरविभेदिन्यै नमः ।

ॐ राक्षसघ्न्यै नमः ।

ॐ रक्षणायै नमः ।

ॐ रक्षोविद्राविण्यै नमः ।

ॐ रतायै नमः ।

ॐ हचिरायै नमः । *

ॐ हचिरूपायै नमः ।

ॐ रोचिषायै नमः ।

ॐ रोमरूपिण्यै नमः ।

ॐ रोमगर्भायै नमः ।

ॐ रोमदेहायै नमः ।

ॐ रोमभूषणतत्परायै नमः ।

ॐ रसायै नमः । ९२०

ॐ रसवत्यै नमः ।

ॐ राज्यलक्ष्म्यै नमः ।

ॐ रावणनाशिन्यै नमः ।

ॐ रावणेज्यायै नमः ।

ॐ रवदतायै नमः । *

ॐ रावणप्रियदायिन्यै नमः ।

ॐ रजोवत्यै नमः ।

ॐ रजःप्राणायै नमः ।

ॐ रजोगुणमय्यै नमः ।

ॐ रवायै नमः ।

ॐ रतिपुष्पप्रियायै नमः ।

ॐ रूंरूं राकिण्यै नमः ।

ॐ रेणुकायै नमः ।

ॐ रयायै नमः ।

ॐ रैं बीजनिलयायै नमः ।

ॐ रैण्णायै नमः ।

ॐ रेणुरूपायै नमः ।

ॐ हाकिन्यै नमः ।

ॐ हक्वाङ्गदस्य भगिन्यै नमः ।

ॐ हक्यरूपायै नमः । ९४०

ॐ रूपभुवे नमः ।

ॐ रौप्यपरायै नमः ।

ॐ रौप्यरौप्यायै नमः ।

ॐ रौप्यगेहविभूषणायै नमः ।

ॐ रौप्यसिंहासनरतायै नमः ।

ॐ रौप्यदानपरायणायै नमः । ९४६

इति श्रीमहोग्राताराक्षोभ्यसंवादे अक्षोभ्यसंहितायां शतार्धसहस्रां नमः ।
ताराविरचितं दिव्यसाम्राज्यमेधाख्यं नामसहस्रं विंशति पटलः नमः ।

*****

# About the Author

(http://Ramamurthy.jaagruti.co.in)

Dr. Ramamurthy is a versatile personality having experience and expertise in various areas of Banking, related IT solutions, Information Security, IT Audit, Vedas, Samskrutam and so on.

His thirst for continuous learning does not subside. Even at the age of late fifties, he did research on a unique topic "Information Technology and Samskrutam" and obtained Ph.D. – doctorate degree from University of Madras. He is into a project of developing a Samskrutam based compiler.

It is his passion to spread his knowledge and experience through conducting classes, training programmes and writing books.

He has already published books as detailed below. Further books are in pipe-line.

| # | Title | Remarks | Pages |
|---|---|---|---|
| | | **Indology Related** | |
| 1. | *Shrī Lalita Sahasranāmam* | English translation of Shrī *Bhāskararāya's Bhāśyam* | 750 |
| 2. | Power of *Shrī Vidyā* | The secrets demystified – with lucid English rendering and commentaries | 80 |
| 3. | ஸ்ரீ வித்யையின் ஶக்தி | ஸ்ரீ வித்யா ரகசியங்கள் | 100 |
| 4. | *Samatā* – **समता** | An exposition of Similarities in *Lalita Sahasranāma* with *Soundaryalaharī, Saptaśatī, Viśṇu Sahasranāma* and *Shrīmad Bhagavad Gīta* | 172 |
| 5. | ஸமதா – **समता** | ஸ்ரீ லலிதா ஸஹஸ்ரநாமம் ஸௌந்தர்யலஹரீ, ஸப்தஶதீ, ஸ்ரீ விஷ்ணு ஸஹஸ்ரநாமம் மற்றும் ஸ்ரீமத் பகவத் கீதைகளில் ஒற்றுமையின் ஒரு வெளிப்பாடு | 266 |
| 6. | *Advaita* in *Shākta* | Advaita Philosophy discussed in Shakta related Books | 80 |
| 7. | *Shrī Lalitā Triśatī* | 300 divine names of the celestial Mother – **English** translation of *Shrī Ādhi Śaṅkara*'s *Bhāśyam* | 193 |
| 8. | ஸ்ரீ லலிதா த்ரிஶதி | 300 divine names of the celestial Mother – Tamil translation of *Shrī Ādi Śaṅkara*'s *Bhāśyam* | 234 |
| 9. | Secrets of *Mahāśakti* | Chandi demystified | 78 |
| 10. | *Daśa Mahā Vidyā* | Ten cosmic forms of the Divine mother | 60 |

| # | Title | Remarks | Pages |
|---|---|---|---|
| 11. | ஸ்ரீ வித்யா பேதங்கள் | ஸ்ரீவித்யா உபாசனையின் படிகள் - கோவை ஶதச் சண்டீ மலர் | 51 |
| 12. | *Shrīvidya* Variances | Variances in Srividya Upasana | 50 |
| 13. | ஸ்ரீ தேவீ ஸ்துதிகள் | பல முக்கிய அம்பாள் ஸ்தோத்ரங்கள் | 133 |
| 14. | Śrī Devī Stutis – श्री देवी स्तुति: | Various important stotras of Sri Devi | 223 |
| 15. | ஷண்மத மந்த்ரங்கள் | பொள்ளாச்சி ஸ்ரீ ஸஹஸ்ரசண்டீ மஹாயாக நினைவு மலர் | 145 |
| 16. | *Śanmata Mantras* – षण्मत मन्त्रा: | Important Mantras relating to Gods of six religions | 87 |
| 17. | தேவதா மந்த்ரங்கள் | அக்கரைப்பட்டி ஸஹஸ்ரசண்டீ மஹாயாக நினைவு மலர் | 32 |
| 18. | ஆதி ஶங்கரரும் ஷண்மதமும் | ஷண்மதங்களைப் பற்றிய ஒரு அறிமுகம் | 32 |
| 19. | ஸ்ரீ ஷண்மத தேவதா அர்ச்சனை | ஸ்ரீ மஹா கும்பாபிஷேக மலர் | 64 |
| 20. | *Vaidhīka* Wedding | Typical Wedding process in English | 56 |
| 21. | வைதீகத் திருமணம் | Typical Wedding process in Tamil | 57 |
| 22. | ஸ்ரீகுரு பாத பூஜா விதானம் | சித்தகிரி ஸஹஸ்ரசண்டீ மலர் | 44 |
| 23. | குரு வார வழிபாடு | | 70 |
| 24. | ஸ்ரீவித்யா ஶடாம்னாய மந்த்ரங்கள் | சித்தகிரி ஸஹஸ்ரசண்டீ மலர் | 60 |
| 25. | *Ekatā* | Oneness among Shiva, Vishnu and Shakti | 277 |
| 26. | ஏகதா - एकता | ஶிவபெருமான், விஷ்ணு மற்றும் ஶக்திக்குள் ஒற்றுமை | 370 |
| 27. | *Vedas* – An Analytical Perspective | A description of Veda, Vedanta, Vedanga, Jyotisha, Shastra, etc. | 240 |
| 28. | வேதங்கள் - ஒரு பகுப்பாய்வு | A description of Veda, Vedanta, Vedanga, Jyotisha, Shastra, etc. | 280 |
| 29. | பரமாச்சார்யாள் நோக்கில் ஸ்ரீ லலிதாம்பிகா | The explanation given by Paramacharya on some of the names in Lalita Sahasranama | 175 |
| 30. | *Ṣaṇṇavati Tarpaṇa* | Repaying Debts to Ancestors | 42 |
| 31. | ஷண்ணவதி தர்பணம் | முன்னோர் கடன் தீர்த்தல் | 48 |
| 32. | *Shrī Mahā Pratyangirā Devī* | Holy Divine mother in ferocious form | 41 |
| 33. | ஸ்ரீ மஹா ப்ரத்யங்கிரா தேவீ | தெய்வீக அன்னையின் பயங்கர வடிவம் | 51 |
| 34. | *Śrī Chakra Navāvarṇam* | Marvels of *Śrī Chakra* | 115 |
| 35. | ஸ்ரீ சக்ர நவாவர்ணம் | ஸ்ரீ சக்ரத்தின் அதிசயங்கள் | 130 |
| 36. | அம்பிகையின் (திரு) அவதாரங்கள் | ஸ்ரீ தேவியின் பல்வேறு அவதாரங்கள் | 142 |
| 37. | Incarnations of Holy Mother | Different Incarnations of *Śrī Devī* | 140 |

| # | Title | Remarks | Pages |
|---|---|---|---|
| 38. | ஸ்ரீ பிரணவானந்தர் - ஒரு சரிதம் | ஒரு அரிய ஸ்வாமிகளின் திவ்ய சரிதம் | 121 |
| 39. | ஸன்யாஸம் - ஓர் அலசல் | ஹிந்து மத ஸன்யாஸ பேதங்கள் - ஒரு பகுப்பாய்வு | 140 |
| 40. | Asceticism – an Analysis | A Study of Hindu *Sanyasam* | 140 |
| 41. | ஶாந்தமும் ப்ரணவமும் | (**ஸ்ரீ** ஶாந்தானந்தரும் **ஸ்ரீ** ப்ரணவானந்தரும்) குரு சிஷ்யருக்கு உபதேசங்கள் | 120 |
| 42. | ஸ்ரீ ஸஹஸ்ராக்ஷரீ வித்யா | 2020 சாதுர்மாஸ்ய மலர் | 84 |
| 43. | *Shakta Upanishats* | *Upanishats* about *Sri Devi* | 385 |
| 44. | ஶாக்த உபநிஷதங்கள் | *Upanishats* about *Sri Devi* | 400 |
| 45. | ஸ்ரீ **தேவீ கீதை** | Sri Devi Geeta | 194 |
| 46. | *Śrī Devī Gīta* | Sri Devi Geeta | 180 |
| 47. | *Śrī Gāyatrī Sahasranamam* | 1,000 Divine Names of *Śrī Gāyatrī Mātā* | 392 |
| 48. | ஸ்ரீ **காயத்ரீ** ஸஹஸ்ரநாமம் | ஸ்ரீ **காயத்ரி** மாதாவின்1,000 திவ்ய நாமங்கள் | 450 |
| 49. | ஸ்ரீ ஸௌந்தர்யலஹரீ | ஸௌந்தர்யலஹரீ ஒரு உள்-அறிவு | 250 |
| 50. | *Śrī Soundaryalaharī* | *Soundaryalaharī* an Insight | 200 |
| 51. | *Śrī Vārāhī Devī* | Holy Divine Mother with a hog face | 96 |
| 52. | ஸ்ரீ வாராஹீ தேவீ | பன்றி முகத்துடன் கூடிய புனிதத் தெய்வீக அன்னை | 106 |
| 53. | Śrī Vijaya Bhairavar | A Terrifying, Sacred, Divine form of Lord Shiva | 164 |
| 54. | ஸ்ரீ விஜய பை$_4$ரவர் | ஶிவபெருமானின் ஒரு திகிலூட்டும் புனித தெய்வீக உருவம் | 188 |
| 55. | ஸ்ரீ ப$_4$த்$_3$ர காளீ | ஸ்ரீ தேவியின் ஒரு திகிலூட்டும் புனித தெய்வீக உருவம் | 226 |
| 56. | *Śrī Bhadra Kālī* | A Startling, Sacred and Divine form of *Śrī Devī* | 224 |
| 57. | ஸ்ரீ தாரா – நீல ஸரஸ்வதீ | 2nd Devi of Dasha Maha Vidya | 182 |
| 58. | *Śrī Tārā Devī* – Blue *Saraswatī* | 2nd Devi of Dasha Maha Vidya | 174 |
| | | **Applied Samskrutam Based** | |
| 59. | *Paribhāshā Stora*–s | An exploration of *Lalita Sahasranāmam* | 96 |
| 60. | பரிபாஷா ஸ்தோத்ரங்கள் | ஸ்ரீ லலிதா ஸஹஸ்ரநாமம் - ஒரு ஆய்வு | 135 |
| 61. | *Shrī Cakra*, An Esoteric Approach | Mathematical Construction to draw *Shrī Cakra* | 64 |
| 62. | ஸ்ரீ சக்கரம் வரையும் முறை | ஸ்ரீ சக்கரம் வரைய கணித கட்டுமானம் | 84 |
| 63. | Number System in Samskrutam | An overview of Mathematics based on Samskrutam | 123 |
| 64. | ஸமஸ்க்ருதத்தில் எண்ணியல் | ஸமஸ்க்ருதத்தில் பொதிந்துள்ள எண் கணிதம் | 140 |

| # | Title | Remarks | Pages |
|---|---|---|---|
| 65. | *Vedic* Mathematics | 30 formulae elucidated | 146 |
| 66. | Vedic IT | Information Technology and Samskrutam | 162 |
| | | **IT Based** | |
| 67. | Orthogonal Array | A Statistical Tool for Software Testing | 180 |
| | | **Banking Based** | |
| 68. | Retail Banking | A guide book for Novice | 213 |
| 69. | Corporate Banking | A guide book for Novice | 232 |
| 70. | Dictionary of Financial Terms | A Guide Book for all – Demystifying Myriad Global Financial Terms | 215 |
| 71. | GRC in BFS Industry | (**G**overnance, **R**isk Management and **Com**pliance by Banking & Finance Industry) | 200 |

*****

www.ingramcontent.com/pod-product-compliance
Lightning Source LLC
Chambersburg PA
CBHW062138160726
48282CB00027B/868
* 9 7 8 9 3 8 2 2 3 7 9 1 4 *